GOD OF COVENANTS

GOD'S UNCHANGING NATURE IN CHANGING COVENANTS

SCOTT MITCHELL

I would like to thank my wife Rhonda who is a constant inspiration and encouragement to me in all I do in service to the Lord. Her love and support is a great strength to me in life and ministry.

"Everyone in heaven will be fully blessed, but not everyone will be equally blessed. Every believer's cup will be full and running over, but not everyone's cup will be the same size. We determine in time what our capacity for appreciating God will be in eternity... By our temporal obedience we determine our reward in eternity (cf. 2 Cor. 5:10)" 1

NORMAN GEISLER

CONTENTS

PREFACE

This is an updated version of my original book. I added a chapter near the end of the book entitled, "How Can I Apply The Old Testament to My Christian Life?" because it added a missing and important element. After the initial writing, it became clear that I did not have a chapter that specifically addressed how to apply Old Testament passages, which all Christians attempt to do. Thus, without this chapter I believe the book was incomplete. It is my hope and prayer that the Lord will use this added chapter to help aid Christians in their use of the whole Bible for life application.

Scott Mitchell

BIBLE VERSIONS AND ABBREVIATIONS

Unless otherwise stated, scripture quotations are from the KJV (King James Version, 1611).

Other Versions:
ESV (English Standard Version, 2001)
HCSB (Holman Christian Standard Bible, NT 1999)
ISV (International Standard Version, NT 1998)
NET (New English Translation, 2005)
NKJV (New King James Version, 1982)
WNT (Weymouth New Testament, 1903)

Longer book titles of the Bible abbreviated as follows:
Genesis – Gen.
Exodus – Ex.
Numbers – Num.
Deuteronomy – Deut.
Chronicles – Chron.
Jeremiah – Jer.
Ezekiel – Ez.
Daniel – Dan.
Zachariah – Zach.
Matthew – Matt.
Romans – Rom.
Corinthians – Cor.
Galatians – Gal.
Ephesians – Eph.
Philippians – Phil.
Colossians – Col.
Thessalonians – Thess.

Timothy – Tim.
Revelation – Rev

FORWARD

Scott Mitchell and I have never met face to face. On hundreds of occasions in the last few years, however, we have encountered one another *heart to heart*.

Scott and I met after I watched a YouTube video in which he was interviewed about his first book. I was impressed by what Scott had to say, and even more, by his gracious way of expressing himself. I contacted him by email to offer my thanks, which led to a great friendship from afar, and even more, a wonderful fellowship in the living Word, the Lord Jesus Christ, and the written Word, the Bible.

In this book, you will read the words of a man who loves his Savior, and who loves people. You will also read the words of one who gives all glory for such love to the Lord Jesus. A clear and definitive declaration of the Covenant of God's grace in Christ awaits in the pages that follow, along with a thorough explanation of the Covenant of Law, as given through Moses. Scott will help the reader better understand the Biblically-revealed dispensations of history wherein an unchanging God worked in necessarily different ways to fulfill His ultimate purpose in Christ. This will result in a far more effective and sanctifying relationship to the Word of God, leading to the same with the God of the Word.

Allow me to suggest that the reader not rush through this book. Clearly written and understandable, it presents truths that require and encourage serious consideration of the issues raised. More importantly, Scott offers multitudes of Scriptural references that inspire, inform, and confirm his perspectives. Take time to ponder all, and determine to allow for an unhurried journey through the dispensations that will prepare heart and mind for better understanding of all other Biblical subjects.

Finally, keep this book handy after reading it. It will serve as an excellent reference volume for years to come. God has blessed us with a special gift through Scott's words, and most importantly, one that will enable us to more devotedly and intelligently seek to love, trust, obey, communicate, and honor our blessed Lord Jesus.

Glen Davis [2]

TO KNOW GOD AND THE BIBLE

When it comes to theological topics in the Bible, there seems to be no end to the potential controversy surrounding them. Among Christians that hold the Bible to be the word of God, at least the controversies are more refined and tend to be more cordial. Indeed, this is because the Bible instructs believers to address these issues as brethren – which most of whom take the Bible seriously try to obey. Christians are all on the same team and should remember it when theological controversies arise within the framework of orthodoxy. People become passionate about these issues, which is understandable because of the nature of the topics. However, it is important to remember that these discussions do not remain isolated to Christians, but inevitably find their way beyond the believing community of church people.

Public discussions between Christians should be done with some measure of discretion and exercise of Christian graces. If not, it can leave a sour taste in the mouths of the unbelieving community, and this can be a difficult recovery. In other words, friendly fire does not make the injury any less damaging. The world does not need to see Christians fighting against one another in a way that neutralizes the ability to share the gospel effectively. There are theological topics that need addressing within the Body of Christ – hence this book – but reasoning with people is better than shooting them. Jesus reminds us, "By this shall all men know that ye are my disciples, if ye have love one to another" (John 13:35).

Well-reasoned discussions can be beneficial to both believers and unbelievers. It ultimately provides a venue to promote the truth to believers who need more enlightenment on a subject and has apologetic value to unbelievers. Promoting bad theologies becomes a problem within the Christian community and can adversely affect efforts to promote the Gospel to those outside who are listening. Paul charged Timothy to instruct those within the church: "As I urged you when I went into Macedonia—remain in Ephesus that you may charge some that they teach no other doctrine, nor give heed to fables and endless genealogies, which cause disputes rather than godly edification which is in faith" (1 Tim. 1:3, 4, NKJV). Today, many unnecessary "disputes" make their way beyond the walls of the church. This can reflect very poorly on who God is and have a direct effect on evangelism. Paul reminds us, "And the servant of the Lord must not strive; but be gentle unto all men, apt to teach, patient, in meekness instructing those that oppose themselves; if God peradventure will give them repentance to the acknowledging of the truth" (2 Tim. 2:24-25).

Atheists, agnostics, skeptics, pantheists, polytheists, and everyone in-between make claims about the God of the Bible and aspects of theology. Unfortunately, Christians who broadcast thoughtless opinions on social media platforms without any discretion can actually bolster skeptical claims of unbelievers. This in turn can also have a destructive effect within the believing community among those with weak or new faith. We do not need Christians giving unbelievers ammunition to reject Jesus or fragile believers reasons to doubt the Gospel. This is not to say we should not have conversations about theology in the presence of unbelievers. Indeed, the evangelistic realm of apologetics requires this very thing. Moreover, it requires the discussion of some of the more difficult topics that many Christians prefer not to discuss.

It can be a daunting task to provide answers for some of the more challenging Bible difficulties, especially to skeptics. Once the door is open, people chime into these theological conversations and make claims – usually very biased opinions. Discussions can be helpful and productive, but education and growth in biblical knowledge should be the goal. If not, communication can quickly deteriorate into unproductive contentions that are theologically damaging in the end. James provides the best direction in relation to this: "My dearly loved brothers, understand this: everyone must be quick to hear, slow to speak, and slow to anger" James 1:19, HCSB). Following this instruction alone would prevent many problems that are the result of these types of conversations.

Many unbelievers speak and write as if they know God personally, as all kinds of claims and pontifications about Him tend to abound. Strangely, many who make claims have never picked up a Bible, which certainly muddies the water when discussing theological topics. Others who do not even believe God exists have some strong opinions as to why He does what He does or how He should do it. These scathing opinions are typically laced with very disrespectful and biting criticisms. There is an obvious problem with this kind of reasoning – it is entirely self-defeating and nonsensical. How can people accuse God of actions that are immoral or open to criticism if He does not even exist? Nonetheless, the point is that not everyone agrees with certain views of the Bible and especially the God revealed in it. This becomes a source of controversy from both within and without the community of Christians. I have found myself in these discussions countless times over the past forty years since I picked up a Bible and began to read it myself, and more so the past thirty-three years since I became a pastor. However, I have noticed that 90% of the disagreements would evaporate if those in the discussion had a more complete understanding of what the Bible actually taught, so that the points argued would be biblically accurate instead of what it is so many times – ignorantly fabricated claims. Thus, the reason for this book is to add some overall context to an area of discussion that appears to be greatly misunderstood.

The lack of familiarity with what the Bible teaches and a limited comprehension of foundational doctrines tend to spark the lion's share of these disagreements – at least as it relates to theological topics. However, no matter the belief of the participants in the discussion, it always reduces itself to who God is, what He is like, and how He acts. This focus really drives the topics and the direction of many discussions. The Bible is the means to that discussion most times, but the discussion itself is not limited to what the Scriptures teach. People too often have their own ideas about the God of the Bible and argue based on what they *believe* or *think*, not what the Scriptures actually say. If they are ignorant of the Scriptures, they base their views on how they would act if they were God. However, since they are not God, this quickly ends in a foolish philosophical discussion of those who imagine they are gods themselves. Indeed, this emphasizes the need for some basic Bible education before any actual conversation or debate ensues.

Others tend to argue based on what they have heard the Bible says about God – often mistakenly – and again, this becomes more of an educational issue. Then there are those who have read some of the Bible and picked up some sound bites from particular verses and argue their views on God based on these limited pieces of knowledge or a Scripture verse here or there. This can be the most challenging of the discussions because so many times these folks believe they understand the Bible based on some verses they read, when in fact they have misunderstood the Bible because they read it like a fortune cookie. In other words, they read a verse or story and isolate it from the rest of the Bible to come up with their own interpretation without any reference to context or overall theme of what the author is teaching. When this occurs, they have developed their own idea about the God of the Bible based on *how* they read it. This is why we should read the Bible carefully, thematically, and systematically.

The cults are notorious for misreading the Bible and coming to some crazy conclusions that are not even within the realm of what the Scriptures teach. Unfortunately, some Christians can be guilty of similar methods, which results in some very unorthodox views about both God and the Bible itself.

JEHOVAH'S WITNESSES – TORTURED TEXTS

As an example of how scripture may be misinterpreted and used to teach something entirely foreign to what it is actually saying, here is a case in point. Jehovah's Witnesses (JW) will not receive blood transfusions because of some verses in Acts chapter 15 (also Leviticus chapter 17) that talk about Gentiles keeping themselves from blood. This example is ideal because it commits so many theological, contextual, covenantal, and interpretative errors. There is no way to conclude that blood transfusions are against the Bible from Acts 15. It must be read into the text.

The discussion in Acts 15 is popularly known as the Jerusalem council. After expanding the Gospel to the Gentiles through their first missionary journey, Paul and Barnabas had come to Jerusalem to meet with church leaders. They discovered there were some believing Pharisees that said the Gentiles needed to obey the ritual of circumcision and obey Moses Law to be saved. Paul and Barnabas had a sharp contention with them that did not last long since the topic was so clearly not part of NT theology. From there the discussion came to James, the Lord's half-brother, who was the pastor of the church, along with the other apostles and leaders. They weighed the issue and concluded that circumcision and obedience to Moses Law was not a requirement to have Jesus as their Lord and Savior. However, what was at stake in this discussion was the fellowship of the Jewish and Gentile believers because of the confusion created by legalistic Jews.

The Gospel started at Jerusalem with only Jewish believers. The addition of Gentiles in the community of believers throughout Asia Minor was a challenge regarding their fellowship with the Jews. This is reflected in Paul's letter to the Galatians. Things are much different today because of the ethnic diversity in the church throughout the world, being mostly composed of Gentiles. Early in the development of the church, a Jew would not typically be comfortable having fellowship with a Gentile because of their food choices and casual connection with idol's temples (1 Cor. 8; 10:16-33). Gentile eating habits, food choices, and preparation practices were unclean in comparison to Jewish practices. Just because a Jew believed in Jesus and was part of the church did not mean they changed their diet or cultural living practices to blend comfortably with Gentiles. Thus, to keep the Gentiles from practices that would divide them from Jews, they wrote a letter to them saying:

> The apostles and elders and brethren send greeting unto the brethren which are of the Gentiles in Antioch and Syria and Cilicia: Forasmuch as we have heard, that certain which went out from us have troubled you with words, subverting your souls, saying, Ye must be circumcised, and keep the law: to whom we gave no such commandment: It seemed good unto us, being assembled with one accord, to send chosen men unto you with our beloved Barnabas and Paul, Men that have hazarded their lives for the name of our Lord Jesus Christ. We have sent therefore Judas and Silas, who shall also tell you the same things by mouth. For it seemed good to the Holy Ghost, and to us, to lay upon you no greater burden than these necessary things; That ye abstain from meats offered to idols, and from blood, and from things strangled, and from fornication: from which if ye keep yourselves, ye shall do well. Fare ye well. (Acts 15:23-29)

There is no way to pull blood transfusion out of this text. To interpret a modern medical practice into it by removing the word blood from its context makes the text teach something foreign to it. The Gentiles were to understand that they were not obligated to circumcision and following Moses Law, and they should modify their eating and living practices so the Jews would more comfortably fellowship with them. Over time, believing Jews would loosen up in their own practices, but initially, the leaders asked Gentiles to make accommodations, and as a result strengthen the Body of Christ. Meanwhile, God was moving the center of Christian missions and expansion to Antioch in Syria from Jerusalem. But the JWs are more interested in following Charles Taze Russell's interpretation of the Scriptures than the Scriptures themselves.

The other Scripture verses used by JWs to instruct against blood transfusions is from Lev. 17:10-16. This law was specifically for the nation of Israel under the Mosaic Covenant (which JWs are not part of, nor any other group) and its intent was to keep Jews from eating blood, not from particular medical practices. Not only are JWs mistaken in their application of these verses in Leviticus, but also use them as a foundation for the verses above mentioned in Acts 15. They combine them to make the point that God does not want His people to have any blood, and in their view, this means blood transfusions. Tragically, many JWs have lost their life by rejecting a needed and most likely live saving blood transfusion. If this were the only side of the story, it would be disturbing enough. However, the JW organization uses the deaths of these adults and children to market it as a sales pitch to motivate others to follow these "martyrs of the faith".

> In former times thousands of youths died for putting God first. They are still doing it, only today the drama is played out in hospitals and courtrooms, with blood transfusions the issue.[3]

This is a psychological practice practiced by many cults; they develop extreme practices that help members demonstrate their loyalty to the organization over any other allegiance. Moreover, they do this by making their allegiance to God and their organization one and the same. This is a prime example of reading the Bible, ignoring the context and making an application based on some words in the text alone and not the text itself.

To clarify, the issue at heart in Leviticus 17 is atonement.

The principle behind atonement is life for life. Since the wages of sin is death, symbolized by the shedding of blood, so "without the shedding of blood is no remission." Forgiveness does not come because the penalty of sin is *excused*, but because it is *transferred* to a sacrifice whose lifeblood is poured out. [4]

The verse that captures the essence of the atonement is, "For the life of the flesh is in the blood: and I have given it to you upon the altar to make an atonement for your souls: for it is the blood that maketh an atonement for the soul" (Lev. 17:11). This verse and surrounding verses are entirely unrelated to blood transfusions, which do not have even a remote application to the text. It has been well said, "if you torture a text long enough you can get it to say anything", but this is beyond torture. In this case, the text was executed and another one has replaced it. JWs have created an application by connecting the word "blood" in the text to their own belief on blood transfusions. Apart from the word "blood" in Lev. 17 there is nothing that remotely infers a connection to medical procedures used to save lives. The book of Leviticus teaches the sanctification of the nation of Israel through laws and sacrifices under the Mosaic Covenant. The issue for the Jews abstaining from blood is the sacredness of life given by God centered in the blood. It was supposed to be respected for sacrifice and not eaten as a common food choice as it was among the surrounding pagan nations.

Moreover, JWs teach that Jesus raised from the dead in a divine spirit body, which they define as something more akin to Casper the Friendly Ghost.[5] They completely misunderstand and misinterpret the atoning death of Christ and His resurrection.

The Bible says that Jesus "was put to death in the flesh but made alive [resurrected] in the spirit."—1 Peter 3:18; Acts

13:34; 1 Corinthians 15:45; 2 Corinthians 5:16. Jesus' own words showed that he would not be resurrected with his flesh-and-blood body. He said that he would give his "flesh in behalf of the life of the world," as a ransom for mankind. (John 6:51; Matthew 20:28) If he had taken back his flesh when he was resurrected, he would have canceled that ransom sacrifice. [6]

Actually, Jesus specifically addressed this issue on the road to Emmaus with Cleopas and his companion. They were so excited about the event that they walked with, talked with, and even ate with Jesus. They went to Jerusalem and found the eleven apostles to recount their experience:

And as they thus spake, Jesus himself stood in the midst of them, and saith unto them, Peace be unto you. But they were terrified and affrighted, and <u>supposed that they had seen a spirit</u>. And he said unto them, Why are ye troubled? and why do thoughts arise in your hearts? <u>Behold my hands and my feet, that it is I myself: handle me, and see; for a spirit hath not flesh and bones, as ye see me have</u>." (Luke 24:36-39) (underline added)

Jesus directly contradicts the JWs teaching on His resurrection body. Moreover, Jesus addressed this issue with the Jews that required a sign from Him, "Jesus answered and said unto them, Destroy this temple, and in three days I will raise it up" (John 2:19). Then John explains exactly what Jesus meant in his following comment, "But he spake of the temple of his body" (John 2:21). Not only do JWs misinterpret the significance of the bodily resurrection of Christ, they create a fabricated reason for Jesus not taking His body back in the resurrection. Jesus taught that when He gave His flesh for the life of the world (John 6:51), He referred to His substitutionary sacrifice, but did not mean He would not rise in His same body three days later. On the contrary, Jesus said "destroy this temple", and as John commented, He meant His own body. Had He not risen in the same body that died, He would not have conquered death, but avoided its consequences. However, the central theme of Peter's sermon on the day of Pentecost specifically addresses this point (Acts 2:24-32). The fact that Jesus' body did not "see corruption" (2:31), should be a clear indication that the body Jesus died in was raised again. If JWs were correct, Jesus would not be a substitutionary sacrifice for anyone, which the Bible makes abundantly clear He was (Isaiah 53; John 6:33, 51; Rom. 4:25; 2 Cor. 5:21; 1 Peter 3:18, 4:1).

Paul taught regarding resurrected bodies, they are "sown a natural body; it is raised a spiritual body. There is a natural body, and there is a spiritual body." (1 Cor. 15:44). Unfortunately, JWs (and some other heretical groups) read the word spiritual as immaterial instead of immortal because it does not fit their theology. Paul makes a contrast between the natural body on earth that dies (mortal) and the spiritual body that lives forever in heaven (immortal). The contrast is not between a material and immaterial body, but a mortal and immortal body. This is a key distinction that is theologically necessary; to lose it creates a heresy. What the JWs entirely miss is that if the same body that died did not come back to life, sin had not been conquered, because death is the result of sin and Jesus paid the price to defeat sin and death (Gen. 2:17; Rom. 5:12, 21, 6:23; 1 Cor. 15:26, 56). This is why the disciples on the third day believed that Jesus raised from the dead, because His body was not in the grave. Neither the Romans, Jews, nor disciples took the body. If the Romans took it, they would have produced it and the same with the Jews – it would have ended all controversy and Christianity would have been dead before it even began (no pun intended). The disciples obviously did not take the body, since many of them went to their death claiming they saw Jesus rise from the dead. As it has been very aptly said, "people will die for what they *believe* is true, but no one will die for what they *know* is a lie".

Therefore, not only do JWs fail to understand what Paul plainly states on the text on the resurrection, they also clearly do not understand the point of the resurrection itself. This is because they have theological errors that drive their application into further error – hence the concern expressed in this book. Paul further said that Jesus "shall change our vile body, that it may be fashioned like unto his glorious body" (Phil. 3:21). If believers are to have the same type of resurrected bodies as Jesus, our resurrected body will be physical, and material when glorified. Even Job understood this and was he lived chronologically closer to Adam, which means his book is technically the oldest in the Bible. Therefore, he understood the teaching Adam brought from the Garden of Eden related to this subject. He said, "And though after my skin worms destroy this body, yet in my flesh shall I see God" (Job 19:26). There is no way for Job to have worms destroy his body and then in that same body stand before God. Only if God brings back the same body in glorified form – which is answered by the resurrection of Christ.

MORMONS – MORE TORTURED TEXTS

Having given an example from the JWs, I would like to provide one more example from Mormon teaching, which will emphasize the point. Mormons teach that the name Joseph mentioned in Ezekiel 37 referring to the tribe of Joseph actually refers to the book of Mormon by Joseph Smith – yes, you read that correctly. First, let us look at the verses:

> The word of the Lord came again unto me, saying, Moreover, thou son of man, take thee one stick, and write upon it, For Judah, and for the children of Israel his companions: then take another stick, and write upon it, For Joseph, the stick of Ephraim and for all the house of Israel his companions: And join them one to another into one stick; and they shall become one in thine hand. And when the children of thy people shall speak unto thee, saying, Wilt thou not shew us what thou meanest by these? Say unto them, Thus saith the Lord God; Behold, I will take the stick of Joseph, which is in the hand of Ephraim, and the tribes of Israel his fellows, and will put them with him, even with the stick of Judah, and make them one stick, and they shall be one in mine hand. And the sticks whereon thou writest shall be in thine hand before their eyes. And say unto them, Thus saith the Lord God; Behold, I will take the children of Israel from among the heathen, whither they be gone, and will gather them on every side, and bring them into their own land: And I will make them one nation in the land upon the mountains of Israel; and one king shall be king to them all: and they shall be no more two nations, neither shall they be divided into two kingdoms any more at all. Neither shall they defile themselves any more with their idols, nor with

their detestable things, nor with any of their transgressions: but I will save them out of all their dwelling places, wherein they have sinned, and will cleanse them: so shall they be my people, and I will be their God. (Ez. 37:15-23)

The clear and obvious teaching of the passage is that God will bring the divided kingdom of Israel (10 northern tribes often called Ephraim since it was the dominant tribe) and Judah (2 southern tribes of Judah and Benjamin referred to as Judah) together in the future. Ephraim and Manasseh were the sons of Joseph. These boys took the place of Joseph in the prophetic blessing by Jacob of the tribe's inheritance in Genesis 48. Thus, speaking of Joseph refers to the northern kingdom because his son Ephraim being the dominant tribe was given preeminence as the firstborn by Jacob – though not born first (Gen. 48:13-20; ref. Jer. 31:9). Contrary to this, Mormons claim:

The prophecy of the two sticks has reference to the power of the Book of Mormon (stick of Joseph) and the Bible (stick of Judah) working together to gather the House of Israel. ... For all of these messages the Lord provided a specific sign: the bringing together of the Book of Mormon and the Bible into "one stick, and they shall be one in mine hand." (Ezekiel 37:19) [7]

How anyone can connect the Book of Mormon to the stick of Joseph in Ezekiel is beyond imagination. However, this is a great example of the severe problems of an allegorical method of Bible interpretation. This method allows any change of the text from what it actually teaches to anything you want it to teach. This Mormon example is a case in point. The Book of Mormon has no connection to the Bible or any OT prophecy whatsoever. Any imagined association with the name Joseph (referring to the tribe of Israel) in Ezekiel 37 and Joseph Smith and the Book of Mormon are the result of a wild imagination at best, at worst calculated deception. These types of Bible interpretations lead to false teachings and deceptive living, or as Paul says, "deceiving spirits and doctrines of demons" (1 Tim. 4:1). Pastor Chuck

Smith of Calvary Chapel Costa Mesa said years ago,

> It is almost laughable it is so ridiculous and idiotic for Joseph Smith to claim that his name is in the Bible and he was prophesied in the book of Ezekiel for the stick of Joseph was to be the Book of Mormon that God would give to him and joined together with the Bible would be the continuation of the Bible and God's Word for man in these last days. That is so completely far-fetched that a person would have to lay his brains on the shelf to accept any kind of an interpretation of the Scripture that way. I mean, God told us what He was talking about. God said, "These two sticks are the two nations and when they come, join them together because there will only be one nation when they come back into the land." Now I would have to say that anybody that can interpret that into the Scripture I would not want to be following their Biblical expositions or trust myself to their teaching. When you can gather that kind of stuff out of this Scripture, you can make red read green. I mean, that's as far-fetched as anything could ever be. And if you're a Mormon here tonight, it's just straight from the shoulder. Look at it and question in your mind the things that you're being taught. For you know that they have taught you that this stick with Joseph on it was actually a prophecy concerning Joseph Smith. But if you can find that in this verse or in this passage or in its context, then you can find snow in hell. I mean, it's just not there.[8]

The point of the example is that isolated texts when allegorized can say anything our imaginations can stir up. No matter what subject we are reading about in the Bible, we must first understand it within the context of the book in which it is written. After that, we can cross-reference the subject to other books of the Bible – once we understand the context of the cross references. If we fail to put this effort into our Bible study, we will inevitably have conclusions that are misleading or false. Lazy study habits and false ideas about divine revelation

19

– mainly because of not knowing the Bible in the first place – have resulted in many false and aberrant views within the Christian church over the past 2000 years. However, with all the available information on the Bible and good online teachers at our fingertips, it is hard to imagine such crazy teachings and beliefs continue to circulate. However, maybe this is actually part of the problem. There is such a plethora of study material on the internet, it is only natural that people will gravitate toward teachings or teachers they are predisposed to prior to any Bible study at all. This ensures they will reinforce false or aberrant dispositions since they are finding what they like instead of finding out what the Bible says first. For example, I may be attracted to a certain Bible teacher because of style or presentation ability, but this is unrelated to the truth of the Bible. Some of the best Bible teachers I have ever read or heard were not great orators or masters of verbal presentation, many would be considered quite boring. But this is part of the problem we face in this culture. We tend to accept something is true because of *how* it is presented and not because of *what* is presented. In other words, our culture tends to determine the truth based on the appeal of the presentation instead of its content. Unfortunately, isolated Bible texts mixed with skilled communicators ignorant of solid Bible doctrine are a bad combination for those wanting to learn what the Bible teaches – especially about God.

The Bible is clear on what it teaches if we understand the context around the topic. Thus, it behooves us to read the Bible, come to some basic understanding of it, and then choose carefully the books and teachers we allow to speak into our lives. Years ago in the 1990's we would get a caravan of people from our church to drive to a Christian book warehouse that ran fantastic sales on returns, incomplete commentary sets, damaged books, and other books they were trying to clean out of their inventory. I used to harp on everyone to buy by author and not title. We often had new Christians among us, so they tended to grab books by title – which claimed to be the answer to everything possible a Christian would want. Therefore, we would put lists of authors together to narrow the focus for the group. I loved those trips and got some great deals as I built up my library. I once called Pastor Chuck Smith the week before we were going to make one of these treks to a warehouse sale. As I asked him questions on Bible commentaries listed as sale items in the warehouse catalog, he gave some great advice and saved me a lot of money. One commentary I thought was going to be a great set because of the price, he warned me would waste my time because as he said, "you have to read a great deal to get very little out of it". I always appreciated the time and wisdom he was willing to share. He went to be with the Lord almost 10 years ago, but I still miss his wisdom and example. Other pastors have provided me with similar advice on books and commentaries over the years that has been invaluable. But I only take advice from pastors that I respect for their Bible knowledge and experience. I have had recommendations from other pastors that I know that I would never even consider because of their viewpoints. These latter pastors are not heretics or even aberrant in their teachings, but they lack a sound method of teaching that makes me uncomfortable because of how they treat a text. Therefore, I do not have respect for their method. They tend to gravitate to others that practice this same loose expositional style, and I am not interested in going down that road. There are too many good, sound, careful expositors to settle for questionable ones. I would not take the advice of a questionable carpenter, plumber or electrician to build a house. So why would I take the advice or follow the directions of a questionable Bible expositor – no matter how well meaning they are? Building a spiritual life is far more important than building a house. One has eternal meaning and consequences; the other is only temporary at best. Yet more people seem to be concerned about the temporary aspects of life rather than the eternal aspects. Paul gives us the direction on this matter so we do not have to guess. He said, "While we look not at the things which are seen, but at the things which are not seen: for the things which are seen are temporal; but the things which are not seen are eternal" (2 Cor. 4:18).

GETTING FOCUSED

The topic of both Law and Grace is prevalent throughout the Bible. This book analyzes this challenging subject as it relates to the God who made these covenants of both the Mosaic Law and Gospel of Grace. Regarding the topic of God Himself, it should be evident to anyone who reads the Bible that He is the only God in existence – considering the first verse of the Bible. There are statements in Scripture that touch on certain topics, but do not necessarily exhaust them. Yet, concerning the wonderful, graceful, merciful, longsuffering, loving God that it reveals, there is more than ample information on this major topic. At times God speaks through His messengers to reveal information about His nature and character, and other times they speak about Him from their own observation and relationship with Him. Yet all the statements of Scripture are *God-breathed* words of Divine revelation; this includes statements of writers in narrations or other statements quoted that are false statements. What I am not saying is that the Bible has errors; what I am saying is that God made sure even false statements made were accurately represented and what He wanted recorded; it is the context that will bear out whether or not a statement itself is true or false. There are many lies spoken in the Scriptures by Satan and others in the narrative sections. That does not mean the Bible is teaching lies, but it demonstrates what lies are and how they deceive. In other words, they are there for our learning and benefit. As Paul warned the Corinthians, "Lest Satan should get an advantage of us: for we are not ignorant of his devices" (2 Cor. 2:11). Many of those devices of the devil are revealed in Scripture.

Moreover, all the authors of Scripture are in harmony regarding everything they say about God. There are some 40 authors over a period of 1500 years, and *most* authors did not know one another since they lived in different times. This is more the case in the OT, but the NT the authors did in fact know one another for the most part. This advantage with NT writings provided a cohesive strength and security that enabled ease for verification, accuracy and consistency. This close attention was also paid to copies of original manuscripts when they were circulated to churches. Yet all these men – OT and NT—had no contradictions of what they revealed about God, His nature, character, or His acts. This would be an impossible task to accomplish among a small group of students from the same classroom with the same teacher on the same subject – as a high school Bible teacher I know this to be empirically true – even though you press to have each student maintain consistency in their understanding and beliefs. Yet we see these men writing over the centuries with a thematic harmony that would stagger and stymie any statistician – and has! Remember, this is only considering their writings on the subject of God, never mind the precision on predictive prophecy and its fulfillment, which would never be possible apart from divine revelation. This is why Peter says, "no prophecy of the scripture is of any private interpretation" (2 Peter 1:20). If Bible prophecies originated from man, they would have failed in their predictions since they would have been at best a wild guess. We see this in self-proclaimed prophets and seers over the centuries and even in books written by those who think they know when Jesus will return, though each one has failed miserably. How could it be any other way? Jesus Himself said He did not know in His human nature the time of His own return (Matt. 24:36), so how can these prophets of their own imagination (Jer. 23:16-22) know more than Jesus? Further, these harmonizing themes and multiple prophecies written with the integrity and accuracy as they have been over the centuries, could not have been maintained if it were just human invention. Contradiction, confusion, and miscalculation would have ensued at many points over time, especially in the realm of prophecy. This is because man sees from a glitch of time within its overall duration, but God sees the entire duration of time from outside of it. Moreover, having created the time-space continuum, God is not part of the material universe He created, but is separate from it and has no difficulty communicating what will happen futuristically to those are bound by time's limitations. This is indeed a single attribute of the God of the Bible and the first one mentioned in this book. This should give us pause when we begin to utter claims about the God of the Bible. He is beyond what we can even imagine in so many ways, and I conclude this based on what the Bible teaches about God. In other words, I am extrapolating a conclusion based on what the Scripture does say about God to realize I cannot totally comprehend Him (I would be concerned if I could). As Solomon said in his dedication of the temple he built, "But will God in very deed dwell with men on the earth? behold, heaven and the heaven of heavens cannot contain thee; how much less this house which I have built!" (2 Chron. 6:18). Now that is wisdom!

The Bible is very specific about who God is. From the first verse, His existence is without question and assumed without qualification. For why would anyone who authored a writing find the need to defend his or her existence? Certainly, any writing itself bears witness to the author's existence. I am assuming I do not have to defend my existence; if I did not exist, you would not be reading this book. Very simply this is what we have in the Bible. We have the words of God as communicated through the pens of human authors. Over the centuries human authors recorded God's words as He disclosed more and more detail of who He is to the people He communicated. We call this progressive revelation. This revelation of God provides the knowledge of His nature, characteristics, acts, and desires for His crowning masterpiece of creation – *man*!

Having said all that, we are faced with discovering the God of covenants and His relation to them. Covenants change, but God does not. Requirements change with each covenant, but again, God does not. God in His essential being is the same and does not change (Malachi 3:6a; Heb. 13:8), He is immutable because He *is* God. This is a characteristic of God's nature, which is why He is always faithful (Psalm 89:3; Jer. 33:20, 21; Lam. 3:23; Malachi 3:6b; 2 Tim. 2:13); it is we who lack faithfulness. As we learn the covenants of the Bible with their criteria, we discover not only what it means to be in a covenant relationship with God, but also how faith is applied so we can have a successful relationship with the God of Covenants.

COVENANTS

If there is one subject that continues to confound Christians and non-Christians, it is the difference between the Mosaic Law and the Gospel of Grace. Among Christians, differing theologies have resulted from varied understandings of these two covenants, strangely, even by well-educated theologians. We read them, we listen to them, we trust them, yet many of them differ on various aspects of their theology. It can be a daunting task to follow well-respected Bible teachers and theologians that we hope accurately present the Bible. Does this leave any hope for the average Bible reader? I think it does if we pay attention to some very simple common sense principles of Bible study and do not allow preconceived notions to cloud our perspectives. We all must be aware that we can have wrong views, and that we can have mistaken interpretations of the Bible. This is what keeps us open to learn and recognize that no fallen human has all the answers. Humility is an important aspect of Bible study – God knows all, but we do not. Thus, it is our goal to learn.

The Bible's clear teachings many times become obscured by what we have been *told* it says, or by what we *think* it should say, without actually reading it. This is a common error and it can result in confusion and or disillusionment, if our expectation finds no confirmation when we read it. Our study of God's Word should not result in error or disillusionment, but rather discovery of truth and clarity. There should be no place where we are more confident than sitting down with the Scriptures and allowing them to teach us, to minister to us, and to strengthen us in our relationship with the Lord Jesus. One of the particular places that preconceived ideas can throw us off is in our attempt to understand the Mosaic Law. We can have a tendency to read the teachings of the New Testament (NT) back into the Old Testament (OT), blending them improperly and ending up confused. It is easy at times to get lost in the weeds. At these times, it is important to take a step back and look at the big picture first, then move into more detail. What I attempt to do in this book is distinguish between the historical, theological, dispensational, and covenantal aspects that the Bible lays out for us. At first this may appear as a complicated and difficult endeavor. However, a methodical presentation can both simplify and clarify to resolve any unnecessary confusion – this is my goal. Once understood, the covenants become very clear, distinguishable, and recognizable.

The reason why we should not minimize this attempt to understand what the Bible teaches about covenants is to ensure a proper understanding of God's desired relationship with Christians today. Additionally, it is vital that Christians grasp issues surrounding the biblical covenants to aid those investigating the claims of Jesus Christ. Imagine the confusion that would result from a Christian trying to live under the Mosaic Law. It would not only diminish the experience of a Christian's new life in Christ, but it would put them in a place where they were attempting sanctification through a covenant to which the church has no relationship. Therefore, there is an inextricable connection of this subject and the life application of Christians. In other words, we must understand this subject for our own personal development and a proper understanding of the God we worship. This is for our own benefit and the benefit of those wanting to know about Jesus Christ. I have watched firsthand the result of Christians attempting to live under the Law of Moses – it's not pretty! Moreover, when Christians begin to delve into the Law, they are uncomfortable making the journey alone and want to drag other unsuspecting believers along for the ride. In the end, it creates a disruption in the lives of many people personally and can severely distort the Gospel they share publicly. Within a church fellowship, this disruption can at times cause unrecoverable damage.

For those attempting to make sense of God and the Bible, this could not be a more significant issue. There is a great amount of misinformation and criticism about the Bible. Unfortunately, much of the criticism is directly against God. Misunderstanding biblical covenants can result in drawing perspective lines right back to the God of covenants resulting in His mischaracterization, both of His nature and purposes. How are we to make any real sense of God, the covenants in the Bible, and the laws and commands it gives among such a variance of views? The answer is through a logical analysis of the Bible's revelation of God, the Abrahamic Covenant, the Mosaic Law, and the New Covenant in Christ's blood. This is important for a Christian's spiritual growth, and it provides them with both an evangelistic and apologetic foundation. If Christians are confused as to who God is, how are they ever going to answer critics or those who simply have questions during a gospel presentation? Indeed, it is incumbent upon us who preach the Gospel and engage in any aspect of Christian apologetics – even just answering our neighbor's questions – to know our God and be able to present Him accurately to others.

In this book, the similarities and differences of the Mosaic Law and Gospel of Grace will be identified and explained – with the hopeful result of coming to know the God of covenants as revealed in the Bible. I will focus mostly on the two covenants of Law and Grace because this is where the main confusion lies for most people. However, to put them into perspective, contrasts and comparisons of these covenants require proper understanding. Additionally, God instituted two covenants with the nation of Israel in the OT, not just one. First was the Abrahamic Covenant where God promised Abraham descendants, land for them to dwell in, and a redemptive blessing that would reach all the nations of the world. This redemptive blessing is developed progressively with the result of the Savior of the world coming through Abraham's descendants. The second is the covenant of the Law given by Moses at Mt. Sinai. This covenant came hundreds of years after the promise and had a different purpose and design than the Abrahamic Covenant. However, each covenant needs to be understood within their respected intention to grasp the workings of God through the nation of Israel.

Further, there are more than two covenants in the Bible as we will observe, but specifically our focus is how the Old Covenant of the Law (Heb. 8:7, 8) contrasts with the New Covenant of the Gospel of Grace. The best way to bring this out is to allow the Bible to say what it wants without imposing a predetermined perspective. I am a stickler for expositional Bible study, which means exegesis[9] is critical and eisegesis[10] is to be avoided at all costs. We will only focus on the practice of exegesis as we move through this book.

The question is when and how are these covenants fulfilled in Israel? For Israel, the short answer is when they recognize Jesus of Nazareth as their promised and prophesied Messiah (Jer. 29:12-14; Hosea 5:15; Zach. 12:10; Matt. 23:38, 39). The promises of the land, descendants, and redemptive blessing to the world will find ultimate fulfillment in the Messianic Kingdom for the nation of Israel. Only when they are in the land and their promised Messiah sits on the throne of David (Isaiah 9:6, 7), will all that they were promised be realized. However, this needs to be developed.

Moreover, since the Law was given only to Israel, how does that relate to the Gospel of Grace and the church (the Body of Christ)? Should Christians add the Law to the Gospel, or keep it separate? In other words, can the Law be part of the Gospel? - If so, how? Alternatively, does each covenant have a different purpose altogether? These questions find their answers in the Scriptures; the Bible provides clear answers so we do not have to venture a guess. Again, this also needs to be developed.

LAYING A FOUNDATION

How do we lay a proper foundation? It is necessary to begin with God, since all else is derived from Him and what He does. God is the author of Scripture and when we know His nature and character, it puts the revelation of the Bible in perspective. Having said that, we can only know what God reveals of His nature and character by studying the Bible. This is unique in one sense because God used multiple authors to communicate these details about Him. Certainly, you will gain some knowledge of how I personally think and reason from reading this book. When reading Scripture, we learn similar things about God and how He thinks and reasons. We cannot fully understand His thoughts (Isaiah 55:8, 9), but we can know what He wants us to know about His thought process and viewpoints. We discover His perspective on various topics such as morality, evil, sin, man, Satan, redemption, justice, love, hate, life, death, and a host of other subjects. It is through the pens of human authors that He ensures us that the revelation of Himself is true and comprehendible. Using human authors ensures a comprehensible and at times personal perspective, since it has to be understandable to the author first. Human authors can provide their own view (humanly speaking), yet record exactly what the Holy Spirit wanted to be communicated to the audience they targeted. It is a masterful work really, the very thing that unbelievers so often attack as a weakness in the claim of divine inspiration is its very strength – human instruments. The fact that God used the pen of human authors with all their various and diverse intellectual capacities, emotional natures, personality traits, and educational levels provides us with a full range of perspective to the God communicating through them. God used people just like us who were uniquely borne along by the Holy Spirit (2 Peter 1:21) to produce (see 2 Tim. 1:16, *inspiration* is literally the word "God-breathed") an inerrant, infallible, authoritative revelation of what He wants us to know about Him, us, life, death, sin, redemption, and many other subjects.

Therefore, we must start with God Himself. He is the most important subject of the Bible since all creation is the product of His handiwork. We find this necessary sequence of God defined first in systematic theologies. A systematic theology is a single book or series that takes topical information out of each book of the Bible and systematizes it for condensed subject study. In other words, verses in each book of the Bible on a given subject are combined together with explanation in a chapter of a systematic theology. In a typical systematic theology, it would begin with first a Bibliology (the doctrine of the Bible), then proceed to Theology Proper (the doctrine about God), then Anthropology (the doctrine of man), Hamartiology (the doctrine of sin), Angelology (the doctrine of angels), Christology (the doctrine of Christ), Soteriology (the doctrine of salvation), Pneumatology (the doctrine of the Holy Spirit), Ecclesiology (the doctrine of the church), and finally Eschatology (the doctrine of last things). There is an interesting historical and logical parallel in this development. Historically, the NT canon of Scripture was established in the 1st century, which is the foundation for the doctrinal development of the NT. Each doctrine is then built upon the knowledge of the previous one. This is true of both the historical and logical aspects of doctrine. Historically, each century required a response of the church against error and each response built on the previous knowledge and understanding of the doctrines laid down. With each new challenge to the church in history, Scripture was analyzed for a response to the challenge of that age. Logically, a systematic theology is established the same way – doctrines building upon the previous one laid down. Thus, there is a foundation and developed structure built. The following list is an example of how the logical development matched the historical development of doctrines. It becomes clear that each doctrine needs to be understood before the next one is logically developed.

Bibliology – the doctrine of the Bible

Apologetics would accompany this endeavor to give evidence of God in the 1st and 2nd century

Theology Proper – the doctrine of God

The Trinity (unity and plurality of God)

Anthropology – the doctrine of man

Man has a free will and is responsible to God

Hamartiology – the doctrine of sin

The effects of sin upon man and creation

Angelology – the doctrine of Angels

The roles of angelic beings that are loyal to God and those in rebellion to God

Christology – the doctrine of the Person of Christ

The Second Person of the Trinity, equal to God the Father

Soteriology – the doctrine of the Work of Christ

Christ's work is substitutionary for man

Pneumatology – the doctrine of the Holy Spirit

The Third Person of the Trinity, equal to God the Father and Son

Ecclesiology – the doctrine of the church

The church is not the nation of Israel, but a separate group ordained by God

Eschatology – the doctrine of last things

God has a plan and purpose for both Israel and the church that are different and conclusive

The necessity of the order is evident. The canon of the Bible must be established before any doctrine can be studied and received true. The doctrine of God must be understood in order to understand the trinity and God's relationship to man. The doctrine of man would need to be known for the doctrine of sin to have a context. The doctrine of the Person of Christ would have to be known to comprehend what His work was in the redemption of man. The doctrine of the church – separate from Israel – must be understood to establish how these groups would relate to the doctrine of last things. It becomes easy to understand why the order makes sense for proper understanding.

In 1897, James Orr delivered The Elliot lectures at Western theological seminary in Allegheny, PA. The book published from those lectures is entitled The Progress of Dogma. Orr makes this remark:

> Has it ever struck you, then... what a singular parallel there is between the historical course of dogma, on the one hand, and the scientific order of the text-books on systematic theology on the other? The history of dogma, as you speedily discover, is simply the system of theology spread out through the centuries ... and this not only as regards its general subject-matter, but even as respects the definite succession of its parts. The temporal and the logical order correspond.[11]

This observation by Orr is very insightful; I am unaware of anyone else who observed this interesting connection. The parallel of history and the logical necessity of the doctrinal layout of systematic theologies is surely not a coincidence. Though the analysis of a systematic theology is beyond the scope of this book, it is important to see that there is a logical development of one doctrine to the next. For example, we cannot truly understand what the Bible teaches about man until we understand what the Bible says about man's Creator – God! This is why God will be our starting point.

THE GOD OF THE BIBLE

God the Creator

The Bible begins with a simple sentence that provides a wealth of information about God. The first verse of the Bible says, "In the beginning, God created the heavens and the earth" (Gen. 1:1). Simple enough, but we must examine what it says explicitly (directly) and also observe what it informs us of implicitly (indirectly).

"In the beginning" tells us that time started – there can be no beginning or starting point apart from time. Therefore, the word "beginning" relates directly to the start of time. If the "heavens and earth", or the universe itself, is eternal there would be no beginning and thus no time. In other words, we would never have arrived at today if the universe were eternal. Speaking of the existence of time in relation to eternity – which has no time – creates a conundrum. We understand time because we are part of it and our very existence connects to it. However, the thought of eternity, though conceptually understandable to our minds, is not truly comprehensible to us because we are not able to experience it while we are *in* time. God knows all about it, He created it! In order for Him to create time, it would be necessary for Him to be beyond time and not contingent[12] with it. In other words, He is not a product of time and did not need time for His own existence. Thus, the Bible reveals that the eternal God created time, as it says God "in the beginning created..." This also tells us there is more than time that started "in the beginning" along with time.

[In Genesis 1:1] the Hebrew puts the emphasis on the word "beginning." Other ancient religions did not see a real beginning or a God great enough to create the entire universe out of nothing. If they discussed creation, it was always creation out of something else, such as earth, air, fire, and water, slime, or a giant's body. Ancient people's view of history was cyclical, with everything repeating itself forever, without any ultimate goal or eternal hope.

But the Bible shows a linear view of history, with a real beginning and a future consummation and an end to the history of this world that will bring glory to God and blessing to all believers as well as judgment to those who reject God's grace.[13]

Building upon this verse we note that God "created the heavens and the earth" at the "beginning". The Hebrew word used for "created" is *bara*, it is a word used *only* in connection with God and it means "to create from nothing."

"Created" (Heb.) is always used of God's divine creative activity, never of human activity. The word is also used of what He creates to bring judgment. (See Num. 16:30, where "if the Lord make a new thing" is literally, "if the Lord [Yahweh] creates a creation.") Thus the use of bara' draws attention to the fact that the creation in the beginning was totally new. There never had been a creation or a created universe before.[14]

There were no preexisting materials when God created the universe, even the space the universe exists in, "the heavens"; He created "in the beginning". God created the earth at that time, so we understand that time, space, and matter all started when God created the universe from nothing. How did He do it? The Psalmist tells us, "By the word of the LORD were the heavens made; and all the host of them by the breath of his mouth. ... For he spake, and it was done; he commanded, and it stood fast" (Psalm 33:6, 9). God spoke everything into existence from nothing (ex nihilo[15])! This aligns with Genesis chapter 1 and the repeated phrase, "And God said" (Gen. 1:3, 6, 9, 11, 14, 20, 24, 26). Only God has the power and capability to accomplish this.

This is an amazing description of God's capability. For God to make all that exists, it means He is beyond all that exists and is not part of what He created, nor does He require it for His own existence (i.e. non-contingent). Therefore, God is infinite and everything that He made is necessary finite – since it had a beginning and God did not. In other words, God cannot be what He created and since He created time, space and matter, it necessitates that He is beyond time, space, and matter. As Dr. Norman Geisler has said many times in presentations and publications, "everything that has a beginning requires a beginner." Thus, the Infinite, Eternal Beginner is God! "All things were made by him; and without him was not any thing made that was made" (John 1:3). He is the original uncaused cause, since everything else operates according to the law of causality, which law He created when He created the universe. We can know these things about God logically before we even pick up a Bible because what we know about reality and the nature of the universe allows us to work backward from effect (the universe) to cause (God). We use this same method when attempting to discover logically the effect of anything caused (law of causality). Just because we may not be able to see the cause of certain things does not mean they do not exist. Jesus gave the example in John 3:8 to Nicodemus when He said, "the wind blows where it wishes, and you hear the sound of it, but cannot tell where it comes from and where it goes" (NKJV). We know the wind by its effects. The same with God, we know Him by His effects – creation – but not directly. The effects of creation (Psalm 19; Rom. 1:19-21) are evidence of His existence, but to know Him personally requires us to place our faith in Jesus Christ.

God's Nature

Genesis 1:1 provides us with more information about God that can be reasoned by what we know to be true logically. For example, since God is separate from His creation, just as a carpenter is separate from the table he makes (he is not part of the table), we conclude that God is eternal and infinite compared to the created universe that had a beginning and therefore finite. However, beyond the logical necessity of our reasoning about God's existence from what we can know, the Bible reveals the God that is the creator of the universe in His nature and character. What general revelation of the creation provides us through logic and reason, special revelation (Bible) adds to and gives the specifics for a detailed understanding of reality. The ultimate source of all reality is God.

"God is Spirit," Jesus said to the Samaritan woman at the well in John 4:24, "God is Spirit, and those who worship Him must worship in spirit and truth." God does not have a physical body; the essence of His Being is spirit. Since God created all that exists, He is beyond His creation and exists independently from it, which logically concludes that He is Self-Existing (does not need the universe to maintain His own existence). Since God is beyond the physical universe, He necessarily is spaceless (beyond the physical space that makes up the universe), timeless (i.e. eternal), immaterial (not part the material universe), all-powerful (omnipotent, or has the capability to create and maintain the universe), purposeful (because He created intentionally, i.e. He has a will), intelligent (the created universe and life has evidence of intricate design and complexity), and relational or personal (created man to offer him fellowship with Himself). All these attributes that we can reason from the effects we can observe and discover through reason align perfectly with what the Bible teaches about God.

Or, as Dr. Frank Turek says,

> If you are used to conceiving of God as a big angel or an old man in the sky, then drop the word *God* for a minute and simply think of the God of the Bible as the Source and Sustainer of all things. The Source and Sustainer of all things is:
>
> **Self-existing**: not caused by another; the foundation of all being
>
> **Infinite**: unlimited; the completely maximized or actualized Being

Simple: undivided in being; is not made up of parts

Immaterial: spirit; not made of matter

Spaceless: transcends space

Timeless: transcends time; eternal; had no beginning and will have no end

Omnipotent: all powerful; can do whatever is logically possible

Omnipresent: everywhere present

Omniscient: all knowing; knows all actual and possible states of affairs

Immutable: changeless; the anchor and standard by which everything else is measured

Holy: set apart; morally perfect; is perfectly just and loving

Personal: has mind, emotion, and will; makes choices.

These attributes and others are coexistent, infinite, and unified in the Source and Sustainer. If you want to get a sense of what the Source and Sustainer is like, meditate on these attributes while removing all limits from your mind. That's what the Bible means by "God."[16]

The Bible clarifies these attributes of God. Much of it we learn just from the explicit examination and necessary implications of Genesis 1:1. Indeed, the Bible assumes God's existence no differently than we would assume there is an author to any book. Moses penned the first five books of the Bible and when he wrote Genesis, God had to communicate to him how the universe began since no one but God was there. In Job 38:4, God asked Job, "Where were you when I laid the foundations of the earth? Tell Me, if you have understanding" (NKJV). Not only was Job not there, no one was there but God.

This is important because it reveals that the God of the Bible is characteristically different from what various world religions believe about their gods or their concepts of god from various pagan sources. The following section provides a list of various beliefs regarding some form of god as maintained by all the major world religions. The various world religions fit the categories of the following seven major worldviews. Understanding these worldviews enable us to examine the sharp contrast between the gods of the world and the God of the Bible. Many people who claim that all roads lead to God or to heaven, are ignorant of or simply ignore the vast contrasts between the views held by the major world religions. The claim is nonsense and violates the law of non-contradiction (two things cannot be opposite and true at the same time in the same sense) and is a logical absurdity. Let us examine the views.

The Seven Major Worldviews

There are numerous belief systems around the world, from atheism to theism, and everything in-between. It is not possible to list the particular nuance of every single view, however they can all be condensed to seven major worldviews because of how the beliefs correlate to the major theme regarding the god they worship. A worldview is how a person interprets what they believe about reality. Worldviews are important because they are the context from which each person acts in accordance with that view. In other words, we apply in life what we believe to be true and real. A person's view of reality affects their everyday life. Understanding this is not simply an academic exercise, it hits home more than most people realize – that is reality.

A Barna Poll done in 2017 among practicing Christians in America yielded some disturbing results. The poll revealed that only 17% of Christians had a biblical worldview.[17] As disturbing as the low percentage results showed, it was what 83% of those polled did believe that was shocking. Essentially, the vast majority of Christians are making daily decisions based on secular and not biblical reasoning. Tragically, much of the beliefs held not only lacked any biblical perspective, but also held to philosophies that are antagonistic to Christianity (talk about an enemy in the camp). If that is not shocking enough, a more recent Barna poll from May of 2021[18] said, "only 6% of Americans are holding on to and believing a biblical worldview."[19] What is interesting in this poll is that 51% of all adults polled believe they have a Biblical Worldview, but only 6% actually did based on the answers given.[20] Is it any wonder why so many American churches are in the deteriorated spiritual condition we see them in today? If Christians *do not* know what the Bible teaches, they *will not* know the God they worship. "Perhaps we might say that many believers have a faulty worldview because they have a faulty *Word* view."[21] This has resulted in a mix of non-biblical beliefs in Christian thinking that is confusing to many and dishonoring to God. It is heartbreaking that many of God's people do not know Him as the Bible reveals Him, or more specifically, how He wants His people to know Him. However, it becomes even more tragic because in today's Christian world of information and Bible study resources, this is completely unnecessary.

For example, some Christian leaders teach that God in the OT is the same as the god of Islam[22] – this is not Christian theology; it is blasphemy! It reveals ignorance of the Bible to the highest degree and a disrespect shown to God by not only comparing Him to a pagan deity, but also making the claim He *is* the same pagan deity as Allah. God asked a question to Israel referring to the pagan gods they were worshiping in conjunction with their worship of Him, "To whom will you liken Me, and make Me equal And compare Me, that we should be alike?" Isaiah 46:5, NKJV). The question is rhetorical; there is no comparison – which is the point! God has no equal (Isaiah 40:18, 25) and defies comparison. The comparison alone is wicked, but to claim that God *is* an actual pagan god or that the pagan god *is* Jehovah is a blasphemy of highest degree. Therefore, to prevent any confusion among Christians and help them understand what major non-biblical worldviews consist of, the following descriptions of each worldview will help.

Pantheism = *pan* means *all* and *theism* means *god*. Thus, pantheism means *all-is-god*. Pantheists (such as in Hinduism, the New Age Movement, Christian Science and other eastern religions) maintain that god is all and in all. This is not logically possible since matter had a beginning, and if a god had a beginning, he could not be God. God could not be part of what He has made, since He would have to exist before anything else. If God is not separate from His creation, that would mean He somehow made Himself and that is not a logical possibility. Since everyone and everything in this view is god, then god is learning, changing, and obviously limited in multiple areas. These definitions alone would disqualify pantheism from a possibility of representing ultimate reality – God.

It is an interesting fact that people with this kind of worldview think that life is an illusion (i.e. is not reality). They believe that the life beyond this world moves them into a higher level of spiritual being (which they believe is *real* existence) as they are morphed into the larger experience of this pantheistic god. However, the question for them is, how do they know that this life is an illusion? A person does not know they are dreaming until they wake up, and they could not know they are hallucinating – or in an illusion until they are out of it. Since they are all stuck in their perceived illusion, they cannot know what they believe to be true is true. Moreover, the logical absurdity of pantheism should be self-evident, since the view is riddled with self-contradictions.

People that follow the fallacy of these pagan concepts of god do not think through their beliefs with the reasoning process God gave them. They either ignore or disregard the evidence God has provided them in nature and obvious reality. As Paul the apostle said in Romans 1:19b-21, "…what may be known of God is manifest in them, for God has shown it to them. For since the creation of the world His invisible attributes are clearly seen, being understood by the things that are made, even His eternal power and Godhead, so that they are without excuse, because, although they knew God, they did not glorify Him as God, nor were thankful, but became futile in their thoughts, and their foolish hearts were darkened" (NKJV). In addition, David said in Psalm 19:1-4a, "The heavens declare the glory of God; and the firmament sheweth his handywork. Day unto day uttereth speech, and night unto night sheweth knowledge. There is no speech nor language, where their voice is not heard. Their line is gone out through all the earth, and their words to the end of the world." The Bible is consistent in what it teaches us about creation. It reveals both God and creation, but the creation is not God. Just think about it, if you have to be told that you are god or somehow you come to that conclusion on your own, all evidence should tell you that you are not god or any aspect of god. If that is how you are thinking, you really need to rethink things – or better – let the Bible do your thinking for you.

Panentheism = *pan* means *all, en* means *in* and *theism* means *god*. Thus, panentheism means *all-in-god*. Panentheism is similar to pantheism with the exception that the panentheistic god has two parts (called poles - one connected with the world, and the other beyond the world). The idea is that god is learning and developing along with the world, which makes this god limited, since there is a learning process and a development that is ongoing. Similar to pantheism, this is a logical inconsistency and unable to be actual reality as we understand the world and universe around us. The same logical absurdity that applies to pantheism applies here.

Polytheism = *poly* means *many* and *theism* means *god*. Thus, polytheism is *many-gods*. This is another pagan worldview. Many religious groups believe in multiple gods. A few examples are Hinduism (which are also pantheistic), Scientology (much of their beliefs are based in Hinduism), and Mormonism.[23] Though Hinduism views everything *is* god, at the same time they also believe that over 300 million gods exist. This combination of two contrasting beliefs only adds to the existing logical conflicts within Hinduism. Like Mormonism (aka, The

Church of Jesus Christ of Latter Day Saints), Hindus believe that men can become gods. This poses a logical and philosophical problem (not to mention a biblical contradiction) because unless we have a God that is beyond all else that exists, everything else is part of the creation itself.

To reason that there are multiple gods, there would have to be something different in each god to distinguish them from each other. Therefore, in order for multiple gods to exist, there must be a difference between each god's will, characteristics, perspectives, knowledge, understanding, etc. If there is any difference between gods-which means one god has something the other god lacks – each one is necessarily limited or finite in some way. Any concept of a god that is finite embodies no perfection and thus is not a god at all. This applies to Hinduism, the New Age Movement (based on Hinduism), Scientology, and Mormonism, since they all believe humans *become* gods (Hollywood has nothing on these scripts). Their views are more like a science fiction movie or Greek mythology with their many gods of very human and limited characteristics. One would have to ask which god – if any – in their list of gods is the ultimate, infinite, and perfect God. Some of these groups see a supreme God above all the other gods, but this view includes a main God creating other gods, which is contrary to what the biblical God does. As God said through the prophet Isaiah to Israel, "Ye are my witnesses, saith the LORD, and my servant whom I have chosen: that ye may know and believe me, and understand that I am he: before me there was no God formed, neither shall there be after me" (Isaiah 43:10, underline added). Since there can only be one Being that is infinite, eternal, and embodies all perfection, without equal, polytheism is not logically or biblically possible. This infinite Being by definition would be the only God that exists. This is the God revealed in the Scriptures.

Finite-godism = is just as the term says – the belief that god is *finite*, meaning, he is not all powerful, all knowing, etc. Thus, this god is not perfect or infinite as the God revealed in the

Bible. A book written by Harold Kushner (a Conservative rabbi) in 1981 called *When Bad Things Happen to Good People* was a #1 best seller read by millions. What was Kushner's conclusion as to why there is evil in the world? He concluded that God is finite and unable to prevent all the evil. In other words, since he believed God was loving and good, it would be (according to Kushner's conclusions) contrary to God to continue to allow evil in the world. However, since there is the existence of evil in the world, he saw the limitation on God's part as unable to prevent it. Unfortunately, Kushner did not think things through. For, had he believed what the Bible says about God, he would have realized that God *is* all powerful, all knowing, infinitely loving and good. God's *apparent* lack of intervention in the world to stop all evil is not because of His lack of capability, but His magnificent ability to provide man his exercise of free will, while still maintaining His purposes and plan on track. God will rid the world of evil, just not at this point. The existence of hell is part of the plan of God in relation to evil. Those who will not come to Jesus Christ while God allows man's rebellion against Him, will one day be quarantined in hell for eternity. Thus, what Kushner was misinterpreting was God's patience with sinning humanity, in attempts to provide opportunity for repentance.

God chose not to annihilate sin but rather to defeat it. He chose to defeat it progressively instead of instantaneously. There are many possible reasons for this, but two prominent ones involve (1) the freedom God gave to humans and (2) God's desire to produce a more godlike (godly) product in the process. Defeating evil without destroying freedom, while at the same time perfecting free creatures – this appears to be at the heart of God's plan.[24]

...evil will yet be defeated (in the future). The fact that God is all-good and all-powerful guarantees this conclusion. Further, since God is all-wise, we can be sure that he has chosen the best means to that end (defeating evil).

Consequently, while this present world is not the best of all possible worlds, nonetheless, it must be the best means to the best world. Thus, a world in which evil is permitted is the best kind of world to permit as a means to produce the best kind of world – one that has no evil in it. that world is our promised destiny. [25]

There are times that God acts to intervene in the affairs of man, but He also has the sovereign capability to control all of human destiny and work it out according to the prophetic timetable He established and recorded in the Bible. If God prevented or eliminated all evil in the world, He would have to eliminate man – who is evil by nature. Kushner had a secular view of good and evil, not a biblical one. He also failed to realize the contradiction in his view. People need to think through the issue at hand. Many want God to remove all evil, yet people do not want God to interfere with their lives as they do things that are out of harmony with His will, or things the Bible defines as evil. Indeed, you cannot have it both ways. If God decided to stop all evil in the world, he may start with those very people who are questioning His ability to do so. In that case, I am sure they would continue their protest, complaining God was not allowing enough time for evil to have its expression.

In the end, the Bible makes it clear that God's infinite sovereign ability enables Him to remove all evil; it is a matter of timing, not capability. He is going to do it on His timetable revealed in the Bible and not on man's arbitrary schedule. If God was finite in any way, He could not have created the universe or have the ability to maintain it since He would lack the necessary characteristics. If God lacked perfection, He could not be the Initial Uncaused Cause of the whole universe. Any mention of the God of the Bible and finite abilities is a logical contradiction. The Bible reveals a God possessing all perfection and is infinite in every way. In other words, He is the ground of all perfection and all reality is grounded in His nature.

Atheism = *a* means *not* and *theism* means *god*. The negative *a* in front of *theism* is *atheism*, meaning *no-god*. Much of our culture is atheistic today, so it is important to understand their position. I recently posted a video series about atheism. I quoted the atheist.org website and responded to their claims against the Bible. I did the series because I realized that their claims against the Bible, accusing it of multiple contradictions and falsehoods, deserved proper answers. I received many responses from atheists that were very emotional and angry – though the video series was mainly for folks in our church to educate them. I was surprised at the lack of logic used in their criticisms of the Bible. There were so many strawman arguments I was a little nervous that someone was going to light a match nearby. After reading their claims, it is no wonder much of the atheism promoted today *appears* to counter the claims of the Bible. They are far more dogmatic than their arguments can maintain, but people do not realize that. Most of the arguments against the Bible were verses stripped from its context and isolated to say something completely different from what the text taught. In reality, atheism is defeated out of the gate because it has no justification for any of its claims – even its own ability to reason or use logic to defend its position. Logic, reason, thinking, etc. are all non-material aspects we possess as humans. Though many atheists (by definition materialists, i.e. only the material universe exists) will attempt to say that consciousness and thinking are illusions or tricks of the mind played upon us, they fail in their claim. Similar to the Hindu criticism, how do atheists know they are deceived or tricked by some illusion of their mind? Especially if their mind – the very thing used to examine the evidence – is the very thing tricking them? Moreover, these non-material aspects of our being (logic, morality, reasoning, thinking, consciousness, etc.) are "believed" to have come from purely material causes in nature and evolution. However, non-material aspects as mentioned cannot come from purely random material processes in nature, not to mention the philosophical problem. As C. S. Lewis noted,

Supposing there was no intelligence behind the universe, no

creative mind. In that case, nobody designed my brain for the purpose of thinking. It is merely that when the atoms inside my skull happen, for physical or chemical reasons, to arrange themselves in a certain way, this gives me, as a by-product, the sensation I call thought. But, if so, how can I trust my own thinking to be true? It's like upsetting a milk jug and hoping that the way it splashes itself will give you a map of London. But if I can't trust my own thinking, of course I can't trust the arguments leading to Atheism, and therefore have no reason to be an Atheist, or anything else. Unless I believe in God, I cannot believe in thought: so I can never use thought to disbelieve in God.[26]

The belief that Darwinian evolution can produce whatever evolutionary scientists need to make their case is a "natural selection of the gaps" fallacy as I call it. It is claiming that the process of Darwinian evolution by natural selection has the miraculous ability to develop anything the atheist needs. Evidence is not necessary in this case, only claims.

Atheism is a self-contradictory system of belief that is not scientific, logical, or reasonable – contrary to their aggressive marketing claims. A statement like this would raise the blood pressure of an atheist because the one thing they believe they use is logic, reason, and science. Most atheists claim they are atheists because of their trust in science. However, the word science simply means knowledge. The word is used as if it is the ultimate reality that all should bow to. However, scientists search for causes of the effects they examine and their worldviews can drastically alter their conclusions. Science (knowledge) changes as new things are learned and technology aids in this search for causes. Therefore, as scientists pursue their proofs for the truth of life's existence, etc., they are really on a search for causes (or a cause) that creates the effects observed in the world today. The entire scientific method is based on observable evidence of cause and effect; the experiment/hypothesis is tested repeatedly to eliminate any possible variant that could change the effect. This is how scientists learned that gravity will have the same effect everywhere in the world, regardless of belief system, because after all the testing and evidence, gravity still has the same effect on all matter within our earth's atmosphere and the planetary relationship in our solar system and beyond.

The problem with atheism is that it cannot account for life or the universe itself. If God does not exist, there is no explanation for why the universe exists in the first place. The universe cannot be eternal because it had a beginning; many atheistic scientists have come to this conclusion, which is why they promote the "big bang" theory.[27] But no matter what theory atheists promote, whether big bang or something else, the universe had a beginning and this required someone to "begin it." Remember, if nothing exists, it cannot make itself. That would be the most illogical, unscientific and unreasonable belief a person could maintain.

Many atheistic scientists today try sleight of hand to make their case, but it still fails to provide true scientific evidence. In a book called, *A Universe from Nothing: Why There Is Something Rather than Nothing*, the author Laurence Krauss attempts to actually make that case. Krauss argues in his book that the universe came from a form of quantum existence, which is something instead of nothing-even quantum physics is something. Sadly, it is another best seller that has promoted a theoretical solution to the reason the universe is here without God creating it, yet, Krauss docs start with something. Only God can start with nothing and make everything – including Lawrence Krauss's quantum vacuum.

If this type of information interests you, I would recommend the book by Frank Turek called, *Stealing from God: Why Atheists Need God to Make Their Case*.[28] Turek does a great job showing how atheists need to use the biblical worldview to argue their case for atheism – another colossal self-contradiction by atheists for sure – though unfortunately, they do not seem to recognize their flaw. Turek does a masterful job at revealing this conflict within the atheistic belief system.

Deism = this is the same as theism (discussed next), except with no miraculous intervention in the world by God. In theism, God makes the world and universe and intervenes in it through miraculous intervention at the times of His choosing. In Deism, God created the world and universe and is separate from it as in theism, but does not interact with it after creation, but just lets it go. There is no logical basis for this position, and there is no evidence to support this view. If God did not interact with the world we live in, how would anyone know what He does or does not do? It assumes knowledge of God that the deist cannot have based on their claim, again another self-defeating position. The deist would have to know God by His interaction with the world for him to determine that God does not interact with it, which is not possible in their view. Therefore, deism does not answer any questions logically, nor does it work with how the Bible describes God. Deism only seems to satisfy those who understand that a theistic God is required for the universe to exist, but do not appear to want a relationship with Him. Apparently, they are comfortable with the belief that God is not interested in them, so they can ignore Him.

None of these belief systems previously mentioned maintain a view of God that is in line with the Bible. Only Judaism and Christianity understand the perfection in God required for God to *be* God.

Theism = is the belief in one God that is separate from creation as the Bible teaches. This is the view that makes logical sense and is most reasonable to conclude, even before you open a Bible. It is a simple thought process; since man and the universe exists with the ability to logically reason what we can know – as we have done – then it is evident that God exists otherwise there would be no time, space, and matter (the universe), nor the existence of man and the other variations of life on earth. Having said that, the only God that would not violate simple reason and the logic of the law of non-contradiction is the theistic God. This self-evident law (non-contradiction[29]) along with other self-evident laws (excluded middle[30] and identity[31]) make it clear that God cannot both exist and not exist at the same time in the same sense. Theism correlates to the biblical God.

These seven major worldviews are simplified and summarized in the following chart[32]:

VIEW	THEISM (God made all)	PANTHEISM (God is all)	ATHEISM (No God at all)
ASSOCIATED RELIGIONS	Judaism, Christianity, Islam	Zen Buddhism, Hinduism, Taoism, Christian Science	Buddhism, Humanism, Confucianism

Theism Today

There are only three theistic religious groups in the world today. By a simple elimination of Pantheism and Atheism, the only logical, reasonable and scientifically supported belief system would be Theism. Panentheism, finite-godism, and polytheism cannot even be seriously considered as possibilities, as the above information illustrates. Pantheism is self-contradictory at numerous points as we have seen above and Atheism suffers from the same – and an even worse deficiency – there is no one to bring everything into existence (either Someone made everything or no one made everything – which is more reasonable?).

Therefore, only the religions of Judaism, Christianity, or Islam could fall under the theistic belief (as the previous chart shows). The God who created the universe has the capability to use miracles to recognize His communication with man to ensure a confirmed method – His fingerprints if you will. In short, the miraculous credentials needed to substantiate God's working today would only point to Christianity. Judaism had this in the past during the time of Moses and the other OT prophets as they spoke the word of God and recorded it book by book. The Bible contains about 300 miracles and we find three major concentrations of them throughout the OT and NT. Moses (representing the Law Covenant) has the first concentration and miracles authenticate him as God's confirmed representative. Elijah and Elisha (representing the prophets) have the second concentration. The third is Jesus and the apostles (representing the New Covenant). This does not mean there were no miracles apart from these representatives of God; these are where we find the three greatest concentrations of them. In the past Judaism was substantiated by the miracles God worked by Moses and the other prophets. The messengers of God (prophets) verified God was speaking through them by the miracles that accompanied their messages and ministries. But Israel anticipated a New Covenant that would replace the Law of Moses (Jer. 31:31-33). This New Covenant in Christ's blood (Matt. 26:28) enabled the birth of the church that began on the day of Pentecost (Acts 2). As the Holy Spirit came upon those in the upper room (Acts 2:1-4), the apostles and others would perform miracles to validate that God was speaking through them and the work of God had moved from the Law of Moses to the Gospel of the Grace of God. The point is that God used miracles to validate through whom He spoke. Signs substantiated the sermons, miracles the messages. Thus, the eternal, infinite God reached into the finite limits of time to make His identifying marks so man would know which God is the true God.

Not just any miracle will validate a messenger of God. Miracles are not magic tricks or performance shows. A miracle is a supernatural intervention in the natural world. A miracle is an event that would not (or could not) have been produced by purely natural forces. Miracles are not magic, they are not providence, and they are not satanic signs or purely physiological effects. They are always to confirm truth and spark faith, "God also bearing witness both with signs and wonders, with various miracles, and gifts of the Holy Spirit, according to His own will" (Heb. 2:4, NKJV). Thus, they are signs to connect God's involvement with the truth of His word. They are not done for the amusement of people or deceptive means. Jesus would not do any miracles for Herod (Luke 23:8, 9), since Herod wanted a show and that is not the reason for miracles. Jesus would not even answer Herod, as Constable observes,

> He clarified here that his interest in Jesus was only as a miracle worker. He had no interest in talking with Him about spiritual matters. It was evidently about His miracles that Herod questioned Jesus. Jesus did not respond because Herod had rejected the implication of His miracles, namely, that Jesus had come from God with a message for humankind. Herod had made his feelings toward prophets clear by decapitating John the Baptist. Jesus had nothing to say to someone such as this.[33]

The miracles we see in the Bible are God's intervening into human activity to validate His spokesmen, fulfill prophecy, advance His purposes, and reveal His character. There was nothing selfish, theatrical, or unproductive in God's miracles.

Today, only Christianity has the clear marks and fingerprints of God's miraculous working power in both the NT revelation and His accompanying signs to substantiate His working. Thus, miracles accompanied the NT revelation and confirmed the OT by miracles and predictive prophecy, a feature enjoyed by no other religious writings, only the Bible has such remarkable credentials. The fulfilled prophecy in the NT from the OT becomes the connecting thread of the entire Bible. The OT anticipates the NT prophetically, and then the NT confirms the OT by its fulfillment. The harmonization of the entire Bible is not only remarkable, but provides the credentials through miracles to follow God's spokesmen.

Islam never fit the criteria of a religion that provided any substantiating evidence they were from God. Therefore, Judaism (only in the past) and Islam (never) will not fit the criteria necessary today for the miraculous accompaniment of evidence of the living God's involvement of man for verifiable credentials. Regarding Islam, there is an unsurmountable problem because there is no verification of the Quran as a writing from God. There is no miraculous verification and there is no predictive prophecy to test it – i.e. no evidence! The only reason Muslims believe the Quran is a book from God is because Mohammad said it was – that is a claim, but it is not evidence. The fact that Mohammad was illiterate does not bode well for any evidence regarding the Quran, though they claim it is miraculous that an illiterate person could birth the Quran. As a matter of fact, the Quran coming some 600 years after the writing of the NT with no verifiable credentials – while the NT provides all the proof necessary that it is the final word from God to man (see Hebrews 1:1-3) – is a further indictment against the Quran. Muslims, along with Mormons, claim the Bible was corrupted, with the conclusion of each group offering their own writings in place of the Bible. Certainly a very convenient attempt to eliminate the competition by slander without evidence. Furthermore, which group should we believe (Muslims or Mormons)? They both claim to have holy books that arose hundreds of years after the Bible to supersede the Bible, yet there is no evidence to support either of their claims. They are simply claims, and neither vociferousness nor enthusiasm can substitute for evidence.

Moreover, there is a problem with the Quran which is called either the Islamic dilemma or Quranic dilemma. The Quran states in Surahs (chapters of the Quran) 3:3-4; 10:94; 18:27; that Christians should believe and obey the Torah and Gospel because Allah has said it is true and to follow it, for there is no corruption in it. This becomes an unresolvable issue for Muslims since the Bible was complete over 600 years before the Quran and contradicts the Quran. Moreover, Muslim's claim that the Bible is corrupt since it does contradict the Quran. But the Quran says the Bible is not corrupt, which creates further unresolvable problems since the Quran says that Christian's should make judgments based on the truth of the Bible as given by Allah (Surah 5:47). Here is the dilemma that cannot be resolved. If the Bible is inspired, authoritative, and preserved without corruption as the Quran claims, *Islam is false* because the Bible contradicts the Quran that came after it along with the other teachings of Islam. If the Bible is false and corrupted as Muslims claim, *Islam is false* because the Quran affirms the inspiration, authority, and preservation of the Bible, which makes the Quran false. You cannot have it both ways.

So that we understand the difference between the God of the Bible and the god of the Quran, the comparison chart below will help. Christians must understand that there is a marked difference and there is no way to make the God of the Bible and the god of the Quran the same, or somehow equal. The Bible teaches that God is a Trinity. This is vital to a proper understanding of the true God, which is why we will examine it in some detail (next).

GOD OF THE BIBLE	GOD OF THE QURAN
Trinity (3 Persons in 1 God)	No Trinity (1 Personality)
Wants a personal relationship with man	Does not want a personal relationship with man
Has a Son	Has NO son
Sent His Son to redeem man	Sent no one to redeem man
Man is saved by God's grace through faith	Man is saved by good works evaluated at death

Performed miracles to confirm His prophets	Performed NO miracles to confirm his prophets
Speaks about His love for man continually	Doesn't speak of his love for man continually
God wants to be called Father	Allah doesn't want to be called father
Gives predictions for evidence of His word	Doesn't give predictions for evidence of his word

It is possible to go on and on about the differences between the God of the Bible and the god of the Quran. However, the only comparison is that they are both called God, but the similarity ends there. They are different in nature, character, workings, speaking, relating, eternal plans, etc. This issue needs to be clear because there are many Christians that are ignorant of what the Bible teaches about God and end up comparing the two *as if* they are the same God. This is not only an ignorant mistake, but also a tragic error that dishonors the God of the Bible in attempts to compare Him to a pagan god. The God of the Bible has no equal and is not comparable. God said through Isaiah the prophet, "To whom then will you liken Me, Or to whom shall I be equal? says the Holy One" (Isaiah 40:25), and "To whom will you liken Me, and make Me equal And compare Me, that we should be alike?" (Isaiah 46:5). Both rhetorical questions that require the answer of *no one*! If Christian's compromise the truth in attempts to win Muslims to a saving knowledge of Jesus Christ, it will never happen by changing the very message that Muslims need to believe to save them. If they are looking to the god of Islam to be their deliverer by a different name (calling Allah Jehovah or Jesus), nothing but confusion and frustration will be the result.[34] Jeroboam, the first king of Israel in the divided kingdom put golden calves in the cities of Dan and Bethel and called them Jehovah (1 Kings 12:28) – that too ended in disaster and a history of idolatry and ultimately judgment

(2 Kings 18:10-12). Altering the truth to bring someone to the truth is nothing but the end justifies the means, which the Bible condemns. Telling lies never brings people to truth and deceiving people is not a confidence builder.

Concerning these differences between Jehovah and Allah, there is no way to harmonize them. Especially when it comes to the Person of Jesus Christ the Son of God, both the Bible and Quran could not be at more of an impasse. The Quran describes Jesus Christ as a prophet that was taken to heaven without death and a substitute was killed in his place on the cross (Surah 4:157). Islam further teaches that Jesus was not the Son of God because god has no son. Finally, it states that Jesus did not redeem the world through His sacrifice on the cross. Therefore, the Quran and Islam deny the central teachings of both the OT and NT. Moreover, since you cannot have two claims that are opposite and true at the same time in the same sense – violating the law of non-contradiction – only one claim (Bible or Quran) can be true. In this regard, the Bible holds all the cards. Therefore, if the Bible is true (which it is), then every other book that teaches anything contrary to it is false. Jesus prayed to the Father, "Sanctify them through thy truth: thy word is truth" (John 17:17). That word "truth" in the prayer was not a verb, but a noun. God's Word (Bible) is the absolute truth and reality! All else is to be measured against it.

God: A Trinity

The word *trinity* was first used in the second century by an early church father named Tertullian. He used the Latin form, *trinitas,* to describe the nature of God (the Father, Son, and Holy Spirit all being co-equal, co-eternal, etc.). If we go back to Genesis 1:1, we find that the Hebrew word for God, "Elohim", is actually a masculine plural noun. What we should observe is the plural use of the word "God" connects in the verse with the singular verb "created". This is unusual for grammar, but tells us something more than appears on the surface.

The Jews believed in what theologians call the "majestic plural" in reference to a single God having a plural word describing Him. They say the use of a plural noun describes the excellence of God in His awe and majesty beyond that of any pagan idea of God. Since the Bible reveals that only one God exists, using a plural noun does not create a multiple of gods in this case, but it is the most expressive way to demonstrate the power and majesty of the one true God! It is almost like using capital letters in English to describe God and using small letters for a false or pagan god; though not exactly the same thing, the comparative concept is similar. Furthermore, as we move forward in the study of Scripture, we find the expression of the plurality in the Godhead throughout the OT in this majestic plural. Again, the plural use is used a number of times in the OT and developed in doctrine of the trinity in the NT.

It will be made clear as we move through the verses listed below that the plurality in the Hebrew word *Elohim* was put there by the biblical writers because the Holy Spirit moved them to do so (2 Peter 1:21). What the Jews believed in the OT about the word Elohim representing the one God is true, but what is also true is the allowance of multiple Persons in the Godhead by the use of the term Elohim. This OT use of Elohim anticipates the triune revelation of God in the NT where the trinity is later developed. The NT explains the OT in many aspects, while the OT contains prophecies that anticipate the NT.

There is only one God revealed in the Bible, and that God created all things. Introducing a second god of any kind immediately makes that god a false god by definition! Many cults do not realize this and try to make Jesus Christ a second or a lesser God than God the Father.[35] But no matter what kind of word gymnastics or grammatical trickery is used, it will never agree with what the Bible teaches regarding the one and only Being identified as God. One thing to remember when reading the following verses, the word LORD (all caps) is the name for God, which we know as Jehovah or Yahweh. This is explained more fully below under the section "Names for God".

There Is Only One God

Genesis 1:2: "And the earth was without form, and void; and darkness was upon the face of the deep. And the Spirit of God moved upon the face of the waters." (The Holy Spirit was involved in creation and God is the creator.)

Deuteronomy 4:35, 39: "Unto thee it was shown, that thou mightest know that the LORD He is God; there is none else beside him. ... Know therefore this day, and consider it in thine heart, that the LORD He is God in heaven above, and upon the earth beneath: there is none else."

Deuteronomy 6:4: "Hear, O Israel: The LORD our God is one LORD." (The Hebrew word "one" speaks of compound unity and though God is "one LORD [Jehovah]", the unity is within the "one LORD".)

Deuteronomy 32:39: "See now that I, even I, am he, and there is no god with me: I kill, and I make alive; I wound, and I heal: neither is there any that can deliver out of my hand." (Revealing the absolute sovereignty of God and the fact that it is unchallenged, since there is no other god.)

2 Samuel 7:22: "Wherefore thou art great, O LORD God; for there is none like thee, neither is there any God beside thee, according to all that we have heard with our ears."

1 Chronicles 17:20: "O LORD, there is none like thee, neither is there any God beside thee, according to all that we have heard with our ears."

Nehemiah 9:6: "Thou, even thou, art LORD alone; thou has made heaven, the heaven of heavens, with all their host, the earth, and all things that are therein, the seas, and all that is therein, and thou preservest them all; and the host of heaven worshippeth the." (One God and He is the one that created all things)

Isaiah 43:10-11: "Ye are my witnesses, saith the LORD, and my servant whom I have chosen: that ye may know and believe me, and understand that I am He: before Me there was no God formed, neither shall there be after me. I, even I, am the LORD; and beside me there is no savior."

Isaiah 44:6, 8: "Thus saith the LORD the King of Israel, and his redeemer the LORD of hosts; I am the first, and I am the last; and beside me there is no God. Fear ye not, neither be afraid; have not I told thee from that time, and have declared it? ye are even my witnesses. Is there a God beside me? yea, there is no God; I know not any."

Isaiah 45:21: "Tell ye, and bring them near; yea, let them take counsel together: who hath declared this from ancient time: who hath told it from that time? have not I the LORD? and there is no God else beside me; a just God and a Savior; there is none beside me."

Isaiah 46:9: "For I am God, and there is none else; I am God, and there is none like Me."

Hosea 13:4: "Yet I am the LORD thy God from the land of Egypt, and thou shalt know no god but me; for there is no savior beside me."

Joel 2:27: "And ye shall know that I am in the midst of Israel, and that I am the LORD your God, and none else: and my people shall never be ashamed."

Malachi 2:10: "Have we not all one father? hath not one God created us?"

Mark 12:32: "And the scribe said unto him, Well, Master, thou hast said the truth: for there is one God; and there is none other but he."

John 17:3: "And this is life eternal, that they might know thee the only true God, and Jesus Christ, whom thou hast sent."

Romans 3:30: "Seeing it is one God, which shall justify the circumcision by faith, and uncircumcision through faith."

1 Corinthians 8:5-6: "For though there be that are called gods, whether in heaven or in earth, (as there be gods many, and lords many,) But to us there is but one God, the Father, of whom are all things, and we in him; and one Lord Jesus Christ, by whom are all things, and we by Him." (The context is that of Christians who know the truth that there is only one God, though people in paganism believe in and call many things god.)

Ephesians 4:6: "One God and Father of all, who is above all, and through all, and in you all."

1 Timothy 1:17: "Now unto the King eternal, immortal, invisible, the only wise God, be honour and glory for ever and ever."

1 Timothy 2:5: "For there is one God, and one mediator between God and men, the man Christ Jesus"

James 2:19: "Thou believest that there is one God; thou doest well: the devils also believe, and tremble."

Since there is only one God, we should understand that the Bible also allows for plurality in the Godhead as mentioned. This plurality of Persons in the one God is implied in the OT, but is not explained and expanded upon until the NT. It took the first coming of Jesus Christ to reveal the Father to us, and in this we also discover that Jesus is both God and man. The NT explains the partial revelation of God in the OT by literally putting flesh on Him and allowing Him to live out the prophecies regarding the Messiah. Many prophecies demonstrated that the anticipated that the Messiah would be God:

OT MESSIANIC ANTICIPATION	NT MESSIANIC FULFILLMENT
Genesis 1:1-2	John 1:3; Acts 14:15; Col. 1:16
Exodus 3:14	John 8:58
Psalm 2:7	Heb. 1:5
Psalm 110:1	Mark 12:35-37

| Isaiah 7:14 | Matt. 1:23 |
| Daniel 7:13 | John 5:27 |

OT Verses Reveal Plurality in the Godhead

OT verses that allow for the plurality in the Godhead (see underlined parts for emphasis):

Genesis 1:26: "And God said, Let us make man in our image, after our likeness." (Only man is made in God's image, not angelic beings – Gen. 1:27, 9:6 and 2 Corinthians 4:4, this verse cannot be speaking of anyone other than God using the "us" and "our." Some following verses have the same feature.)

Genesis 3:22: "And the LORD God said, Behold, the man is become as one of us, to know good and evil:"

Genesis 11:7: [God said] "Go to, let us go down, and there confound their language, that they may not understand one another's speech."

Deuteronomy 6:4: "Hear, O Israel: The LORD our God is one LORD." (The Hebrew word for "one" speaks of compound unity.)

Isaiah 6:3: "And one cried unto another, and said, Holy, holy, holy, is the Lord of hosts: the whole earth is full of his glory." (The Seraphim praise God and there are three repetitions of the words "holy" spoken in praise for the Father, Son, and Holy Spirit.)

Isaiah 6:8: "Also I heard the voice of the Lord, saying, Whom shall I send, and who will go for us?"

Isaiah 44:6: "Thus saith the LORD the King of Israel, and his redeemer the LORD of hosts; I am the first, and I am the last; and beside me there is no God." (Speaking of the Father and the Son.)

Proverbs 30:4: "Who hath ascended up into heaven, or descended? who hath gathered the wind in his fists? who hath bound the waters in a garment? who hath established all the ends of the earth? <u>what is his name, and what is his son's name, if thou canst tell</u>?"

Daniel 7:13: "I saw in the night visions, and, behold, <u>one like the Son of man came with the clouds of heaven</u>, and came to the Ancient of days, and they brought him near before him." (Speaking here of the Father and the Son. Jesus claimed the title "Son of man" in John 5:27, this described who He was and why He claimed all authority to be the final Judge of man, see Daniel 7:14.)

NT Verses That Allow For the Plurality in the Godhead

Matthew 28:19: "Go ye therefore, and teach all nations, baptizing them in <u>the name of</u> the Father, and of the Son, and of the Holy Ghost." (The word "name" is singular, but combines the Father, Son, and Holy Spirit in the one name.)

John 10:30: "I <u>and my Father</u> are one." (This is NOT saying that the Father *IS* the Son, but that they are one in nature and Being. It is better understood as "I and the Father, *We* are One".)

NT Verses That Show Jesus is God

John 1:1: "In the beginning was the Word, and the Word was with God, and <u>the Word was God</u>."

John 1:3: "<u>All things were made by him</u>; and without him was not any thing made that was made." (God is the Creator; Jesus created all things.)

John 1:18: "No man hath seen God at any time; the only begotten Son, which is in the bosom of the Father, he hath <u>declared him</u>." (The Greek word "declared" means to reveal, no one but the Son could have seen the Father, therefore no one but the Son could reveal Him.)

John 3:13: "And no man hath ascended up to heaven, but

he that came down from heaven, even the Son of man <u>which is in heaven</u>." (Being Deity the Son is in heaven, as man Jesus the Messiah is on earth.)

John 5:18: "Therefore the Jews sought the more to kill him, because He not only had broken the Sabbath, but said also that God was His Father, <u>making himself equal with God</u>." (The Jews understood that Jesus claimed that God was His own unique Father, which made Him equal with God. The Son would have to be of the same nature and essence as the Father to make such a claim and the Jews understood perfectly what He meant, which is why they tried to stone Him because they believed such a claim was blasphemy. Jesus could have removed the entire controversy by declaring to them that they misunderstood him and He was not claiming equality with God. However, on the contrary Jesus in the rest of John chapter 5 makes it clear that He is equal with God and explains what that means by way of testimony, witnesses, and ultimately the writings of Moses.)

John 5:23: "That all men should honour the Son, <u>even as they honour the Father</u>." (No one but God the Son can have equal honor with God the Father.)

John 5:25: "Verily, verily, I say unto you, the hour is coming, and now is, when <u>the dead shall hear the voice of the Son of God</u>: and they that hear shall live." (The Son of God has authority over death; it is subject to His word – He can speak life into existence, an attribute of God alone.)

John 6:33: "For the bread of God is he which cometh down from heaven, and <u>giveth life</u> unto the world." (These are not claims a sinful man can make, only the God-man.)

John 8:58: "Jesus said unto them, Verily, verily, I say unto you, Before Abraham was, <u>I am</u>." ("I Am" is the description of Himself that God revealed to Moses in Exodus 3:14.)

John 10:30: "I and my Father are one." (This is NOT saying that the Father IS the Son, but that they are one in nature and Being. It is better understood as "I and the Father, We are One.")

John 20::27: "And Thomas answered and said unto him, My Lord and <u>my God</u>." (Thomas – a monotheistic Jew – called Jesus God.)

Matthew 28:17: "And when they saw Him, <u>they worshipped Him</u>." (Jesus' disciples worshiped Him and Jesus received that worship. However only God is to be worshiped; Matthew 4:10.)

Colossians 1:15-17: "Who is the image of the invisible God, the firstborn of every creature: For <u>by him were all things created</u>, that are in heaven, and that are in earth, visible and invisible, whether they be thrones, or dominions, or principalities, or powers: all things were created by him, and for him. And he is before all things, and by him all things consist." (Jesus is the Creator of all things and is "before all things," which means He has the preeminence and priority over all He created. He is also holding together [consist] Creation. Only God the Creator can hold together all atomic particles.)

Colossians 2:9: "<u>For in him dwelleth all the fulness of the Godhead bodily</u>." (This can be said only of God in human flesh.)

1 Timothy 3:16: "And without controversy great is the mystery of godliness: <u>God was manifest in the flesh</u>." (Paul again calls Jesus God.)

Titus 2:13: "Looking for that blessed hope, and the glorious appearing of <u>the great God and our Saviour</u> Jesus Christ." (Again Paul calls Jesus God.)

Revelation 5:11-14: "And I beheld, and I heard the voice of many angels round about the throne and the beasts and the elders: and the number of them was ten thousand times ten thousand, and thousands of thousands; Saying with a loud voice, Worthy is the Lamb that was slain to receive power, and riches, and wisdom, and strength, and honour, and glory, and blessing. And every creature which is in heaven, and on the earth, and under the earth, and such as are in the sea, and all that are in them, heard I saying, Blessing, and honour, and glory, and power, be unto him that sitteth upon the throne, and unto the Lamb for ever and ever. And the four beasts said, Amen. And the four and twenty elders fell down and <u>worshipped him</u> that liveth for ever and ever." (John saw in heaven that all worship the Lamb of God as God; again, only God receives worship – especially in heaven!)

Verses That Show the Holy Spirit is God

Genesis 1:2: "And the earth was without form, and void; and darkness was upon the face of the deep. And <u>the Spirit of God moved</u> upon the face of the waters." (God created all things and the Holy Spirit was involved in creation.)

2 Samuel 23:2-3: "<u>The Spirit of the LORD spake by me</u>, and his word was in my tongue. The God of Israel said, The Rock of Israel spake to me, He that ruleth over men must be just, ruling in the fear of God." (David calls 'the Spirit of the LORD' - Holy Spirit – God.)

Job 33:4: "<u>The spirit of God hath made me</u>, and the breath of the Almighty hath given me life." (God created man.)

Psalm 104:30: "Thou sendest forth <u>thy spirit</u>, they are created: and thou renewest the face of the earth." (The Holy Spirit is involved in creation.)

Psalm 139:7: "Whither shall I go from <u>thy spirit</u>? or whither shall I flee from thy presence?" (Only God is omnipresent - everywhere at the same time - the Holy Spirit is omnipresent.)

Isaiah 6:3: "And one cried unto another, and said, <u>Holy, holy, holy</u>, is the Lord of hosts: the whole earth is full of his glory." (The Seraphim praise God and there are three (3) words 'holy' spoken in praise for the Father, Son, and Holy Spirit.)

Matthew 28:19: "Go ye therefore, and teach all nations, baptizing them in the name of the Father, and of the Son, and of the Holy Ghost." (The word 'name' is singular, but combines the Father, Son, and Holy Spirit in the one name.)

John 16:12-13: "I have yet many things to say unto you, but ye can not bear them now. Howbeit when he, the Spirit of truth, is come, he will guide you into all truth: for he shall not speak of himself; but whatsoever he shall hear, that shall he speak: and he will show you things to come." (God is the One that speaks the truth of God's Word and communicates that to man; Jesus says the Holy Spirit is God.)

Acts 5:3-4: "But Peter said, Ananias, why hath Satan filled thine heart to lie to the Holy Ghost, and to keep back part of the price of the land? While it remained, was it not thine own? and after it was sold, was it not in thine own power? why hast thou conceived this thing in thine heart? thou hast not lied unto men, but unto God." (Peter says the Holy Spirit is God.)

Acts 28:25: "And when they agreed not among themselves, they departed, after that Paul had spoken one word, Well spake the Holy Ghost by Esaias the prophet unto our fathers." (Paul says the Holy Spirit is God.)

1 Corinthians 2:10-11: "For God hath revealed them unto us by his Spirit: for the Spirit searcheth all things, yea, the deep things of God. For what man knoweth the things of a man, save the spirit of man which is in him? even so the things of God knoweth no man, but the Spirit of God." (Only the Holy Spirit-who is God-can know and communicate the things of God to man.)

1 Corinthians 12:4-6: "Now there are diversities of

gifts, but the same Spirit. And there are differences of administrations, but the same Lord. And there are diversities of operations, but it is the same God which worketh all in all." (The Holy Spirit is equal to the Father and Son the way they are listed together.)

2 Corinthians 13:14: "The grace of the Lord Jesus Christ, and the love of God, and the communion of the Holy Ghost, be with you all. Amen." (The Son, Father, and Holy Spirit are equal in extending God's grace, love, and communion.)

Hebrews 3:7-9: "Wherefore as the Holy Ghost saith, To-day if ye will hear his voice, harden not your hearts, as in the provocation, in the day of temptation in the wilderness: When your fathers tempted me, proved me, and saw my works forty years." (This quote from Psalm 95:8-10 shows that God was speaking here; ascribed to the Holy Spirit.)

Hebrews 9:14: "How much more shall the blood of Christ, who through the eternal Spirit offered himself without spot to God, purge your conscience from dead works to serve the living God?" (This is only a work that God can do through the Holy Spirit, and only if He is God. Infinite and eternal are characteristics of God's nature; and the offering of Christ is a work of God.)

2 Peter 1:21: "For the prophecy came not in old time by the will of man: but holy men of God spake as they were moved by the Holy Ghost." (The word of God comes from God, who is the Holy Spirit.)

These verses attribute to the Holy Spirit the characteristic of personhood by calling Him "He," and thus speaks of Him as a Person. Acts of the will and intelligent direction are attributes of the Holy Spirit. This is important because the Holy Spirit is not just a force or energy. He is a Person – the third Person of the Godhead, equal to God the Father and God the Son.

We must not confuse function and role with nature and essence of Being. Jesus submitted to the Father willingly to offer Himself for us, but that did not make him *less* than God the Father. His role is different from the Father and the Holy Spirit in relation to the work of man's redemption. The willing submission of the Son in the incarnation does not make Him less than God the Father; it is a different function and role. In relation to man, the Son took on a role to secure man's redemption (Jesus took on human flesh; the Father and Holy Spirit did not). Likewise, the Holy Spirit has a different role in relation to how the Godhead interacts with man, but that doesn't change Who He is, only the role He performs in His ministry. Husbands, wives, and children have different roles in a family, but are all equally human – even though some operate with more authority or in different roles. This is not a great comparison, but I am trying to make clear the distinction between role and nature. This confusion in recognizing varied roles within the Godhead as they relate to man has resulted in cults and "ism" groups greatly distorting the Bible and its God. The Bible is simple; there is one God and three Persons in that One God. The Bible does not use the word trinity – as stated earlier, the term was originally used by the early church father Tertullian in the second century.

It is important to note that there are several terms not in the Bible that are applied today to various concepts or positions, etc. For example, the Bible does not use the term "grandparents", though there are many grandparents mentioned in Scripture. There are countless examples used to describe beliefs associated with concepts or doctrines the Bible teaches but the words are not found in the Bible itself (some positive, some not so flattering), such as Creationism, Legalism, Charismatic, Fundamentalism, Evangelicalism, Cessationism, Dispensationalism, Covenantalism, et al. In English and Greek NT translations, the term "rapture" is not used, but in the Latin Vulgate (Latin version of the Bible), it is. The English word "rapture" is from the Latin word "raptio", and this is derived from the Latin text "rapiemur." This is the word St. Jerome (Latin vulgate translator) used for our English translation of "we will be caught up" in 1 Thess. 4:17. The Greek word "harpazo" is the actual word translated into English as "caught up." Terminology should not be an obstacle as long as it accurately represents what the Bible is teaching. This is a normal practice for various doctrines, subjects, beliefs, and concepts described in the Bible and explained in conventional form for understanding and discussion.

Visual Example of the Trinity

The Trinity is three divine Persons in one God. It is not three separate Gods, nor is it one God manifesting Himself in three different ways. The three divine Persons *are* God! The best comparison example is the triangle, it has three corners but it is *one* triangle. It *is* a triangle because it has three corners in a closed shape. You cannot remove a corner of the triangle and have it still *be* a triangle. Similarly, you cannot remove or separate any of the divine Persons from God and still have God.

Unique to the persons of the trinity, the Son "added" humanity to Himself in the incarnation, but He did not cease from being God at any time. It is important to note that the human nature the Son added did not combine with the divine nature. This was expressed well in the Athanasian Creed (373 AD):

> Whosoever will be saved, before all things it is necessary that he hold the catholic [true Christian] faith. Which faith except every one do keep whole and undefiled, without doubt he shall perish everlastingly. But this is the catholic faith: That we worship one God in trinity, and trinity in unity; Neither confounding the persons; nor dividing the substance. For there is one person of the Father: another of the Son: another of the Holy Ghost. But the Godhead of the Father, and of the Son, and of the Holy Ghost is all one: the glory equal, the majesty coëternal. Such as the Father is, such is the Son, and such is the Holy Ghost. The Father is

uncreated: the Son is uncreated: the Holy Ghost is uncreated. The Father is immeasurable: the Son is immeasurable: the Holy Ghost is immeasurable. The Father is eternal: the Son eternal: the Holy Ghost eternal. And yet there are not three eternals; but one eternal. As also there are not three uncreated: nor three immeasurable: but one uncreated, and one immeasurable. So likewise the Father is almighty: the Son almighty: and the Holy Ghost almighty, And yet there are not three almighties: but one almighty. So the Father is God: the Son is God: and the Holy Ghost is God. And yet there are not three Gods; but one God. So the Father is Lord: the Son Lord: and the Holy Ghost Lord. And yet not three Lords; but one Lord For like as we are compelled by the Christian verity to acknowledge every Person by himself to be God and Lord: So are we forbidden by the catholic religion to say, there are three Gods, or three Lords. The Father is made of none; neither created; nor begotten. The Son is of the Father alone: not made; nor created; but begotten. The Holy Ghost is of the Father and the Son: not made; neither created; nor begotten; but proceeding. Thus there is one Father, not three Fathers: one Son, not three Sons: one Holy Ghost, not three Holy Ghosts. And in this Trinity none is before or after another: none is greater or less than another. But the whole three Persons are co-eternal together, and co-equal So that in all things, as aforesaid, the Unity in Trinity, and the Trinity in Unity is to be worshiped. He therefore that will be saved, must thus think of the Trinity. Furthermore, it is necessary to everlasting salvation, that we believe also rightly in the incarnation of our Lord Jesus Christ. Now the right faith is, that we believe and confess, that our Lord Jesus Christ, the Son of God, is God and Man. God, of the substance of the Father, begotten before the worlds: and Man, of the substance of His mother, born in the world. Perfect God: perfect Man, of a reasonable soul and human flesh subsisting. Equal to the Father as touching His Godhead: inferior to the Father as touching His Manhood.

And <u>although He be God and Man; yet He is not two, but one Christ. One, not by conversion of the Godhead into flesh; but by assumption of the Manhood into God. One altogether, not by confusion of substance; but by unity of person. For as the reasonable soul and flesh is one man; so God and Man is one Christ.</u> Who suffered for our salvation: descended into hades: rose again the third day from the dead. He ascended into heaven: He sitteth on the right hand of God, the Father almighty: From whence He shall come to judge the quick and the dead. At whose coming all men must rise again with their bodies; And shall give account for their own works. And they that have done good shall go into life everlasting; but they that have done evil, into everlasting fire. This is the catholic faith; which except a man believe truly and firmly, he cannot be saved.[36] (underline added)

I included the entire creed so the viewpoint from those in the fourth century would be clear. The word "catholic" in the creed is not a reference to the Roman Catholic Church, but to the universal church, in other words, all true believers universally throughout the world. Additionally, those who come to Christ (i.e. whoever will be saved) do not necessarily understand every detail in this creed at the time they place their faith in Christ. Though it would certainly question whether or not a person actually has legitimate faith if they reject any of the points made in the creed. The creed is an excellent statement of faith regarding the nature of God as revealed in the Bible. The points are very well stated and expressed in a succinct manner. The key point regarding the current topic is the underlined portion. When it says, "He [Jesus] is not two, but one Christ. One, not by conversion of the Godhead into flesh; but by assumption of the Manhood into God," this is very well put. This is because Jesus has two natures (human and divine), yet is only one Person – the Son. People get this confused all the time. The way to avoid the confusion is to ask a question when talking about Jesus, which is "which nature?" i.e. is the question related to the human or divine nature of Jesus? The human nature would answer why Jesus got hungry, tired, did not know the time of His own return, and could be tempted, etc. The divine nature would answer why He has knowledge, authority, receives worship, forgives sins, Messianic title (deity), etc.

The creed makes a statement that is vital to the understanding of the nature of God, "by assumption of the Manhood into God," or another way of saying the same thing, "by adding humanity to deity." The creed is correct when it says, "not by confusion of substance; but by unity of person," i.e. the natures did not mix, but found their unity in the one Person, or, Jesus is one Person with two natures. This is well stated in the creed and made very clear. It is also a point of orthodoxy today, since it accurately represents what the Bible teaches us about the nature(s) of Jesus.

Paul says of Jesus in Phil. 2:6, "being in the form of God," the verb "being" is in the present tense which means that Jesus never ceased to be God, or continued to be deity. The grammar of this verse simply states that Jesus "continued to be God in His very essence." The word "form" in Greek means the revealing of His innermost being was expressed outwardly. Thus, at no time did the Son give up any of His Divinity, on the contrary He only laid aside the prerogatives of *operating* as Deity. Jesus relied upon the Holy Spirit for what He needed to know and do as a man (John 3:34), because He was the ideal Man. This was a willing limitation the Son of God made when He took on a human nature (John 1:14).

Note in the following example that the Father, Son, and Holy Spirit are God, but that they are *not* each other – they are distinct Persons in the Godhead. The Father *is not* the Son or the Holy Spirit, the Son *is not* the Father or Holy Spirit, the Holy Spirit *is not* the Father or Son. The Father, Son, and Holy Spirit *are* God. The following diagram is one of the better conceptual representations of the trinity. Note that the human nature added to the Son does not mix with the divine nature, there is no confusion here.

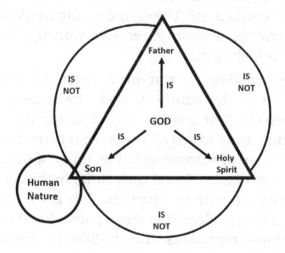

The critical fact that many people overlook regarding the Trinity is the relationship in the Godhead that has existed from all eternity. This relationship God wants to share with man. God is not a singular personality as in Islam. If this was the case, the first relationship God would have experienced was when he created man or some other angelic being to experience relationship. Thus, God would be learning what relationships were all about, since his experience with His creation would be that initial experience. Contrary to this view, the Bible teaches that God was in fellowship within the Godhead from eternity and it is this existing relationship – the embodiment of perfection regarding relationship – which God desires man to enter into and experience with Him. This is essential when trying to understand the nature of God revealed in Scripture since He is infinite, eternal, and perfect. In other words, we define relationships by that which is within the Trinity. This is comparative to the perfection of love, goodness, purity, holiness, morality, etc., attributes grounded in God's nature and where they derive their definitions from and to which we gain our understanding.

For example, when we read that John says, "God is love" (1 John 4:8, 16), though it does mean that God has more love than we do, the emphasis is on the nature of love in God, or that God's nature embodies that which defines love. In other words, if you want to know what true love is, God's nature is the basis and His acts are the demonstration. This is why Paul could say in Rom. 5:8, "But God demonstrates His own love toward us, in that while we were still sinners, Christ died for us" (NKJV). This act of love expresses the nature of love within God. Thus, all of God's acts and commands are an expression of the perfection of His Divine nature. As God created the world in six days, each day He said, "that it was good" (Gen. 1:4, 10, 12, 18, 21, 25), and on day six after He made man in His image, it was said, "it was very good" (Gen. 1:31). Everything God created was good, which includes the relationship He established with man. Thus, evil (see Gen. 3) is the result of taking something of the good that God created and perverting it, corrupting it, or using it in opposition to God's will and purposes. The very intimacy of the relationship that God wanted to have with man was the focus of attack when Satan deceived Eve into rebelling against God, and thereby corrupted the relation. All corruption works the same way; what God created to be good is stolen and repurposed to evil.

John begins his gospel by saying, "In the beginning was the Word, and the Word was with God, and the Word was God." The phrase "the Word was with God" is speaking of the fellowship of the Godhead. The key word is the Greek word "pros" translated into English "with." As the Classic Greek grammarian A.T. Robertson says, "*With God (pros ton theon).* Though existing eternally with God the Logos was in perfect fellowship with God. *Pros* with the accusative presents a plane of equality and intimacy, face to face with each other."[37] Thus John 1:1 can be paraphrased, "the Word (Jesus) was face to face in intimate fellowship with God the Father and the Holy Spirit."[38] It is this fellowship enjoyed in the Godhead throughout eternity that is offered to man through Jesus Christ. "Thus John's statement is that the divine Word not only *abode* with the Father from all eternity, but was in the living, active relation of communion with Him."[39]

In Jesus' high priestly prayer in John 17, He expresses the oneness that He desires of His followers, that is, to be in the fellowship Jesus enjoyed with the Father. This is the fellowship God intends for believers to have as they place their faith in Jesus Christ. Jesus is in fellowship with the Father and the Holy Spirit, thus to be "in Christ" offers that same opportunity. This is revolutionary and something never heard of or even conceived of by any other religious system or religious belief. Paul expressed it like this, "That Christ may dwell in your hearts by faith; that ye, being rooted and grounded in love, May be able to comprehend with all saints what is the breadth, and length, and depth, and height; And to know the love of Christ, which passeth knowledge, that ye might be filled with all the fulness of God" (Eph. 3:17-19). We have the opportunity to take advantage of this fellowship and intimacy that "passes knowledge." It is not something that we can fully comprehend with our limited capacities, but we can enjoy. Furthermore, to "be filled with the fullness of God" is certainly beyond our thinking, but this was Paul's prayer for believers to have this intimacy with God to the "fullness." At this point, it is important to realize that a misunderstanding of the Christian's relationship to the OT covenant of Law can undermine the fullness mentioned by Paul. It is only under the NT covenant that this intimate fellowship is possible because of the work of Christ on the cross, resurrection, and His subsequent ascension to heaven.

How wonderful of our God to offer this kind of fellowship with Him to have access and opportunity to relate to the Living God is beyond what many Christians allow themselves to enjoy. Nevertheless, this is what God intended for man to enjoy from the beginning of creation. In this sense, the Trinity is the most necessary and essential aspect of God's nature and

Being that we need to understand. God did not have His first experience of what a relationship was when He created Adam, but He desired Adam to enter into the same experience that the Trinity was already enjoying in its perfection. God enjoys this relationship as His very nature expresses and defines the love and graciousness that He wants to share with His creation. Therefore, He created Adam (and all people) with the capacity to have this relationship by making man "in His own image" (Gen. 1:27, 9:6, 2 Cor. 4:4).

Denial of The Trinity (doctrinal errors/heresy)

With the above said, some historical background is useful now. In 313 A.D., the Roman Emperor Constantine proclaimed the Edict of Milan (aka the Edict of Toleration). This edict effectively made Christians a protected class after over 200 years of severe persecution by Rome. Since open persecution against Christians became *illegal*, church leaders had the freedom to gather and clarify doctrinal issues since the church was unable to all "get on the same page" over the years of persecution. In 325 A.D. they held their first church council in Nicaea, a city in the Galatian region of Asia Minor (modern day western Turkey). Over 300 bishops (pastors), representing Europe, North Africa, Asia Minor, and the Middle East attended. This was their first opportunity to discuss the Person of Jesus Christ so all churches could be in doctrinal agreement. Varying views regarding certain doctrines had been taught in Christian congregations and were represented by these bishops.

In the end, there were two major views that needed a decision. The first was a position by a man named Arius from North Africa. He held that Jesus Christ was *created* by God the Father, meaning He was a god, but one in lesser status. Opposite him was the second position by Athanasius, a man also from North Africa. He held that Jesus Christ was one in *substance* (essence) with the Father, meaning they were equal in nature and eternal in the One God of the Bible. In attempts to help Athanasius and put down the view of Arius, a man named Sabellius, also believed to be from North Africa, put forth his own view. He believed that God was a single Being (no trinity) and only manifested Himself as Father, Son, or Holy Spirit. Sabellius did not solve anything, but unfortunately just complicated the issue. In attempting to prevent the heresy of Arius, Sabellius created a different heresy. Swinging the pendulum to the opposite extreme or developing a position to exclude a wrong view does not make it true. This is never a good method for determining the truth. When it comes to the Bible, the truth is what it simply teaches it in the proper context.

A creed (called the Nicene Creed) resulted from this meeting of the bishops in Nicaea. It states that God the Father and Jesus Christ were of the same *substance* (essence) as one key result of this council. Because the view that Athanasius championed was represented in the creed, the result was the classification of both Arius' and Sabellius' views as *heresies*.[40] The Nicene Creed says this:

> We believe in one God the Father Almighty, Maker of heaven and earth, And of all things visible and invisible. And in one Lord Jesus Christ, the only-begotten Son of God, Begotten of the Father before all worlds; God of God, Light of Light. Very God of very God, Begotten, not made, Being of one substance with the Father; By whom all things were made; Who, for us men, and for our salvation, came down from heaven, And was incarnate by the Holy Ghost of the Virgin Mary, And was made man. He was crucified for us under Pontius Pilate; And suffered and was buried; And the third day he rose again, According to the Scriptures; And ascended into heaven, And sitteth on the right hand of the Father; And he shall come again, with glory, to judge the quick and the dead; Whose kingdom shall have no end. And I believe in the Holy Ghost, The Lord, and Giver of life; Who proceedeth from the Father and the Son; Who with the Father and the Son together is worshiped and glorified; Who spake by the

Prophets. And I believe in one holy catholic and apostolic Church; We acknowledge one baptism for the remission of sins; And we look for the resurrection of the dead; And the life of the world to come.[41]

It is important to understand the basics of these historical views; it lays a proper foundation when analyzing heretical views today. A better understanding of church history and its doctrinal development would prevent many cults and ism groups from gaining traction today. We call a proper biblical view *orthodox*, which means *right opinion*. *Wrong opinions* (about biblical teachings) are called *unorthodox*. The following are some *unorthodox* views regarding the Trinity represented at the Council of Nicaea and previously mentioned.

Arianism – viewed the supremacy of God the Father to that of the Son, who was the first created god at the beginning. This would reduce Jesus Christ the Son of God to a second god, which defines Him biblically as a false god. Since the Bible teaches that there is only one God, introducing another god creates a polytheistic situation that is a heresy. A number of cults hold this view today; the most well-known are Jehovah's Witnesses. They teach that Jesus was Michael the Archangel.

Sabellianism – the belief that God Father, Son, and Holy Spirit are three different *modes* of God, opposed to a Trinitarian view of three distinct Persons within the Godhead. This view also called Modalism, teaches that God presents Himself in different *modes*. The view also holds that the Holy Spirit is not a separate Person of the Godhead, but instead describes God in action. This again is a view at variance with the Bible because it tries to make the Father and the Son the same person, manifesting themselves with different masks/faces (Father or Son) at different times. It contradicts John 1:1 where the Word (the Son) is "face to face in fellowship" with God (the Father and Holy Spirit). It also makes nonsense of the various passages where Jesus is communicating with the Father. Further, it ignores the passages of Scripture that represent the Holy Spirit as a Person of the Godhead with a will, intellect, and other equal characteristics of the Father and Son. Modalism also attempts to remove the clearly stated distinction in passages that reveal the plurality of God, along with verses that list the separateness of the Persons of the Godhead. Like other heresies, this confuses the *nature* of God with the operating *activities* we see God perform in relation to man's redemption and interaction with the world. The most popular cult today that holds to this view is the United Pentecostal Church International (UPC) or Oneness Pentecostals (aka Jesus Only Movement). Unitarianism also views God as a form of modalism.

It is very unfortunate that basic church history is not part of much of Christian education. That is not to say that all in church history is good doctrinal teachings, or even correct practices. However, knowing both the good and the bad gives a better perspective in relation to issues today. So much of the problems in the church we see today is nothing more than repackaged old heresies and aberrant practices. There is much to be gleaned from knowing the major issues that arose over the centuries and what the conclusions were. Many Christians could avoid weird and false teachings if they could recognize that in many cases, these issues were put to bed many years ago. Indeed, it is never too late to begin that education.

God's Characteristics

There are particular characteristics of God conveyed in the Bible to provide an understanding of who God is. For example, many people have heard the verse "God is love" (1 John 4:8). This does not mean that God only possesses love to the exclusion of other attributes. We learn He can be angry (1 Kings 11:9) or grieved (Gen. 6:6), He also is righteous (2 Chron. 12:6), forgiving (Ex. 34:7), just (Zeph. 3:5), merciful, gracious, longsuffering, and abundant in goodness and truth (Ex. 34:6) – and this is not an exhaustive list. Thus, what the Bible means when it says, "God is love" is that God is infinite in His love. As previously mentioned, this does not mean He has an infinite amount in quantity, but that He embodies the perfection of what love is. Therefore, if you want to understand what love really is, God possesses and represents the ideal of love. He defines it by His very nature and expresses it in His actions. John tells us right after 1 John 4:8, "In this was manifested the love of God toward us, because that God sent his only begotten Son into the world, that we might live through him" (1 John 4:9). So John makes it clear that the love that we understand is His nature, finds its expression in sending Christ so that we might have spiritual life. This love is a selfless, giving, sacrificial love exercised to the benefit of others. That is why it is always wrong to take our understanding of love – which is faulty, selfish and misguided – and try to assign that type of love to God. We do not come to understand God's love based on our own views of love. Using God's absolute standard of love we can understand how corrupt our love is by comparison. He is the standard, not us.

The Scripture tells us that God loves us (John 3:16 and many other verses). However, the *reason* why God loves us is because of who He is, not who we are! His love is not because there is something lovable in us, but because He is a loving God – it is *His* nature! We cannot alter the love of God for us, for we did not create it and therefore we cannot change it. Thus, when God expresses His love to us it is because it resides in Him and He is going to love us though we are undeserving of it. To understand this will be the difference between having a solid relationship with God, or to be carried about with emotional variances always wondering if we measure up to His love and grace – which we never will. Romans 5:8 says, "But

God demonstrates His own love toward us, in that while we were still sinners, Christ died for us" (NKJV). This verse is so vital to our understanding of God's love. It tells us two very important facts. First, the *demonstration* of God's love – the cross – is the unchangeable historical event that reveals God's gracious offering of His Son for us. This love did not just start with the cross of Christ, for God knew He would do this for us from before the foundation of the world (Acts 2:23; Rev. 13:8). Second, this plan and *demonstration* was accomplished for us while we were in our sinful state, separated from God by our sin. In other words, we did not deserve God's love or Jesus' sacrifice for us on the cross. Yet God in His love for us knew, planned, and sent His Son to the cross for lost sinful humanity. We never asked for it, we could never have planned it, and we in our sinful rebellion do not think we need it. Yet God knew He would have to set His plan in motion before He ever created Adam. This is the grace of God.

The same truth exists regarding the other characteristics of God. When it says He is *just*, it means that He is absolutely just because He is the embodiment of perfect justice. Therefore, if you want to know what justice is, God is the standard, just as He is with love, grace, mercy, anger, etc. God is the source of all reality and therefore the source of all the attributes He placed in man when He made man in His own image. In other words, we need to measure ourselves against the nature of God. Any other measurement is an arbitrary moving target. This is why it is so important to understand what the Bible teaches about God because God is *revealing* Himself through His Word! We see God's love *explicitly* in the Bible and *implicitly*; both are there for our learning.

For example, Jonah did not want to go to Nineveh when God told him to go (Jonah 1). He eventually went to Nineveh (Jonah 2), but he was not pleased when he saw the *mercy* extended to the Assyrians; he was hoping for judgment (Jonah 3). He ended up angry because he knew that God was "a gracious God, and merciful, slow to anger, and of great kindness" (Jonah 4:2).

God's merciful response to the Assyrians caused great anxiety in Jonah. He hated them for their wickedness, much of it experienced by the Jews. Jonah was a loyal patriot of Israel and a successful prophet that God sent to the rebellious northern kingdom (2 Kings 14:25). Though Jonah's attitude is not acceptable, it is certainly understandable. When God sent him to the Assyrians, it was like asking him to reach out to wicked and cruel terrorists that had done much harm to the Jewish people. However, God's desire is to bring people to repentance and faith, not destroy them. The lesson of Jonah is simple. If God is willing to show mercy to a corrupt pagan nation that repented of their wickedness, would He not do the same for northern Israel (10 tribes during the divided kingdom) who were living like a wicked pagan nation at the time under idolatrous kings? The word love is not in the book of Jonah, but God's love is implied by His actions. Though God disapproved of the wickedness of the Ninevites and was willing to judge them for it (Jonah 3:4), He loved these pagans enough to get His prophet there and respond with mercy at their repentance. Did the Ninevites deserve the mercy shown? – No! But God loved them because of the love in Him, not in them.

God is able to have all the attributes spoken of; yet, because He is perfect and infinite, He can work them in harmony with His will and truth without compromise. There is no conflict in the various attributes of God; He is a marvelous and wonderful God. Though He is beyond our full comprehension, He is not beyond our apprehension as we receive that revealed in His word.

God's Names

We learn much about God from the names He is known by in the Bible. Some are general terms for God while others are particular *compound names* He is known by to help with relationship. The following provides the English reader with some helpful information.

God: is the translation of **Elohim** (plural) occurring over

2500 times in the OT, **Eloah** (singular or dual) and **El** (singular). Each term is the generic term for God. Its usage is determined by the context of the passage for a correct understanding.

Elohim: This is the general name for God in the Hebrew OT. It is in the plural form (known by the "im" on the end), but generally used with a singular verb when it refers to the true God. Genesis 1:1 is an example, "In the beginning, God (Elohim) created (singular verb) the heavens and the earth." There are a few exceptions.

Eloah: "Although the plural *Elohim* is ordinarily used for God, the singular form *Eloah* is found in fifty-seven passages, most of which are in the Book of Job. Only six times is *Eloah* applied to any but the true God. The Aramaic form *Elah* is found thirty-seven times in Ezra, once in Jeremiah, and forty-six times in Daniel. Of the eighty-four passages where it occurs, seventy-two refer to the True God. The Assyrian form is *Ilu*."[42]

El: This is the singular form of Elohim. "The more simple and elementary form *El*, which is frequently adopted either alone or in dependence on another substantive, to express power or might, is used of the True God in 204 passages, and of others in eighteen passages. It is found especially in Job, the Psalms, and Isaiah."[43]

El Shaddai: means Almighty God and speaks of God's great power.

Adonai (translated in the English Bible as Lord): means Lord or Master. It can be related to God or man; it is determined by the context. It is used with God as "Lord God" to identify the true God of Israel.

It is first used of God in Genesis 15:2; Genesis 15:8; Genesis 18:3, &c. It is rare in the Pentateuch and historical Books, but frequent in the Psalms, Isaiah, Jeremiah, Ezekiel, Daniel, and Amos. The words which we read in the 110th Psalm and the first verse, if literally translated, would run thus: - 'Jehovah said unto my Master [According to the present Masoretic punctuation the word is in the singular - Adoni, not Adonai.] sit thou on my right hand until I make thine enemies thy footstool;' and our Saviour's comment might be rendered, 'If David call him Master, how is he his Son?'[44]

YHVH or JHVH, Yahweh or Jehovah (translated in the English Bible as LORD – all caps): the Name for God used as a compound name is connected with other terms to describe a relational characteristic of God. The Jews would not spell out the Name of God when they translated the OT, so they wrote only the consonants: YHVH or JHVH. This is known as the tetragrammaton, which is from the Greek meaning "having four letters." Thus when you read the English Bible and see the word LORD, you know it is a translation of the actual Name for God. "**Jehovah (יהוה)**, which occurs about 5500 times in the O.T. this name has been preserved by our translators in a few passages, but the word Lord, spelt in small capitals, has usually been substituted for it."[45]

An illustration of the two names (LORD and Lord) is in Psalm 110:1, "The LORD [**JHVH**] said unto my Lord [**Adoni**], Sit thou at my right hand, until I make thine enemies thy footstool." This quote is the most referenced and quoted OT verse in the NT. It is David saying in effect, "God the Father said to God the Son, sit...", a prophecy of the time when the Son will rule the kingdom of God on earth. Later in Psalm 110, it quotes the Son's priesthood, revealing that it is not according to the Levitical line, but follows the order of Melchizedek, which is developed in the NT book of Hebrews. The following are examples of the compound names used in the OT with their meaning.

Jehovah-Elohim: means LORD God (Genesis 2:4)

Jehovah-Jireh: means The LORD Will Provide (Genesis 22:14).

Jehovah-Rapha: means The LORD who Heals (Exodus 15:26).

Jehovah-Nissi: means The LORD our Banner (Exodus 17:15)

Jehovah-M'kaddesmh: means The LORD Who Sanctifies or Makes Holy (Leviticus 20:8)

Jehovah-Shalom: means The LORD our peace (Judges 6:24)

Jehovah-Tsidkenu: means The LORD our Righteousness (Jeremiah 33:16)

Jehovah-Rohi: means The LORD our Shepherd (Psalm 23:1)

Jehovah-Shammah: means The LORD is there (Ezekiel 48:35)

Jehovah-Saboath: means The LORD of Hosts (Armies) (Isaiah 1:24)

El-Elyon: means Most High God (Deuteronomy 26:19)

El-Roi: means God Who sees (Genesis 16:13)

El-Olam: means Everlasting God (Psalm 90:1-2)

El-Gibhor: means Mighty God (Isaiah 9:6)

All these Names of God are expressive of who He is and his capabilities. These Names progressively reveal God in the OT to the nation of Israel. In the NT, we are given one name that is "above every name" (Phil. 2:9), and that is the name of Jesus. All the compound names of the OT find their fulfillment in that one name – Jesus. They are there for our learning and understanding, but Jesus embodies and fulfills all that is revealed about God in the OT (Col. 1:19, 2:9).

God's Attributes

Omnipresence – God the Father, Son, and Holy Spirit are everyplace at the same time. This is not true of any other being.

2 Chronicles 2:6: "But who is able to build him an house, seeing the heaven and heaven of heavens cannot contain him? who am I then, that I should build him an house, save only to burn sacrifice before him?"

2 Chronicles 6:18: "But will God in very deed dwell with men on the earth? behold, heaven and the heaven of heavens cannot contain thee; how much less this house which I have built!"

Isaiah 66:1: "Thus saith the LORD, The heaven is my throne, and the earth is my footstool: where is the house that ye build unto me? and where is the place of my rest?"

Psalm 139:7-12: "Whither shall I go from thy spirit? or whither shall I flee from thy presence? If I ascend up into heaven, thou art there: if I make my bed in hell, behold, thou art there. If I take the wings of the morning, and dwell in the uttermost parts of the sea; Even there shall thy hand lead me, and thy right hand shall hold me. If I say, Surely the darkness shall cover me; even the night shall be light about me. Yea, the darkness hideth not from thee; but the night shineth as the day: the darkness and the light are both alike to thee."

Jeremiah 23:23-24: "Am I a God at hand, saith the Lord, and not a God afar off? Can any hide himself in secret places that I shall not see him? saith the Lord. Do not I fill heaven and earth? saith the Lord."

Omniscience – God knows everything; thus, there is nothing that He does not know. He did not learn anything and does not learn as time advances. He does not accumulate knowledge, but knows all that is knowable or that is even potentially possible in knowledge and future events, and remarkably, He knows it at the same time – from eternity. The nature of God would necessitate this absolute and complete knowledge of time and eternity. This is why God can speak of things to come and communicate them to His messengers with pinpoint accuracy. Interestingly, God even knows what people would do if given the opportunity (see Matt. 11:20-24), though these activities did not actually occur.

Isaiah 46:9-10: "Remember the former things of old: for I am God, and there is none else; I am God, and there is none like me, Declaring the end from the beginning, and from ancient times the things that are not yet done, saying, My counsel shall stand, and I will do all my pleasure."

Psalm 139:1-6: "O lord, thou hast searched me, and known me. Thou knowest my downsitting and mine uprising, thou understandest my thought afar off. Thou compassest my path and my lying down, and art acquainted with all my ways. For there is not a word in my tongue, but, lo, O Lord, thou knowest it altogether. Thou hast beset me behind and before, and laid thine hand upon me. Such knowledge is too wonderful for me; it is high, I cannot attain unto it."

Hebrews 4:12-13: "For the word of God is quick, and powerful, and sharper than any twoedged sword, piercing even to the dividing asunder of soul and spirit, and of the joints and marrow, and is a discerner of the thoughts and intents of the heart. Neither is there any creature that is not manifest in his sight: but all things are naked and opened unto the eyes of him with whom we have to do."

1 John 3:20: "For if our heart condemn us, God is greater than our heart, and knoweth all things."

Omnipotence – God possesses all power and there is nothing beyond His capabilities. Not only is He powerful enough to create the universe, but He also sustains the universe and all creation (Col. 1:17).

Genesis 18:14: "Is any thing too hard for the LORD? At the time appointed I will return unto thee, according to the time of life, and Sarah shall have a son."

Job 42:2: "I know that thou canst do every thing, and that no thought can be withholden from thee."

Jeremiah 32:17: "Ah Lord GOD! behold, thou hast made the heaven and the earth by thy great power and stretched out arm, and there is nothing too hard for thee."

Jeremiah 32:27: "Behold, I am the LORD, the God of all flesh: is there any thing too hard for me?"

Matthew 28:18: "And Jesus came and spake unto them, saying, All power is given unto me in heaven and in earth."

Infinite – God is without end and any limits that time, space, and matter have upon beings that had a beginning (i.e. any created being). When we talk about the infinite nature of His being, it must be understood in the sense that He embodies the perfection of characteristics and capabilities that would in the nature of any other being have some form of limitation. These characteristics of God's nature find their definition in Him as the infinite and ultimate reality.

Job 11:7: "Canst thou by searching find out God? canst thou find out the Almighty unto perfection?"

Job 21:22: "Shall any teach God knowledge? seeing he judgeth those that are high."

Psalm 145:3: "Great is the Lord, and greatly to be praised; and his greatness is unsearchable."

Isaiah 40:13-14: "Who hath directed the Spirit of the LORD, or being his counsellor hath taught him? With whom took he counsel, and who instructed him, and taught him in the path of judgment, and taught him knowledge, and shewed to him the way of understanding?"

1 Corinthians 2:16: "For who hath known the mind of the Lord, that he may instruct him? But we have the mind of Christ."

Eternal – God transcends time, space, and matter. He is the only eternal Being without beginning or end. Thus, He is the uncaused cause of the universe and unique in that He has no equal.

Genesis 21:33: "And Abraham planted a grove in Beersheba, and called there on the name of the Lord, the everlasting God."

Psalm 90:1-2: "Lord, thou hast been our dwelling place in all generations. Before the mountains were brought forth, or ever thou hadst formed the earth and the world, even from everlasting to everlasting, thou art God."

Isaiah 40:28: "Hast thou not known? hast thou not heard, that the everlasting God, the Lord, the Creator of the ends of the earth, fainteth not, neither is weary? there is no searching of his understanding."

Micah 5:2: "But thou, Bethlehem Ephratah, though thou be little among the thousands of Judah, yet out of thee shall he come forth unto me that is to be ruler in Israel; whose goings forth have been from of old, from everlasting."

1 Timothy 1:17: "Now unto the King eternal, immortal, invisible, the only wise God, be honour and glory for ever and ever."

Revelation 1:8: "I am Alpha and Omega, the beginning and the ending, saith the Lord, which is, and which was, and which is to come, the Almighty."

Immutable – God's nature, council, and purposes do not change (subtitle of this book). This means God is always trustworthy and will keep His word. God's acts change from man's perspective and in light of the covenantal relationship, but his nature never changes. This is why God is faithful, true, and trustworthy.

Numbers 23:19: "God is not a man, that he should lie; neither the son of man, that he should repent: hath he said, and shall he not do it? or hath he spoken, and shall he not make it good?"

Psalm 102:27: "Thou art the same, and thy years shall have no end."

Isaiah 46:9b-10: "I am God, and there is none else; I am God, and there is none like me, Declaring the end from the beginning, and from ancient times the things that are not yet done, saying, My counsel shall stand, and I will do all my pleasure."

Malachi 3:6: "For I am the Lord, I change not; therefore ye sons of Jacob are not consumed."

James 1:17: "Every good gift and every perfect gift is from above, and cometh down from the Father of lights, with whom is no variableness, neither shadow of turning."

Hebrews 6:17b-18a: "Wherein God, willing more abundantly to shew unto the heirs of promise the immutability of his counsel, confirmed it by an oath: That by two immutable things, in which it was impossible for God to lie, we might have a strong consolation."

Hebrews 13:8: "Jesus Christ the same yesterday, and to day, and for ever."

Sovereign - As Creator of the universe, God has the absolute right to govern and dispose of the universe as He pleases despite any attempts to frustrate His will. He is the single reigning God of everything that He made (ie. all that exists). This does not mean that God must determine all that will happen in the universe He created such as sin and evil. But it does mean that He has absolute control of all that occurs. God is the only being that has the capability of allowing the existence of free will among His creation (angels and man) without their ability to thwart any of His will or purposes in His ultimate plan. He sovereignly determined that His creation would possess this freedom to act, enabling their actions to be undetermined by Him, which means they are legitimately free will creatures. God's sovereignty does not mean that He must determine all that will happen in order for it to happen. His capabilities are beyond that limited view. God controls all of His creation and though He allows free will, He will accomplish His ultimate plan for His creation. He will achieve His will in light of the freedom given to His creatures (angels and man). It is a mistake to limit God's sovereignty to only what He determines will happen, or properly called theological determinism. If God must determine all things to happen in order for them to happen, this is fatalism and reveals a limited and diminished view of God. Removing man's free will immediately diminishes the biblical revelation and capability of God and the Scriptures must be manipulated to accomplish this view. The Bible does not reveal this about God; it is typically put forth by the determined choice of theologians who assign this activity to God. As A.W. Tozer has insightfully said:

God sovereignly decreed that man should be free to exercise moral choice, and man from the beginning has fulfilled that decree by making his choice between good and evil. When he chooses to do evil, he does not thereby countervail the sovereign will of God but fulfills it, inasmuch as the eternal decree decided not which choice the man should make but that he should be free to make it. If in His absolute freedom God has willed to give man limited freedom, who is there to stay His hand or say, 'What doest thou?' Man's will is free because God is sovereign. A God less than sovereign could not bestow moral freedom upon His creatures. He would be afraid to do so.[46]

God's sovereign control of the universe is clear in Scripture. The following examples should make this very clear.

Job 38:4: "Where wast thou when I laid the foundations of the earth? declare, if thou hast understanding."

Job 38:31: "Canst thou bind the sweet influences of Pleiades, or loose the bands of Orion?"

Psalm 33:11: "The counsel of the LORD standeth for ever, the thoughts of his heart to all generations."

Psalm 115:3: "But our God is in the heavens: he hath done whatsoever he hath pleased."

Psalm 135:6: "Whatsoever the LORD pleased, that did he in heaven, and in earth, in the seas, and all deep places."

Isaiah 45:7: "I form the light, and create darkness: I make peace, and create evil: I the LORD do all these things."

Isaiah 46:10: "Declaring the end from the beginning, and from ancient times the things that are not yet done, saying, My counsel shall stand, and I will do all my pleasure."

Ezekiel 18:4: "Behold, all souls are mine; as the soul of the father, so also the soul of the son is mine: the soul that sinneth, it shall die."

Daniel 4:35: "He doeth according to His will in the army of heaven, and among the inhabitants of the earth; and none can stay His hand, or say unto Him, What doest thou?"

Transcendent – God is beyond the world, He transcends (is beyond) all that He made – which is all that exists other than Him. Many of the previous verses quoted express this attribute of God. Very simply, He is not part of His creation but separate from it. Since God is an infinite being and the Creator of all, we find that He is the grounding of the attributes previously mentioned (i.e. love, justice, morality, et al). In other words, we are not left to ourselves to figure out how to love, be just, know right and wrong, etc., because the definition of all these attributes is in the nature of God. He transcends His creation and provides the absolute measurement for the exercise of these values.

Immanent – God is involved with His creation. He is present in His creation – not part of it, but presently interacts with it. He is distinct from His creation, sustaining it (Col. 1:17), and at times miraculously interacting with it. A few examples of this:

Genesis 3:8: "And they heard the voice of the Lord God walking in the garden in the cool of the day: and Adam and his wife hid themselves from the presence of the Lord God amongst the trees of the garden."

Genesis 11:7: [God said] "Go to, let us go down, and there confound their language, that they may not understand one another's speech."

Psalm 104:10-15: "He sends the springs into the valleys; They flow among the hills. They give drink to every beast of the field; The wild donkeys quench their thirst. By them the birds of the heavens have their home; They sing among the branches. He waters the hills from His upper chambers; The earth is satisfied with the fruit of Your works. He causes the grass to grow for the cattle, And vegetation for the service of man, That he may bring forth food from the earth, And wine that makes glad the heart of man, Oil to make his face shine, And bread which strengthens man's heart" (NKJV).

Psalm 104:19: "He appointed the moon for seasons: The sun knoweth its going down."

Psalm 136:25: "Who giveth food to all flesh: for his mercy endureth for ever."

Psalm 147:8-9: "Who covereth the heaven with clouds, who prepareth rain for the earth, who maketh grass to grow upon the mountains. He giveth to the beast his food, and to the young ravens which cry."

Jeremiah 23:23: "Am I a God at hand, saith the Lord, and not a God afar off?"

Matthew 1:18: "Now the birth of Jesus Christ was on this wise: When as his mother Mary was espoused to Joseph, before they came together, she was found with child of the Holy Ghost."

Acts 9:3-5: "And as he journeyed, he came near Damascus: and suddenly there shined round about him a light from heaven: And he fell to the earth, and heard a voice saying unto him, Saul, Saul, why persecutest thou me And he said, Who art thou, Lord? And the Lord said, I am Jesus whom thou persecutest?"

The many verses in the Bible that say people are filled with the Holy Spirit reveal God is immanent, since the Holy Spirit is God. There are many, thus a sampling makes the point.

Exodus 31:3: "And I have filled him with the spirit of God, in wisdom, and in understanding, and in knowledge, and in all manner of workmanship."

Exodus 35:31: "And he hath filled him with the spirit of God, in wisdom, in understanding, and in knowledge, and in all manner of workmanship."

Numbers 11:25: "And the LORD came down in a cloud, and spake unto him, and took of the spirit that was upon him, and gave it unto the seventy elders: and it came to pass, that, when the spirit rested upon them, they prophesied, and did not cease."

Judges 3:10: "And the Spirit of the LORD came upon him, and he judged Israel, and went out to war: and the LORD delivered Chushanrishathaim king of Mesopotamia into his hand; and his hand prevailed against Chushanrishathaim."

Judges 6:34: "But the Spirit of the LORD came upon Gideon, and he blew a trumpet; and Abiezer was gathered after him."

Judges 11:29: "Then the Spirit of the LORD came upon Jephthah, and he passed over Gilead, and Manasseh, and passed over Mizpeh of Gilead, and from Mizpeh of Gilead he passed over unto the children of Ammon."

Judges 14:6: "And the Spirit of the LORD came mightily upon him, and he rent him as he would have rent a kid, and he had nothing in his hand: but he told not his father or his mother what he had done."

Judges 14:19: "And the Spirit of the LORD came upon him, and he went down to Ashkelon, and slew thirty men of them, and took their spoil, and gave change of garments unto them which expounded the riddle. And his anger was kindled, and he went up to his father's house."

Judges 15:14: "And when he came unto Lehi, the Philistines shouted against him: and the Spirit of the LORD came mightily upon him [Samson], and the cords that were upon his arms became as flax that was burnt with fire, and his bands loosed from off his hands."

1 Samuel 16:13: "Then Samuel took the horn of oil, and anointed him in the midst of his brethren: and the Spirit of the LORD came upon David from that day forward. So Samuel rose up, and went to Ramah."

Isaiah 37:36: "Then the angel of the LORD went out, and killed in the camp of the Assyrians one hundred and eighty-five thousand; and when people arose early in the morning, there were the corpses—all dead" (NKJV).

Luke 1:15: "For he shall be great in the sight of the Lord, and shall drink neither wine nor strong drink; and he shall be filled with the Holy Ghost, even from his mother's womb."

Luke 1:41: "And it came to pass, that, when Elisabeth heard the salutation of Mary, the babe leaped in her womb; and Elisabeth was filled with the Holy Ghost."

Luke 1:67: "And his father Zacharias was filled with the Holy Ghost, and prophesied, saying."

Acts 2:4: "And they were all filled with the Holy Ghost, and began to speak with other tongues, as the Spirit gave them utterance."

Acts 4:8: "Then Peter, filled with the Holy Ghost, said unto them, Ye rulers of the people, and elders of Israel."

Acts 4:31: "And when they had prayed, the place was shaken where they were assembled together; and they were all filled with the Holy Ghost, and they spake the word of God with boldness."

Acts 9:17: "And Ananias went his way, and entered into the house; and putting his hands on him said, Brother Saul, the Lord, even Jesus, that appeared unto thee in the way as thou camest, hath sent me, that thou mightest receive thy sight, and be filled with the Holy Ghost."

Acts 13:9: "Then Saul, (who also is called Paul,) filled with the Holy Ghost, set his eyes on him."

Acts 13:52: "And the disciples were filled with joy, and with the Holy Ghost."

The next verses are examples of divine inspiration, in which God's immanence is necessary.

Isaiah 20:2: "At the same time spake the LORD by Isaiah the son of Amoz, saying, Go and loose the sackcloth from off thy loins, and put off thy shoe from thy foot. And he did so, walking naked and barefoot."

Mark 7:6: "He answered and said to them, "Well did Isaiah prophesy of you hypocrites, as it is written: 'This people honors Me with their lips, But their heart is far from Me'"" (NKJV). (Jesus said that Isaiah was divinely inspired.)

John 12:38: "that the word of Isaiah the prophet might be fulfilled, which he spoke: "Lord, who has believed our report? And to whom has the arm of the Lord been revealed?"" (NKJV). (Jesus again confirms Isaiah.)

Acts 28:25: "So when they did not agree among themselves, they departed after Paul had said one word: "The Holy Spirit spoke rightly through Isaiah the prophet to our fathers."" (NKJV). (Paul recognized that God spoke through Isaiah.)

2 Samuel 23:2: "The Spirit of the LORD spake by me, and his word was in my tongue." (David was aware that God was speaking through him. (2 Peter 1:21))

Mark 12:36: "For David himself said by the Holy Ghost, The LORD said to my Lord, Sit thou on my right hand, till I make thine enemies thy footstool." (Jesus confirmed that God spoke through David by the Holy Spirit, this is divine inspiration. (2 Tim. 3:16))

Acts 1:16: "Men and brethren, this scripture must needs

have been fulfilled, which the Holy Ghost by the mouth of David spake before concerning Judas, which was guide to them that took Jesus." (Peter confirmed the same divine inspiration.)

Finally, Jesus' incarnation and ministry is the focal point of God's immanent work in the world. His birth, life and ministry, death, resurrection, and ascension all confirm God's immanence. A few verses that address the incarnation point this out. Obviously, the Gospels are filled with the life and activity of Jesus, how He fulfilled the OT prophecies regarding Himself as He was well aware (John 5:46; Luke 4:16-21; 24:44); however, the verses are far too many to list. A reading of the Gospels will make this abundantly clear.

Matthew 1:23: "Behold, a virgin shall be with child, and shall bring forth a son, and they shall call his name Emmanuel, which being interpreted is, God with us."

John 1:14: "And the Word was made flesh, and dwelt among us, (and we beheld his glory, the glory as of the only begotten of the Father,) full of grace and truth."

Romans 1:3: "Concerning his Son Jesus Christ our Lord, which was made of the seed of David according to the flesh."

Galatians 4:4: "But when the fulness of the time was come, God sent forth his Son, made of a woman, made under the law."

Philippians 2:6-7: "Who, being in the form of God, thought it not robbery to be equal with God: But made himself of no reputation, and took upon him the form of a servant, and was made in the likeness of men."

1 Timothy 3:16: "And without controversy great is the mystery of godliness: God was manifest in the flesh, justified in the Spirit, seen of angels, preached unto the Gentiles, believed on in the world, received up into glory."

Hebrews 2:14: "Forasmuch then as the children are partakers of flesh and blood, he also himself likewise took part of the same; that through death he might destroy him that had the power of death, that is, the devil."

1 John 4:3: "And every spirit that confesseth not that Jesus Christ is come in the flesh is not of God: and this is that spirit of antichrist, whereof ye have heard that it should come; and even now already is it in the world."

2 John 1:7 "For many deceivers are entered into the world, who confess not that Jesus Christ is come in the flesh. This is a deceiver and an antichrist."

It is this last attribute of God (Immanence) that is so important. We pray because of God's involvement with His creation. The Bible is filled with the interaction of God with believers, and at times unbelievers. We experience the presence of God through the work of the Holy Spirit in our lives. Thus, we experience the personality of God because of His love and involvement with His creation.

What a wonderful God we worship! He is all-powerful and sovereign, yet we are thankfully secure with Him because He loves us. We are not concerned He will exercise His awesome power in a way that would be against His nature, so His will and purposes are a comfort to us – which is why it is so important to know them. We do not always understand why God acts in a particular way, but when we understand His nature and attributes, we are thankful that He is exactly how He has described Himself in the Bible. Circumstances may change, but God never does. This is a comfort to Christians as it was to the nation of Israel (Malachi 3:6), God is always good to His promises and covenants (Heb. 6:6-19).

At times Christians dwell on or overanalyze the issues they *cannot* understand (about God), instead of focusing on what the Bible reveals which they *can* understand. This is something we can all over think at times, but it is not necessary to be filled with anxiety wondering if God has changed – He has not and never will. His nature and characteristics should be a comfort to us, which is why it is so important that we understand what the Bible reveals about God – or better – what God reveals about Himself.

God has an eternal plan of redemption, and He will accomplish it according to His sovereign will. He gives every person an opportunity to be part of that plan by simple faith in Jesus Christ. God is a relational God; therefore, He honors the freedom of each person to love or hate Him. Man is capable of rejecting the love and grace of God through Jesus Christ; otherwise, the very nature of God would be in question. God loves, therefore He desires us to trust Him (faith) and offer our love (relationship) to Him without reservation. People do not want a relationship with someone who is not willing to have one, and God is no different in that way. He is not going to force anyone to love Him or serve Him against their libertarian free will. It is the freedom that God allows which enables the greatest expression of love, since love is only valid when freely given. Very simply, God desires a relationship with man whom He made in His image. If this is God's desire, the only way for this to occur is without coercion. Anything short of the legitimate freedom of the will to engage in a trust-based relationship with God would be an indictment against the very nature of God.[47]

Trust is the foundation of all true relationships. We trust (believe, have faith) that the person we plan to enter a relationship with is truthful and honest in their representation of themselves to us. It is our response of trust in who they say they are that is where the essence of the relationship exists. It is the same with God. He represents Himself in time and records it in Scripture. If we trust (believe, have faith) Him as He reveals Himself, this is where faith comes in. Following laws or rules represents the type of relationship, but observing them can never create the actual relationship. This is why man cannot relate to God through his works, since that is never going to be the basis of a loving relationship. People cannot have a genuine love relationship by following rules, so why would it be different with God? Trust is required; there is intimacy in that aspect of relating. If I tried to relate to my wife by giving and receiving a list of rules to follow each day so our relationship could flourish, it would never get off the ground. I married my wife because I believed who she was and trusted the woman that shared her life with me. My actions now follow a pattern that correlates to loving actions because of my love *for* her, not to gain it. My behavior represents our mutual trust for each other, but rules and laws cannot create what we have in shared trust.

God is looking for people who will trust Him and His redemptive work through His Son Jesus Christ. He has done everything possible other than forcing people to believe against their wills. He created man (knowing man would sin), worked His plan for redemption, carried it out through His Son who gave the ultimate sacrifice, conquered death and the power of sin, and sits at the right hand of God to intercede for those who will place their trust in Him. How do people come to faith in Christ? The Holy Spirit of God convicts them of their sin and need for Christ (John 16:8), the Scriptures contain the power of God to convert those who believe the Gospel (Rom. 1:16), and the church of the redeemed witness the graceful life changing power of God in them (2 Cor. 3:2). Therefore, God has done all that is necessary for the redemption of man. Man has the freedom to trust in (believe) or reject God. Is He trustworthy? That is what individuals must decide for themselves. However, just as it is true among human relationships it is true with our relationship with God. Either we believe who God says He is and how He represents Himself through the Bible's revelation of Him, or we reject it. Is it an important decision? Absolutely! It is the most important decision a person will make in this life, for the consequences become effective now and will carry on to eternal life beyond this world.

THE COVENANTS

The Law and the Gospel

John began his Gospel by revealing that Jesus Christ is God (John 1:1), the Creator of all things (1:2), the provider of physical and spiritual life (1:4), provider of light (knowledge, truth, purity), and this is to everyone (1:9). Though Creator of all, He was not recognized by the world (1:10), and though the Creator of Israel, was not received by them (1:11). The ones that did receive Him as Messiah (God in human flesh) were given spiritual life by grace through faith – to as many as believed - not by any of the works of the Law (1:12-14).

1. In the beginning was the Word, and the Word was with God, and the Word was God. 2. He was in the beginning with God. 3. All things were made through Him, and without Him nothing was made that was made. 4. In Him was life, and the life was the light of men. 5. And the light shines in the darkness, and the darkness did not comprehend it. 6. There was a man sent from God, whose name was John. 7. This man came for a witness, to bear witness of the Light, that all through him might believe. 8. He was not that Light, but was sent to bear witness of that Light. 9. That was the true Light which gives light to every man coming into the world. 10. He was in the world, and the world was made through Him, and the world did not know Him. 11. He came to His own, and His own did not receive Him. 12. But as many as received Him, to them He gave the right to become children of God, to those who believe in His name: 13. who were born, not of blood, nor of the will of the flesh, nor of the will of man, but of God. 14. And the Word became flesh and dwelt among us, and we beheld His glory, the glory as of the only begotten of the Father, full of grace and truth. (John

1:1-14, NJKV)

After this introduction of the Person of the Messiah, John says in verse 17, "For the law was given by Moses, but grace and truth came by Jesus Christ." Was John saying there is no truth in the Mosaic Law? Of course not, the Law would be shown throughout John's gospel to be the very truth that was necessary to receive in order to know who Jesus in fact is (John 5:46-47). What John informs his readers of is that the Law that came through Moses was preparatory to that of the "grace and truth" through Jesus Christ. The Mosaic Law both pointed to and anticipated the Messiah! John explains the preeminence of the revelation of Jesus Christ to that of Moses. Moses could not reveal the Father to Israel as Jesus did, for only the Son of God can reveal God to man, Moses did not possess that capability. Thus, in verse 18, John says, "No man hath seen God at any time; the only begotten Son, which is in the bosom of the Father, he hath declared (revealed) him." It is through the revelation of the Son of God that the Gospel of the Grace of God finds its fulfillment.

To understand properly what John is communicating specifically in John 1:17, we need to back up to verse 16 since verse 17 begins with the word "for." In other words, John is concluding in verse 17 what he states in verse 16. Verse 16 says, "And of his fulness have all we received, and grace for grace." The fullness was introduced previously in verse 14 when John said, "And the Word was made flesh, and dwelt among us, (and we beheld his glory, the glory as of the only begotten of the Father,) full of grace and truth." The grace and truth that was complete in Jesus, is received by those who receive Him, and available to those who want Him. Thomas Constable provides a good explanation of verse 17:

> Whereas Moses was the individual through whom God gave His law to His people, Jesus Christ is the one through whom He has manifested abundant grace and truth. This is John's first use of the human name "Jesus," which occurs 237 times in this Gospel, more than a quarter of the total 905

times it appears in the entire New Testament. The compound "Jesus Christ," however, occurs again only in John 17:3 in John. This evangelist used "Christ" 19 times, more than any of the other Gospel writers (cf. John 20:31). This seems reasonable if John wrote late in the first century A.D. by which time "Christ" had become a titulary (a title turned proper name).

John's statement shows the superiority of the gracious dispensation that Jesus introduced over the legal dispensation that Moses inaugurated (cf. Rom. 5:20-21; Eph. 2:8). The legal age contained grace, and the gracious age contains laws. For example, each sacrifice that God accepted under the old economy was an expression of His grace. John was contrasting the dominant characteristics of these two ages. Law expresses God's standards, but grace provides help so we can do His will. Surprisingly, John used the great Christian word "grace" three times in his prologue (John 1:14; John 1:16-17) but nowhere else in his Gospel.[48]

Thus, John reveals a contrast between the two covenants. Moses reveals the Law that was part of the previous dispensation, "God, who at various times and in various ways spoke in time past to the fathers by the prophets has in these last days spoken to us by His Son" (Heb. 1:1-2a, NKJV). Moses was part of this partial revelation "in time past," but the Son provides the fullness of the revelation of God to man (John 1:18). The important thing to note is that these are not competing covenants, but complementary. They are not to be understood as contradicting, but cooperating to bring about the continued progressive revelation of God to man. The book of Hebrews informs us that the Old Covenant (Mosaic Law) had an expiration date, "For if that first covenant had been faultless, then should no place have been sought for the second" (Heb. 8:7). This second covenant is the New Covenant in Christ's blood (Luke 22:20). The writer of Hebrews references Jeremiah 31:31-34, then concludes the chapter with, "In that he saith, A new covenant, he hath made the first old. Now that which decayeth and waxeth old is ready to vanish away" (Heb. 8:13). Therefore, the New Covenant was prophesied of and anticipated under the Old Covenant. Thus, the old gives way to the new, as John the Baptist (last OT prophet) gave way to Christ (John 3:30). There is no competition or blending of the two covenants, one ends and the other begins.

In the remainder of John's gospel, he reveals the Son through a marvelous selection of incidents and statements from Jesus' life. John is unique in how he reveals the Son, tying together essential truths related to the life of Jesus in a more personal way, and providing connections left open in the synoptic gospels. That he emphasizes the deity of Christ in each chapter is obvious to even a casual reader. This unique description of Jesus from John gives detail to the verse already quoted above, that God has "in these last days spoken to us by His Son" (Heb. 1:2). Indeed, the New Covenant inaugurated by the Son is the result of the Old Covenant running its course and doing its job (Rom. 10:4; Gal. 3:24-25). For John clarifies the complementary nature of the New Covenant to the old, and the move into the next phase of God's plan, when he quoted Jesus saying, "For if you believed Moses, you would believe Me; for he wrote about Me" (John 5:46). It is difficult to miss the fact that John maintains this theme throughout his entire gospel.

At this point, it will be helpful to have an overview of the various eras in the Bible. Whether you agree with the Dispensational perspective or not, it will be helpful to have the overview that follows. This will help see the Bible at a high level and the relationship between covenants and dispensations in more detail.

DISPENSATIONS

God gave the NT apostles and prophets knowledge in the mystery of the revelation (Eph. 3:3) of the current *dispensation*. Paul the apostle explains this to us in his letter to the Ephesian church (Eph. 1:10, 3:2). He taught that God made a new group of believers called "the Body of Christ." This group would be a completely new Body of believers, made up of both Jews and Gentiles without any distinction between them (Eph. 3:6). This plan of God was not prophesied in the OT (Eph. 3:5), but only revealed in the NT and is called a *mystery*. The word mystery, as Paul uses it, does not mean a "who done it" mystery that is solvable by the exercise of keen detective skills; it is information from God not previously revealed, but now disclosed. In other words, a mystery in the manner Paul is using it requires revelation to understand it, since there is nothing in the OT that anticipates it.

It is essential for us to understand how this new Body is distinct, since Paul reveals the fact that the church, the Body of Christ, is *not* the nation of Israel. The nation of Israel gives supremacy to the Jews, and Gentiles can enter the nation by proselytization and committing to live under the Law no different from the Jews. However, they are not on equal terms for all that the Law describes and offers. Under the Mosaic Law, each Jewish tribe received its own allotted land area and this was to be passed on to each successive generation (Joshua 14:1-2). Gentiles could become worshippers of Israel's God under the Law, not by birth, but by entering through ritual. A Gentile convert was called a "stranger" (Exodus 12:48). The point is that the equality Gentiles enjoy in the Body of Christ (the church) that God works through today-though very natural today since the church after 2000 years is mostly Gentiles – was a shock to a

Jew under the Law in the first century.

This was Peter's experience when he went to Cornelius's house in Acts 10. It was a revelation to him at that point that God was extending the Gospel to the Gentiles. The first converts to Christianity were Jewish, and as Peter had to relate his experience at Cornelius's house to the church in Jerusalem, he was almost apologetic as he compared the same experience of the Holy Spirit descending on the Jews, as the experience among the Gentiles (Acts 11:1-18; Acts 2; Acts 10). The Jews experienced a change at Pentecost with the birth of the church, and with the additional work of God's Spirit at Cornelius's house, the Gentiles became involved with the Gospel. This new work of God is entirely different, not an extension of the Mosaic Covenant. The change was a new dispensation. This new dispensation is where the church comes in.

> That Gentiles were to be saved was no mystery (Rom. 9:24-33; Rom. 10:19-21). The mystery 'hidden in God' was the divine purpose to make of Jew and Gentile a wholly new thing-'the Church, which is his [Christ's] body,' formed by the baptism with the Holy Spirit (1Cor. 12:12-13) and in which the earthly distinction of Jew and Gentile disappears (Eph. 2:14-15; Col. 3:10-11). The revelation of this 'mystery' of the Church was foretold but not explained by Christ (Matt. 16:18). The details concerning the doctrine, position, walk, and destiny of the Church were committed to Paul and his fellow 'apostles and prophets by the Spirit' (Eph. 3:5).[49]

Abraham and his offspring were under the dispensation called Promise which has gone by; it ended at the dispensation of the Law because there was a change in condition. However, the promises given to Abraham (Gen. 12) were ratified into the Abrahamic Covenant (Gen. 15), which is still in effect because it is everlasting and has yet to be entirely fulfilled.

> The Dispensation of Promise extends from (Gen_12:1) to (Exo_19:8); and was exclusively Israelitish. The *dispensation* must be distinguished from the *covenant*. The former

is a mode of testing; the latter is everlasting because unconditional. The law did not abrogate the Abrahamic Covenant (Gal. 3:15-18) but was an intermediate disciplinary dealing "till the Seed should come to whom the promise was made"; (Gal. 3:19-29); (Gal. 4:1-7). Only the *dispensation*, as a testing of Israel, ended at the giving of the law.[50]

Genesis chapter 17 uses the word "covenant" 13 times and "everlasting" 4 times to describe it. However, the dispensation of the Law, which came over 600 years later (considering the ages of Abraham, Isaac, Jacob, and the 400 years of Israel in Egypt), ended at the cross and gave way to the dispensation of grace. Both covenants of Abraham and the Mosaic Law were given to Israel alone, no other peoples or nations ever fell under the particulars of the Mosaic Legal System or the promises given to Abraham (nations received the effect of the redemptive aspect). Both of these covenants (Abrahamic and Mosaic) will ultimately be fulfilled in their entirety in the Messianic Kingdom (Rev. 20), which Jesus will establish upon His return (Rev. 19), which will be fulfilled *through* the nation of Israel. Moreover, these covenants will ultimately be fulfilled when Israel comes to faith in Christ (Rom. 11:26-27). These two covenants only have reference to Israel-no other nation, ethnic group, or people can make a claim to them – though many have shamefully tried.

Therefore, to understand what Paul spoke of and what Peter experienced (Acts 2 and 10), we must comprehend what a dispensation is, especially since this NT revelation is a dispensation as Paul makes reference to it as revealed to him and other NT apostles and prophets (Eph. 3:5). The word dispensation is a combination of two Greek words meaning "a house" and "law" or "rule," so literally it is "house law, rule or management" and is often translated as "stewardship." In other words, it is the management over the affairs of a house, to oversee the house according to the laws or rules. Thus, the idea is simply "the law or stewardship of the house." A "dispensation" is not a period or epoch (a common, but erroneous, use of the word), but a mode of dealing, an arrangement or administration of affairs."[51] Thus, God has different criteria of managing man under different conditions, such as under the Law or under the Gospel. The word does not spell out the calendar period, though the "law or rules of the house" will differ through various times. Because of the change in management that occurs throughout history, these changes are called dispensations. The dispensation is changed with the change in criteria of stewardship man is placed under, not a specific period of time. The time element is not the defining factor, the change of rule is. In other words, it is a change in house rules that creates a new dispensation. Thus, the dispensation becomes the conditions or rules God will manage His affairs with man. Though the relationship is always by faith, the rules change based on the dispensation criteria. It also must be noted that a dispensation is not always aligned with a covenant.

The Third Dispensation: Human Government. Under Conscience, as in Innocency, man utterly failed, and the judgment of the Flood marks the end of the second dispensation and the beginning of the third. The declaration of the Noahic Covenant subjects humanity to a new test. Its distinctive feature is the institution, for the first time, of human government -- the government of man by man. The highest function of government is the judicial taking of life. All other governmental powers are implied in that. It follows that the third dispensation is distinctively that of human government. Man is responsible to govern the world for God. That responsibility rested upon the whole race, Jew and Gentile, until the failure of Israel under the Palestinian Covenant (Deuteronomy 28:1-10) brought the judgment of the Captivities, when "the times of the Gentiles" (See); (Luke 21:24); (Rev. 16:14) began, and the government of the world passed exclusively into Gentile hands; (Dan. 2:36-45); (Luke 21:24); (Acts 15:14-17). That both Israel and the Gentiles have governed for self, not God, is sadly apparent. The judgment of the confusion of tongues ended the racial testing; that of the captivities the Jewish; while the Gentile testing will end in the smiting of the Image (Dan. 2) and the judgment of the nations (Matt. 25:31-46).[52]

The Palestinian[53] or Land covenant with Israel is not limited to a dispensation. Since Israel never possessed the land in its promised entirety, it will be accomplished in the millennial reign. Similarly, the Davidic Covenant (2 Sam. 7:8-17) or that of the Messianic Ruler coming from the line of David will also be fulfilled in the millennial reign.

The Davidic Covenant (2 Sam. 7:8-17).

This covenant, upon which the glorious kingdom of Christ "of the seed of David according to the flesh" is to be founded, secures:

(1) A Davidic "house"; that is, Posterity, family

(2) A "throne"; that is, Royal authority

(3) A kingdom; that is, Sphere of rule

(4) In perpetuity; "for ever."[54]

When theologians view the different dispensations that the Bible naturally reveals, they are called dispensationalists. Typically, there are seven dispensations observed. The original Scofield Bible says this about dispensations, "A dispensation is a period of time during which man is tested in respect of obedience to some specific revelation of the will of God. Seven such dispensations are distinguished in Scripture."[55] I agree with Scofield that this is a good explanation of how we should view biblical dispensations. It is vital that the rule change in a given dispensation not be viewed as the change of the criteria for salvation. People are saved from Adam until the end of the Millennial reign by faith alone! The rule change provides conditions of living and this in turn can give the indication of whether or not a person is living by faith or not. But the actual relationship with God is always by faith. This misunderstanding

GOD OF COVENANTS

of the change of conditions has caused some to think that dispensationalists teach that the new condition man is placed under brings a new way to be saved – this is not the case. For example, the Law did not save those under it; God enacted the Law as a means of sanctification for the nation of Israel, not their salvation. Rebelling against the Law may be an indication that a Jew was not living by faith in God, but the two conditions are not equal in relation to a person's individual salvation. The point bears repeating; man has always been and always will be saved by faith alone apart from any works – no matter what dispensation or covenant they live under.

Dispensationalists can have a variety of understandings regarding how many dispensations exist; I will present a typical and more natural view in this book. The advantage of the dispensational view is that the Bible naturally lays this out historically with its progressive revelation. Ignoring the differing eras and the conditions man is placed under by God creates an inherent danger of taking the conditions of the current church period (which we understand), and imposing it back on previous eras that did not have the advantage of the current revelation we live under today. In other words, we can impose the context of the current times back into previous periods. That would be like reading the twenty-first century culture back into the biblical culture of the first or prior centuries. This is a recipe for disaster if we are trying to understand the Bible in its context. The dispensational viewpoint allows us to distinguish the criteria of each era, while keeping the criteria for salvation separate. Correlating a dispensation with salvation criteria will ensure at worst a heresy, or at least some false teaching – which has been the misery throughout church history.

Here in this chart below is a typical example of seven dispensations that naturally identify conditions within the chronological layout of biblical history. Following the chart below is a brief explanation of each of these seven dispensations.

The Seven Typical Dispensations

1	2	3	4	5	6	7
Innocence	Conscience	Human Gov.	Promise	Law	Grace	Kingdom
Before sin	Rom. 2	Noah	Abram	Moses	NT	Jesus reign

1. **The Dispensation of Innocence**: Prior to sin entering into the Garden of Eden, man was in a state of innocence - not having experienced the effects of sin. Thus, the only law Adam and Eve were under was the command not to eat of "the tree of the knowledge of good and evil" (Gen. 2:17). No other obligation was upon man at that time, so the categorization as a dispensation of innocence is very reasonable. Both Adam and Eve ended up expelled from the Garden of Eden after this innocence ended because of their sin. This also ended this dispensation since the command and criteria given prior to Adam and Eve's sin was no longer how God managed people. There is a judgment ending this dispensation; Adam and Eve were expelled from the garden (Gen. 3:23-24).

2. **The Dispensation of Conscience**: After the fall of man (Adam and Eve's sin), each person had the effect of Adam's sin nature passed to them (Rom. 5:12) and lived by the rule of their conscience. This was really the only condition man lived under because God did not place them under any laws or official restrictions. We know God works through man's conscience because man is made in God's image (Rom. 2:14-15) and the Spirit of God worked with man to bring conviction of conscience during this era (Gen. 6:3). This second dispensation ended with the flood judgment, which was the consequence of man's failure under this second stewardship.

3. **The Dispensation of Human Government**: After the flood, God gave Noah new conditions He required man to abide by (Gen. 9:1-9). These conditions established

what we could call human government, since God instructed Noah (a human) to exercise this governing rule over his descendants. He was to make sure that premeditated murder required the judgment of capital punishment. The reason? God told Noah that no one but God has the authority destroy His image in Man; in other words man had no right to commit murder. If they did, they would be forfeiting their own life in the process and the governing agent for God (Noah at this point) would be the one to exact that capital punishment. As you can see, the changes are not based on time periods, but as the rules change under which man lives, the times change as a natural consequence.

It is important to realize at this point that the requirements under which man finds himself are the conditions required by God for a relationship with Him. In every dispensation, *faith* is the salvation condition of how man relates to God; therefore, if faith is genuine there should be an indication outwardly in a proper response to the conditions that God requires. Only God truly knows if a person's faith is genuine because only God can see the heart of man. It would be hard to make a case for genuine faith if a man consistently rebelled against the dispensational conditions. Thus, obedience in every dispensation only has the potential to *prove* faith, never to *create* faith. From Adam to the end of the millennial kingdom in Rev. 20, *faith* is the condition for salvation, never works or human effort.

This third dispensation ends in failure with the judgment at the tower of Babel in Gen. 11. There is no nation free of the infection of idolatry and corrupt rebellion. Thus, God creates a new nation through which to bring His kingdom – lost in Eden under the rule of Adam and Eve. He will bring His kingdom to earth through the offspring of Abraham, Isaac, and Jacob.

4. **The Dispensation of Promise**: After the judgment of

nations at Babel, God began a new nation with a man from Ur named Abram, later named Abraham. God made a promise to Abraham that He would birth a nation through Abraham's descendants, bless the world through this nation (meaning the Savior promised from the Garden of Eden - Gen. 3:15), and give them a land to dwell in so this promise could come to fruition. Abraham believed God's "promise," which resulted in God imputing (transferring) His own righteousness to Abraham (Gen. 15:6). In other words, the nation He creates from Abraham will be the vehicle to bring His word, Savior, and Kingdom to a world lost in sin.

Paul the apostle used the faith that Abraham exercised as the foundation for the doctrine of justification by faith, which he developed in the letter to the Romans and taught in Galatians. The promise made to Abraham would be ratified into an *unconditional* covenant (Gen. 15) and passed on to his descendants that would end up being the nation of Israel. This promise will be in effect until the requirements of the covenant are fulfilled. It is key to distinguish the dispensation of promise from the covenant of Abraham. The dispensation will come and go; the covenant promises will remain through the millennial kingdom, since it will take that particular dispensation of the Kingdom to fulfill it.

5. **The Dispensation of Law**: With the Law given by Moses, we enter into the next stewardship under which God obligates man – Israel in particular. This is a *conditional* covenant and it is through these conditions (Ex. 19:3-8) that the nation of Israel will demonstrate their stewardship to God. This dispensation of Law is explained in some detail in this book and will be further developed, but it is important to know that this stewardship ended at the judgment of the world's sin at the cross. This covenant was only to the nation of Israel, no other people. It is the confusion of how this

covenant is given, what it is used for, and to whom it was covenanted that much of this book is addressed.

6. **The Dispensation of Grace**: This begins with the death, resurrection, and ascension of Jesus Christ. The condition man is placed under is the acceptance or rejection of Jesus Christ by faith alone. As mentioned, in each dispensation man is saved by faith, but the stewardship they are placed under reveals whether or not they are demonstrating such faith. For example, under promise man was saved by faith just as Abraham was (which only God could see), but it was demonstrated (for people to see) by their living in anticipation of the promise made to Abraham. Under the Law, man again is saved by faith, but their faith was seen by their obedience to the Law – God provided the Law as the means of maintaining a relationship with Him, not salvation. It was a means of the sanctification of the nation of Israel, not a way to salvation. Now, under Grace, man is saved by faith in Jesus Christ and that faith is demonstrated by abiding in Christ and obedience to the NT teachings to the church. This can be a bit tricky because it is easy to make the demonstration of faith the criteria for salvation instead of faith alone. Focusing on what a person does can emphasize the works they do to evaluate their salvation. However, this is really bringing the Sanctification process into Justification. Many have done this unintentionally (I believe), yet the results are not pretty. It creates a legalistic-minded Christian that focuses on the salvation standing based on works and not faith. This has caused much damage and deterioration in churches throughout the centuries (Gal. 5:13-15).

7. **The Dispensation of the Kingdom**: This begins with the start of the millennial reign in Rev. 20. Under this

dispensation the condition man will be in is the ideal government with the perfect global ruler, Jesus Christ. He will rule and reign from Jerusalem and man will be required to live under the criteria set down by Christ and His government. Evil will not have free reign as today, but Christ will rule His kingdom with a "rod of iron" (Ps. 2:9, Rev. 2:27, 12:5; 19:15). In other words, an enforced righteousness when necessary.

There are varied conditions under which man is placed as a form of testing for each dispensation. John Walvoord insightfully observed, "Each dispensation recorded in the Bible ends in failure, thus proving that no one under any arrangement can achieve perfection or salvation. Even in the millennial kingdom, with its near-perfect circumstances, humanity will still fail."[56]

The bottom line regarding the overall purpose for these stewardships is that under every condition placed, man fails. Man failed in the first six dispensations so far, and Rev. 20:7-10 predicts the final rebellion at the end of the millennial reign in the last dispensation. As mentioned Jesus will have to rule with a "rod of iron" (Psalm 2:9; Rev. 2:27; 12:5; 19:15), which implies a forced righteousness that is only necessary if sin in the hearts of man still exists. During this current age of grace, the three battles man contends with are against the world, the flesh, and the Devil. During the millennial reign of Christ, the world system will no longer be under the power and sway of the Devil (1 John 5:19), but will be under the power and control of the Messiah and ruled by His righteousness (Isaiah 11:1-10). Moreover, the Devil will be chained (Rev. 20:2) so he will not be there to move around "like a roaring lion, seeking whom he may devour" (1 Peter 5:8). Therefore, those who inhabit the kingdom having survived the tribulation period will still possess their sin nature (the flesh) to contend with which has enough evil of its own. In other words, people who enter the kingdom from the tribulation will not yet have their glorified bodies. Yet, this is enough for man to fail and have a final rebellion break out after the Devil is loosed from his prison (Rev. 20:7). Thus, it was necessary that God, out of love for us and in His marvelous grace to send His Son, take on human flesh, suffer, die, and rise again from among the corpses to conquer death for the salvation of man. There is no capability in man to save himself or succeed in any dispensation, no matter the criteria. God did all the work to redeem man; He did all the heavy lifting so the only condition required by God in our response is faith. Man can respond in faith since he is made in God's image and capable of responding to God. Today, believing in the work of God through Jesus Christ is the result of the conviction of the Holy Spirit and power of the Gospel message. Therefore, God receives *all* the glory and man will praise Him for His marvelous and unending grace, mercy, and love. "Let them praise the name of the LORD: for his name alone is excellent; his glory is above the earth and heaven" (Psalm 148:13).

Through the dispensations there are covenants made by God to ensure that the eschatological purposes He intends for the world are ultimately accomplished. Chafer makes the following observation:

> The kingdom Scriptures of the Old Testament are occupied largely with the character and glory of Messiah's reign, the promises to Israel of restoration and earthly glory, the universal blessings to Gentiles, and the deliverance of creation itself. There is little revealed in the Old Testament Scripture concerning the responsibility of the individual in the kingdom; it is rather a message to the nation as a whole. Evidently the details concerning individual responsibility were, in the mind of the Spirit, reserved for the personal teaching of the King, at the time when the kingdom would be "at hand."[57]

It is important to keep this in mind Israel's relationship to each covenant God makes with them. God's intention for Israel is recognized nationally in His call upon the nation to serve His purposes. However, it is individual to those within the nation as each person exercises personal faith and obeys the covenant to enjoy the blessings promised. Remember, a person is a member of the nation of Israel by their genealogical connection to Abraham, Isaac, and Jacob, but not every member was a genuine believer (Rom. 9:6). This meant that if a Jew did not have personal faith in God, typically this was evident by their lack of adherence to the covenant conditions. Those who were obedient exercised their faith in that respect (Luke 1:5-6). Again, in every dispensation a person is saved by their personal faith. Dispensations are not covenants, they at times correlate to the era, but they are not always functioning the same.

For example, the covenant (unconditional) connected to Noah and his descendants is associated with the flood. God gave the sign of the rainbow to indicate He would never flood the earth again for a judgment (Gen. 9:8-17). It was when Noah got off the Ark that God instituted the dispensation of human government, but this was unrelated to the rainbow covenant. The Davidic Covenant (unconditional) is not its own dispensation, but a specific covenant for David – his offspring the Messiah – to sit on the throne in the millennial kingdom (2 Sam. 7:13, 16, 19; 1 Chron. 17:12; 22:10; Isaiah 55:3; Ez. 37:25). The Abrahamic Covenant (unconditional) has three aspects to it – descendants, land, and redemptive blessing – these describe the dispensation prior to the Mosaic Covenant (conditional); thus the dispensation ended but aspects of the covenant continue. However, the land covenant (Gen. 12:1, 13:14-17; 15:18; 17:7-8; Psalm 105:9-11) is its own covenant, though anticipated in the promise to Abraham and contained in the Abrahamic Covenant. In addition, the redemptive blessing contained in the Abrahamic Covenant becomes its own covenant expressed in the New Covenant. As J. Dwight Pentecost states:

> Thus it may be said that the land promises of the Abrahamic covenant are developed in the Palestinian [land] covenant, the seed promises are developed in the Davidic

covenant, and the blessing promises are developed in the new covenant. This covenant, then, determines the whole future program for the nation Israel and is a major factor in Biblical Eschatology.[58]

When Pentecost states that "this covenant, then, determines the whole future program for the nation", he refers to the Abrahamic Covenant. Since the covenant is ratified in Genesis 15, it is developed along the way within the future covenants. The key is that they are all unconditional covenants (Mosaic notwithstanding), which means that God will perform what needs to be done in order for the development of each covenant. This is why the Jews are referred to as a covenant people since they are the only nation that God made covenants with (Rom. 9:4). Moreover, all the covenants are said to be eternal, as Pentecost remarks in quoting Charles Fred Lincoln:

All of Israel's covenants are called eternal except the Mosaic covenant which is declared to be temporal, i.e., it was to continue only until the coming of the Promised Seed. For this detail see as follows: (1) The Abrahamic Covenant is called "eternal" in Genesis 17:7, 13, 19; I Chronicles 16:17; Psalm 105:10; (2) The Palestinian Covenant is called "eternal" in Ezekiel 16:60; (3) The Davidic Covenant is called "eternal" in II Samuel 23:5; Isaiah 55:3; and Ezekiel 37:25; and (4) The New Covenant is called "eternal" in Isaiah 24:5; 61:8; Jeremiah 32:40; 50:5; and Hebrews 13:20.[59]

The following chart clarifies the relation of Israel's covenants to dispensations.

COVENANT	SCRIPTURES	CONDITION	DISPENSATION
Abrahamic (descendants, land, redemptive	Gen. 12:1-7; 13:14-17; 15:1-21; 17:1-14;	Unconditional	Promise

blessing reaffirmed through Isaac and Jacob)	22:15-18; 26:1-5; 24-25; 28:12-15		
Land	Gen. 12:1; 13:14-17; 15:18; 17:7-8; Deut. 30:1-7	Unconditional	Promise – Millennial
Mosaic	Ex. 19:5-8	Conditional	Law
Davidic	2 Sam. 7:13, 16, 19; 1 Chron. 17:12; 22:10; Isaiah 55:3; Ez. 37:25	Unconditional	Law – Millennial
New	Deut. 30:6; Jer. 31:31-34; Matt. 26:28; Mark 14:24; Luke 22:20	Unconditional	Grace – Millennial

TWO DIFFERENT COVENANTS: LAW AND GOSPEL

The Law of Moses (the Law) and the Gospel of Jesus Christ (the Gospel of Grace) are two covenants in two different dispensations announced by two different messengers of God. Paul tells us in Col. 2:17, the Law was "a shadow of things to come; but the body is of Christ." In other words, the Law was the shadow, but the body that cast the shadow was Jesus. Another way to understand it would be to say that the Law talked about, foreshadowed, and provided examples of Jesus – who He would be and what He would do. But the NT has the reality of the actual person Jesus Christ because He arrived on the scene in human flesh. Therefore, the Law is different in its intent and purpose from what Jesus brought in "grace and truth" (John 1:17). If the covenant of the Law had been adequate in itself to provide for man's *eternal* spiritual needs-there would be no need for another covenant. The mere fact that it anticipated a Savior, represented by various types and shadows, reveals its temporary nature. Thus, the covenant of the Law came through Moses for a *temporary* purpose, but grace and truth (Jesus embodying the very truth of God), the New Covenant in Christ's blood (Luke 22:20) came through Jesus Christ for an *eternal* purpose.

It would be wrong to conclude that there was no grace or truth under the Law. The giving of the Law to Israel was an act of grace, (grace is something God initiates and gives for man's benefit that is entirely undeserved) and the Law certainly reflects the truth of God and His righteousness. The entire Mosaic system of approach through the animal sacrifices and the offer of temporary forgiveness for a sanctifying relationship was God's gracious offer to Israel, not offered to any other nation. Therefore, the Mosaic system of Law is a result of grace.

It should be noted that the whole reason the Law was given to Israel was because of the call of the nation to accomplish God's purpose in the world. It is because of this call that God through the Law gave both provision and protection to the accomplishing of His purposes (Malachi 1:2-5; Rom. 9:4-5). Moreover, the Gospel of Jesus Christ has laws to follow, though called "the Gospel of the Grace of God" (Acts 20:24). Indeed, Jesus and the apostles give instructions and commands (not suggestions) that amount to laws expected for NT believers to follow. The difference is how disobedience is now managed under the New Covenant opposed to the Mosaic Covenant. The bottom line or main point here is that God is always the initiator and man is always the responder no matter the covenant. The mere fact that God initiates a relationship with man – that is entirely underserved – is the grace of God. Without God initiating, there would be no opportunity for man to have any relationship at all with God. Further, God chose Abraham from among the pagans in Ur (Gen. 11:31; Joshua 24:2, 3; Neh. 9:7) to birth the nation of Israel. This nation (Abraham's offspring) would fulfill God's purpose to bring His word and Savior into the world, and ultimately bring the Kingdom of Heaven to the earth during the millennial reign of Christ (Rev. 20). All of these activities God initiated because of His grace.

God originated both the Law and the Gospel of Grace, but they are certainly different in both purpose and function. If they had the same intent and purpose, there would be no need to have both covenants. While the Jews were under the Law, Jeremiah announced there would be a "New Covenant" (Jer. 31:31) in the future, which meant the covenant of Law they were under would eventually end. The key is to understand what the contrasts and similarities are between these covenants and why. Clarifying the distinction between the two covenants will prevent NT Christians from trying to incorporate OT Law requirements that God never intended to continue into the Christian life.

UNDERSTANDING THE LAW

God gave the Law of Moses to Israel as a *conditional* covenant (Ex. 19:5-8), meaning Israel had to fulfill certain *conditions* on their side of the covenant (agreement) in order for God to fulfill His side of the covenant. Though it was not a business contract, the Law operated in a similar way. There are two parties involved in the agreement and conditions must be fulfilled on the side of party #2 (Israel) in order for party #1 (God) to fulfill His part. God was not reluctant to fulfill that which He obligated Himself to in this regard, it was actually His intent and desire to bless the nation (Deut. 28:1-14). But the covenant contained severe damages that would be incurred if party #2 failed in their obligation (Deut. 28:15-68), similar to the damages incurred by a business transaction if the inferior party (#2 in this case) failed. In our example, party #1 (God) is the superior party and #2 (Israel) the inferior. Thus, party #1 holds all the advantage and party #2 possess the opportunity for great prosperity based on party #1's gracious offering, if party #2 can keep their end of the contract obligations. Remember, party #1 was not obligated to offer party #2 anything, and thus this is a gracious offer. Indeed, God was under no obligation to offer Israel the opportunity for blessing under the Law. But if Israel was to have a relationship with the eternal God and creator of the universe, there were conditions that they would have to meet for their very survival.

The unconditional Abrahamic Covenant came prior to the Mosaic Covenant. The Mosaic Covenant did not affect the Abrahamic Covenant; there was a different purpose for its later addition. However, the purpose was in harmony with the Abrahamic Covenant of promise and not contrary to it. When the term *unconditional* is used to describe the Abrahamic

Covenant, it does not mean there were no conditions that if obeyed brought blessing, but it describes the type of covenant relationship to Abraham and his descendants. God's nature is not obscured by the unconditional nature of the Abrahamic Covenant. This means that under the Abrahamic Covenant, if people sin God will not bless the sin, but if people act in accordance with the moral character of God's nature, He can bless and prosper as He chooses. As Pentecost describes:

> There are two kinds of covenants into which God entered with Israel: conditional and unconditional. In a conditional covenant that which was covenanted depends for its fulfillment upon the recipient of the covenant, not upon the one making the covenant. Certain obligations or conditions must be fulfilled by the receiver of the covenant before the giver of the covenant is obligated to fulfill that which was promised. It is a covenant with an "if" attached to it. The Mosaic covenant made by God with Israel is such a covenant. In an unconditional covenant that which was covenanted depends upon the one making the covenant alone for its fulfillment. That which was promised is sovereignly given to the recipient of the covenant on the authority and integrity of the one making the covenant apart from the merit or response of the receiver. It is a covenant with no "if" attached to it whatsoever.

> To safeguard thinking on this point, it should be observed that an unconditional covenant, which binds the one making the covenant to a certain course of action, may have blessings attached to that covenant that are conditioned upon the response of the recipient of the covenant, which blessings grow out of the original covenant, but these conditioned blessings do not change the unconditional character of that covenant. The failure to observe that an unconditional covenant may have certain conditioned blessings attached to it had led many to the position that conditioned blessings necessitate a conditional covenant, thus perverting the

essential nature of Israel's determinative covenants.[60]

When Pentecost mentions "determinative covenants," he means a covenant that God determines to fulfill and does not contain an "if" statement in it so that a human condition is required for the covenant itself to be fulfilled, such as the Mosaic Covenant. An unconditional covenant – such as the New Covenant – does not require man's obedience as a means of fulfilling it, but man enjoys the blessings of it when entered into it by faith in Christ. This distinction with the conditional aspects of the Law becomes vital when we start to examine the contrasts of the Law and Gospel covenants and their associated dispensations. Regarding the Abrahamic Covenant, though determinative in nature, Abraham still needed to obey God (Gen. 12:4, 17:1-14, 23, 15-18). Abraham's faith was the basis of his obedience throughout his life. At the beginning God saw Abraham's heart of faith (Gen. 15:6), which is foundational to Paul's teaching on justification by faith apart from works (Rom. 4:1-4). Later in Abraham's life, his faith was observed in the willingness to offer the very son that the Abrahamic Covenant depended upon for its fulfillment (Gen. 22). James emphasizes this aspect of Abraham's life to example the outward manifestation and fruitfulness of faith (James 2:20-24). This was such a remarkable event, the writer of Hebrews tells us of Abraham:

> By faith Abraham, when he was tried, offered up Isaac: and he that had received the promises offered up his only begotten son, Of whom it was said, That in Isaac shall thy seed be called: Accounting that God was able to raise him up, even from the dead; from whence also he received him in a figure. (Heb. 11:17-19)

Thus, Abraham trusting in the promise received and enjoyed the blessings of the relationship because he walked with God and obeyed Him by exercising his faith in God. Similarly, under the New Covenant in Christ's blood, those who respond by faith to the Gospel are blessed with the benefits of the New Covenant just as Abraham was in believing the promise of God – both covenants are entered by faith and enjoyed by obedience. As Paul made clear, "And the scripture, foreseeing that God would justify the heathen through faith, preached before the gospel unto Abraham, saying, In thee shall all nations be blessed. So then they which be of faith are blessed with faithful Abraham" (Gal. 3:8-9). Abraham is the model of faith linked to the promise of God; those who believe the Gospel of Jesus Christ for justification under the New Covenant are also blessed just like Abraham was in believing the promise of God. Indeed, there are no works involved with the entrance of either of these two covenants.

At the time Moses gave the Law, Israel was under the *unconditional* covenant of promise, which previously God gave to Abraham (Gen. 12 and 15). The covenant promise to Abraham contained three specific points (which covenant continued through the Mosaic Covenant though the dispensations changed). The first promise was that of land, the second of descendants, and the third was of the redemptive blessing to all nations of the world (Gen. 12). These *promises* given to Abraham were later ratified into an *unconditional* covenant as mentioned, meaning God was going to use Abraham and his offspring to accomplish His purposes – i.e. the nation was created to serve God. There were no conditions put upon Abraham or his descendants (Israel) as there were under the Mosaic Law that came later. God made the Abrahamic a unilateral covenant when He alone passed between the divided animal (Gen. 15:8-18) in confirmation of His commitment to accomplish His promise. The only condition Abraham needed was the faith to believe God and respond to the promise. Abraham actually tried to help God in the accomplishing of the promise by impregnating a maidservant (Hagar) picked up in Egypt (Gen. 12:10) because Sarah could not get pregnant at that point (Gen. 16:1-2). However, this only resulted in the persecution from Ishmael (illegitimate son of Hagar) in his relationship to Isaac (promised son through Sarah), which continues through

Ishmael's descendants to the present day against the nation of Israel. Indeed, a lesson in the destructive effects of not trusting God's Word. Abraham's decision to help God was a work of the flesh and showed a lack of faith in God to accomplish His purpose. Ultimately, Abraham did trust God and the nation was born (Rom. 4:16-25).

In order for God to accomplish His promised purpose in His covenant to Abraham, God needed to bring Abraham's descendants into the land He promised them. He would fulfill His redemptive purpose (blessing) through them – specifically bringing the Savior of the world into the world. However, their lack of obedience to the Mosaic Law impeded these efforts creating multiple unnecessary detours along the way. It was during the time Israel was under the covenant of promise, that the Mosaic Covenant was added to define sin (Gal. 3:19). Which they needed to obey to receive God's blessing and success in the land, and for the sanctification of the nation. The Law did not eliminate or disannul the promise (Gal. 3:17), for the Law was a different covenant that contained very specific promises. The Law had a different purpose and goal than the covenant of promise. The promise required belief (Gen.15:6), but the Law required obedience (Deut. 30:9-10). Obedience to the laws was the condition. The nation would receive blessings for obedience and curses for disobedience (ref. Deut. 27 and 28).

The following chart shows Abraham's covenant in contrast to some others:

COVENANT WITH	COVENANT PROMISES	COVENANT TYPE
Abraham (also with Isaac & Jacob)	Land, Descendants, Blessing – Redemptive to all nations	Unconditional
Nation	Blessings and	Conditional

of Israel (Mosaic Cov.)	Curses*	
The Church (New Cov.)	Blessings*	Unconditional

*Chastisement is a disciplinary tool of God with His people under these covenants (Prov. 3:12; Heb. 12:3-17), which is not a curse.

The covenant of promise had the purpose of creating a nation, placing them in the land and bringing the Messiah – Savior of the world – through that nation. The covenant of the Law first had the purpose of managing the nation in its relationship with God. Second, it provided the meticulous details prophetically and characteristically to identify the Messiah. That is why both covenants work in cooperation with each other to advance the nation of Israel while being in stark contrast to each other in their operation.

ISRAEL UNDER TWO COVENANTS

While under the Abrahamic covenant, the Mosaic Covenant was added to the nation of Israel, each operated in parallel. Knowing the reason for the Abrahamic Covenant helps provide the variance in design and necessity for the Mosaic Covenant. The reason for the Abrahamic Covenant was to bring redemption to all nations through Israel (Abraham's "Seed," ref. Gal. 3:16), while the Mosaic Covenant's design was to manage Israel's sanctification until the promised "Seed" arrived (Gal. 3:19). The Mosaic Covenant sanctified the nation through detailed instruction so the nation would know how to approach God, abide in a relationship with Him, manage moral behavior, and understand the criteria necessary to know who the Messiah would be when He showed up. The Abrahamic Covenant contains no conditions; it was a unilateral covenant to which God obligated Himself.

O ye seed of Abraham his servant, ye children of Jacob his chosen. He is the LORD our God: his judgments are in all the earth. He hath remembered his covenant for ever, the word which he commanded to a thousand generations. Which covenant he made with Abraham, and his oath unto Isaac; And confirmed the same unto Jacob for a law, and to Israel for an everlasting covenant: Saying, Unto thee will I give the land of Canaan, the lot of your inheritance: When they were but a few men in number; yea, very few, and strangers in it. When they went from one nation to another, from one kingdom to another people; He suffered no man to do them wrong: yea, he reproved kings for their sakes; Saying, Touch not mine anointed, and do my prophets no harm. (Psalm 105:6-15)

A cursory reading of the OT would inform any reader that Israel was a moral management challenge. Being afforded all the privileges (Rom. 9:4) that a nation could expect from the Creator of the universe did not motivate them to obedience (Rom. 9:29). However, what we observe is that God showed mercy to Israel while at other times brought judgment. What determined this variance of God's method? God extended mercy to Israel for their preservation to fulfill the Abrahamic Covenant, while at other times judgment for their violation of the Mosaic Covenant.

While Israel was under both covenants in the OT, we can observe God working His purpose through each covenant operating in parallel. For example, during the reign of Solomon's son Rehoboam, Israel became a divided nation. It split into the northern kingdom (10 northern tribes referred to as Israel or Ephraim) and the southern kingdom (consisting of Judah and Benjamin referred to as Judah). Out of 20 kings that reigned in Judah, only eight of them were good kings; the rest were evil (the northern kingdom having 20 kings – all of them evil). The last good king who reigned in Judah was King Josiah (2 Kings 22-23; 2 Chron. 34-35). He reigned up until 25 years before Judah went into captivity to Babylon, which was for their rebellion and disobedience of the Mosaic Law. By the time Josiah became king, the Assyrians had already taken the northern kingdom (10 tribes) captive in 722 B.C. because of their flagrant idolatry and disobedience to the Law. Judah followed Israel's example for fifty-seven years when Josiah came to the throne at the age of eight – a boy with a heart after God. By the time he was sixteen years old, he removed all idolatry and its remnants from Judah, even into territories of the northern kingdom. At age twenty-four, he commanded the priests to cleanse and repair the temple which had fallen into disrepair during king Manasseh's fifty-five year evil reign (longest reign of any king). While that work was underway, they found a copy of the Law of Moses among the rubble. They brought it to the king and read it to him. He tore his clothes in consternation as he realized the terrible violations to the Law and rebellion of the nation. The reading of the Law revealed what kind of judgment awaited the nation for their iniquity, and Josiah was in tears concerning the nation's condition. Meanwhile, one of the priests informed a prophetess named Huldah about the situation. Huldah prophesied a message to be brought to king Josiah saying God was going to judge Judah, specifically for its disobedience to the Law (2 Chron. 34:24). However, because Josiah was humble and his heart tender toward God, the judgment would come after he was dead (2 Chron. 34:27-28). The judgment would ultimately bring them to Babylon for 70 years, after which God would bring them back to their land to continue His redemptive program through the nation (Jer. 29:10-11).

In this example we see the two covenants working side by side – one based on the promise related to the program of redemption (Abrahamic Covenant), the other managing and educating the nation regarding their sin and disobedience (Mosaic Covenant). This explains why Josiah was spared the coming judgment, but the nation would have to pay for their violation of the Law and endure the curses of the covenant (Deut. 27-30) after his death. Josiah's obedience received blessing from God (which extended to the nation) his actions brought the nation back into obedience to the Mosaic Covenant, destroying all the idolatry and those serving other gods (2 Kings 23:1-20). However, the nation would not escape the coming judgment of their flagrant idolatry. Josiah's reform could not erase the accumulated sinful violations of the Law, only delay it.

When Josiah was gone, the nation would pay for their accumulated sins and covenant violations from their previous kings. The coming judgment is consistent with God's conditions under the Mosaic Covenant, as was His temporary stay of judgment while the nation committed to obeying the Law under Josiah (2 Kings 23:1-3). The Babylonian captivity was the judgment of God because of the Mosaic Law violations while at the same time, God promised to bring Israel back from Babylon after 70 years (Jer. 29:10) to fulfill the Abrahamic Covenant. Jeremiah prophesied beginning at Josiah and continued through Zedekiah's reign (last king of Judah). He informed Israel that God would eventually bring them to Babylon and back again to the Promised Land, continuing His redemptive program through the nation. This is now all past history. God has accomplished what He promised, having returned Israel to their land after the captivity, revealing His faithfulness to His covenant promises.

This dual covenant exercise is evident through many of the prophets. What we find in the prophet's writings is a repeated theme of both covenants working side by side. As they wrote of warnings and judgments because of their rebellion under the Mosaic Covenant, additionally we find the reassurance God would not abandon them, but fulfill the Abrahamic Covenant promises (Gen. 50:24; Ex. 2:24, 6:8, 32:13, 33:1; Lev. 26:42; Num. 32:11; Deut. 1:8, 6:10, 9:5, 27, 29:13, 30:20; 2 Kings 13:23; Psalm 105:9, 42; Jer. 33:26; Micah 7:20). Many of these ultimate restoration promises are given at the end of (or sprinkled throughout) the prophets messages, and describe certain features about the coming kingdom that God will bring to the earth through Israel (few examples, Hosea 13:9 – 14:1-9; Joel 3:17-21; Amos 9:11-15; Micah 4:1-3; Zeph. 3:13-20; Zech. 6:12-13). This prophesied kingdom will occur *after* they turn to God (by their faith in Jesus as their Messiah) during the coming 7 year tribulation period (Rev. 6-18), at the end of which Jesus will return (Rev. 19) and establish the kingdom on earth for 1000 years as promised (Rev. 20). For the nation of Israel, this time of the millennial reign will fulfill the Mosaic Covenant in that the Jews will receive Jesus as Messiah (Matt. 23:37-39), who the Law pointed to in shadow and type. The kingdom could have possibility arrived had Israel not rejected Jesus (John 1:11; Matt. 12). It was offered initially by John the Baptist, Jesus, and His disciples (Matt. 3:1, 2; 4:17; 10:5-7), but it will be fulfilled at Jesus' return. Israel's repentance will create a mourning as they look back and realize their national failure (Zech. 12:10-14), but their recognition of Jesus as their Messiah will fulfill the purpose of the Law (Rom. 10:4; Gal. 3:19 – 4:7).

What a fascinating plan God devised with Israel, and ultimately for the world – who could have imagined? Two covenants working side by side to make sure that the whole world would have the opportunity to receive the Messiah's work of redemption. The Abrahamic Covenant ensured that the Messiah would come to accomplish man's redemption, while the Mosaic Covenant ensured Israel would know whom the Messiah was, why He was coming, and helped prepare them for Him. The Law taught Israel about sin, righteousness, justice, and the necessity of redemption. It also instructed them how they could have access to and maintain a relationship with God. Thus, God made sure He protected Israel under the Abrahamic Covenant – even when disobedient – and He taught Israel the truth under the Mosaic Covenant, guiding sinners to learn how to relate to a holy God. We see these two covenants working in parallel throughout the OT in a beautiful harmony. It answers why at times God extended mercy to fulfill the Abrahamic Covenant and at other times brought judgment because of the Mosaic Covenant. This is why He would have compassion when it served His plan and purposes and why at other times He would not. He would never let Israel be destroyed (Abrahamic Covenant), but He would judge Israel for their sin (Mosaic Covenant). God is always faithful and consistent with the handling of each covenant. Realizing the difference between the two enables us to understand more of why God managed the nation of Israel exactly the way He did.

THE NEW COVENANT

The New Covenant is introduced by Jesus to the apostles in the upper room during the last Passover supper prior to His death (Luke 22:20). This New Covenant replaced the Mosaic Covenant because Jesus fulfilled all its requirements, and therefore it will no longer be necessary (Rom. 10:4). However, for Israel to experience the New Covenant as a nation, which results in the establishment of God's Kingdom on earth and Jesus reigning as King, they need to receive Jesus as their Messiah and King – which they have not done. Yet the New Covenant began without Israel receiving it, so how can we understand our current situation biblically?

Jeremiah prophesied of the New Covenant to Israel when he said,

> Behold, the days come, saith the LORD, that I will make a new covenant with the house of Israel, and with the house of Judah: Not according to the covenant that I made with their fathers in the day that I took them by the hand to bring them out of the land of Egypt; which my covenant they brake, although I was an husband unto them, saith the LORD: But this shall be the covenant that I will make with the house of Israel; After those days, saith the LORD, I will put my law in their inward parts, and write it in their hearts; and will be their God, and they shall be my people. (Jer. 31:31-33)

The New Covenant came, but not as far as Israel is concerned. In their rejection of Christ, they cannot receive the benefits stated by Jeremiah nationally. However, a Jew who personally puts faith in Jesus Christ in this present dispensation is baptized by the Holy Spirit into the Body of Christ (1 Cor. 12:13), no different from Paul the apostle (Rom. 11:1) or any of the other apostles. Though the New Covenant is a covenant promised to Israel, it will be new for individual Jews as they place their faith in Christ and the Mosaic Law will become old. During the present era, the Christian church (Body of Christ) enjoys the New Covenant because of the finished work of Christ. Both believing Jews and Gentiles together make up the church that began on the day of Pentecost (Acts 2). The church is God's people through whom He currently works to reach the world until the rapture takes the church to heaven. After that, the 7 year tribulation period will begin at the signing of an evil and deceptive covenant (Dan. 9:27) with the Antichrist (Beast of Rev. 13), and during that period God will once again work through the nation of Israel to reach the world. Israel will come to faith during the "time of Jacobs's trouble" (Jer. 30:7), as God uses that period to accomplish a number of things. The remnant of Israel coming to faith in Jesus of Nazareth as their Messiah being one of key issues (Matt. 23:39; Joel 2:32; Rom. 10:13).

The New Covenant fulfills the promise made to Abraham in relation to the redemptive blessing that would be for all nations. Thus, we currently see this operating in the church throughout the world (blessing all nations). The covenant benefit of the Holy Spirit living inside Christians, providing them with a new heart and enabling power to a new changed life (regeneration) is promised (Jer. 31:31-34) and fulfilled (Heb. 8:8-12). It requires faith (Gen. 15:6; Hab. 2:4), since it is a promise to be *believed* and not a law to be *obeyed* (Deut. 27:26; Jer. 11:3; Gal. 3:10). It replaces the Mosaic Covenant because that covenant would no longer be required since it did its job in preparing Israel for this New Covenant (Gal. 3:24-25). The Mosaic covenant was established and functions on different principles as the following chart shows:

COVENANT	PRINCIPLE	REQUIREMENT
Abrahamic	Promise – grace	Faith
Mosaic	Law – works	Obedience

New Covenant	Promise – grace	Faith

The New Covenant explained by NT writers such as Paul the apostle correlates the promise to Abraham and the Gospel of grace. Paul always connects promise, grace, and faith together, while contrasting law, works, and obedience (note previous chart). Paul clarifies these relationships in both Romans 4 and Galatians 3. In Romans 4:13-17 he says:

> For the promise, that he should be the heir of the world, was not to Abraham, or to his seed, through the law, but through the righteousness of faith. For if they which are of the law be heirs, faith is made void, and the promise made of none effect: Because the law worketh wrath: for where no law is, there is no transgression. Therefore it is of **faith**, that it might be by **grace**; to the end the **promise** might be sure to all the seed; not to that only which is of the law, but to that also which is of the faith of Abraham; who is the father of us all, (As it is written, I have made thee a father of many nations,) before him whom he believed, even God, who quickeneth the dead, and calleth those things which be not as though they were (bold added).

In his letter to the Galatians, Paul reveals the contrast of works and law with faith and promise. He says, "For as many as are of the **works** of the **law** are under the curse: for it is written, Cursed is every one that continueth not in all things which are written in the book of the law to do [obey] them" (Gal. 3:10). When Paul says "works of the law," he joins works and law together. Faith is opposite, therefore Paul provides the contrast in the next two verses: "But that no man is justified by the law in the sight of God, it is evident: for, The just shall live by faith. And **the law is not of faith**: but [of doing/obeying], The man that doeth [obeys] them shall live in them" (bold added, Gal. 3:11, 12). A person that wants to live under the Law to obtain justification or sanctification must "live in them," in other words, obey them all and live under that system. For they have chosen it as an alternative to the righteousness offered through faith – i.e. they would rather work for it. The curse mentioned in verse 10 is described as applicable for people that are under the Law but do not keep *all* of the Law. It is important to keep *all* of the Law and not selected pieces. Completing the connection in the next two verses Paul explains that Christ paid the price for the man's failure to keep the Law and, therefore, enabled the promised blessing of righteousness transferred ("imputed", used 11 times in Romans 4) because of Christ's redemptive work to come upon people simply by faith – like Abraham (Gen. 15:6).

> Christ hath redeemed us from the curse of the law, being made a curse for us: for it is written, Cursed is every one that hangeth on a tree: That the blessing of Abraham might come on the Gentiles through Jesus Christ; that we might **receive the promise of the Spirit through faith**" (bold added, Gal. 3:13-14).

Again, we see that faith and promise (v. 14) are set in contrast to law and works in the previous verse (v. 10). In verses 13-18 in Galatians 3, Paul proceeds to emphasize faith as the means to receive the promise. In verses 19-29, Paul teaches why God established the Law as a temporary covenant with Israel (i.e. define sin, prepare Israel for faith in Messiah, etc.):

> Why the law then? It was added because of transgressions until the Seed to whom the promise was made would come. The law was ordered through angels by means of a mediator. Now a mediator is not for just one person, but God is one. Is the law therefore contrary to God's promises? Absolutely not! For if a law had been given that was able to give life, then righteousness would certainly be by the law. But the Scripture has imprisoned everything under sin's power, so that the promise by faith in Jesus Christ might be given to those who believe. Before this faith came, we were confined under the law, imprisoned until the coming faith was revealed. The law, then, was our guardian until Christ,

so that we could be justified by faith. But since that faith has come, we are no longer under a guardian, for you are all sons of God through faith in Christ Jesus. For as many of you as have been baptized into Christ have put on Christ. There is no Jew or Greek, slave or free, male or female; for you are all one in Christ Jesus. And if you are Christ's, then you are Abraham's seed, heirs according to the promise. (Gal. 3:19-29, HCSB)

These verses from both Romans and Galatians make the connection of the redemptive promise given through Abraham – who believed it by faith – to those under the New Covenant that believe by faith. Paul says when we exercise faith as Abraham did, we are blessed through the redemptive promise (Gal. 3:9, 13-14) made to him, and because we are Christ's, we are Abraham's seed (in Christ spiritually) and become heirs of this promise (Gal. 3:29). Abraham then becomes our spiritual father (if you will) because we have exercised faith in Christ, Who is the fulfillment of the redemptive promise Abraham initially believed when it was made to him (Gen. 12:2, 15:6; Rom. 4:16).

A chronological comparison of the Abrahamic, Mosaic, and New covenant will be helpful. Having said that, God only works through one people at a time to reach the world – either Israel or the church, but not both. Though both Israel and the church are in the world at the same time, both groups are not active agents of God. The land, descendants, and redemptive blessing of the Abrahamic Covenant continue through to the fulfillment of each of these regarding Israel as a nation. However, the redemptive aspect of the New Covenant is enjoyed now by the church until it is raptured. Following the rapture (removal of the church), the 7 year tribulation period will be a time when God refocuses on Israel. He will separate the true Israel from the false, and during this time of their trial (Jer. 30:7) Israel will be brought to the place where they will cry out for their true Messiah the Lord Jesus Christ (Matt. 23:39).

The following graphic provides a helpful visual of how these covenants relate in a timeline.

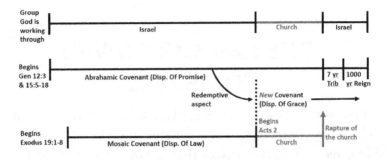

THE LAW ONLY GIVEN
TO ISRAEL

Before moving on, it is essential to understand that Israel was the only nation to ever receive and be obligated to the Mosaic Covenant. The reason this is such a key issue is that so many Christians and others try to take aspects of the Law and impose it on the Christian's experience under the New Covenant. Moreover, the Mosaic Covenant was temporary in nature so it was not *only* a conditional covenant, but it had an expiration date (Heb. 8:6-13).

First, the Law of Moses was given only to Israel (underline added for emphasis), no other nation:

> **Exodus 24:3, 7-8:** "And Moses came and told the people <u>all the words of the LORD, and all the judgments</u>: and all the people answered with one voice, and said, All the words which the LORD hath said will we do… And <u>he took the book of the covenant, and read in the audience of the people</u>: and they said, All that the LORD hath said will we do, and be obedient. And Moses took the blood, and sprinkled it on the people, and said, <u>Behold the blood of the covenant, which the LORD hath made with you concerning all these words.</u>"

> **Deut. 4:5-8:** "Behold, I have taught you <u>statutes and judgments</u>, even as the LORD my God commanded me [Moses], that ye should do so in the land whither ye go to possess it. Keep therefore and do them; for this is your wisdom and your understanding in the sight of the nations, which shall hear all these statutes, and say, Surely this great nation is a wise and understanding people. For what nation is there so great, who hath God so nigh unto them, as the LORD our God is in all things that we call upon him

for? And <u>what nation is there so great, that hath statutes and judgments so righteous as all this law, which I set before you this day</u>?"

Deut. 4:32-40: "For ask now of the days that are past, which were before thee, <u>since the day that God created man upon the earth, and ask from the one side of heaven unto the other, whether there hath been any such thing as this great thing is, or hath been heard like it? Did ever people hear the voice of God speaking out of the midst of the fire, as thou hast heard, and live? Or hath God assayed to go and take him a nation from the midst of another nation, by temptations, by signs, and by wonders, and by war, and by a mighty hand, and by a stretched out arm, and by great terrors, according to all that the LORD your God did for you in Egypt before your eyes? Unto thee it was shewed</u>, that thou mightest know that the LORD he is God; there is none else beside him. Out of heaven he made thee to hear his voice, that he might instruct thee: and upon earth he shewed thee his great fire; and <u>thou heardest his words out of the midst of the fire. And because he loved thy fathers, therefore he chose their seed after them, and brought thee out in his sight with his mighty power out of Egypt</u>; To drive out nations from before thee greater and mightier than thou art, to bring thee in, to give thee their land for an inheritance, as it is this day. Know therefore this day, and consider it in thine heart, that the LORD he is God in heaven above, and upon the earth beneath: there is none else. <u>Thou shalt keep therefore his statutes, and his commandments, which I command thee this day</u>, that it may go well with thee, and with thy children after thee, and that thou mayest prolong thy days upon the earth, which the LORD thy God giveth thee, for ever."

Psalm 147:19-20: "He sheweth his word unto Jacob, his statutes and his judgments unto Israel. <u>He hath not dealt so with any nation: and as for his judgments, they have not known them</u>. Praise ye the LORD."

Malachi 4:4: "Remember ye the law of Moses my servant, which <u>I commanded unto him in Horeb for all Israel, with the statutes and judgments</u>."

Romans 3:1-2: "What advantage then hath the Jew? or what profit is there of circumcision? Much every way: chiefly, <u>because that unto them were committed the oracles of God</u>."

Romans 9:4: "<u>Who are Israelites, to whom pertain the adoption, the glory, the covenants, the giving of the law, the service of God, and the promises</u>."

Gentiles were never obligated to the Mosaic Law as Paul explains:

Acts 14:16: "Who [God the Creator] <u>in times past suffered all nations to walk in their own ways</u>."

Ephesians 2:12: "That at that time [prior to the church] <u>ye were without Christ, being aliens from the commonwealth of Israel, and strangers from the covenants of promise, having no hope, and without God in the world</u>."

Second, everything in the Law began with Israel's acceptance of the covenant. This includes the Ten Commandments and the 613 additional ones that comprise the entire Mosaic Covenant. Some may be surprised that the Ten Commandments were given only to Israel and are part of the Mosaic system and not a separate isolated list of commands for all nations to observe. This issue is so vital for Christians to understand in their relationship to God it cannot be over emphasized.

The Law began in Exodus 19:3-9 when God offered the Law to Israel through Moses (underline added for emphasis):

And Moses went up unto God, and the LORD called unto him out of the mountain, saying, <u>Thus shalt thou say to the house of Jacob, and tell the children of Israel</u>; Ye have seen what I did unto the Egyptians, and how I bare you on eagles' wings, and brought you unto myself. Now therefore, <u>if ye will obey my voice indeed, and keep my covenant, then ye</u>

shall be a peculiar treasure unto me above all people: for all the earth is mine: And ye shall be unto me a kingdom of priests, and an holy nation. These are the words which thou shalt speak unto the children of Israel. And Moses came and called for the elders of the people, and laid before their faces all these words which the LORD commanded him. And all the people answered together, and said, All that the LORD hath spoken we will do. And Moses returned the words of the people unto the LORD. And the LORD said unto Moses, Lo, I come unto thee in a thick cloud, that the people may hear when I speak with thee, and believe thee for ever. And Moses told the words of the people unto the LORD.

The Law continued to the end of the book of Deuteronomy (underline added for emphasis):

And this is the blessing, wherewith Moses the man of God blessed the children of Israel before his death. And he said, The LORD came from Sinai, and rose up from Seir unto them; he shined forth from mount Paran, and he came with ten thousands of saints: from his right hand went a fiery law for them. Yea, he loved the people; all his saints are in thy hand: and they sat down at thy feet; every one shall receive of thy words. Moses commanded us a law, even the inheritance of the congregation of Jacob. ...And of Levi he said, Let thy Thummim and thy Urim be with thy holy one, whom thou didst prove at Massah, and with whom thou didst strive at the waters of Meribah; Who said unto his father and to his mother, I have not seen him; neither did he acknowledge his brethren, nor knew his own children: for they have observed thy word, and kept thy covenant. They shall teach Jacob thy judgments, and Israel thy law: they shall put incense before thee, and whole burnt sacrifice upon thine altar. (Deut. 33:1-4, 8-10)

Therefore, if the Law was given only to the nation of Israel in its entirety and not to the church, how are we to understand what is written in the OT? First, Paul provides us the answer:

"Now all these things [OT judgments on Israel rehearsed in 1 Cor. 10:1-10] happened to them as examples, and they were written for our admonition, upon whom the ends of the ages have come" (1 Cor. 10:11, NKJV). And to the Romans he said, "For whatever things were written before were written for our learning, that we through the patience and comfort of the Scriptures might have hope" (Rom. 15:4, NKJV). Thus, we understand that the whole Bible was written *for* us (Christians), but not *to* us. It was written for us that we could learn from the examples we find in the OT in God's relationship to Israel in regard to their failures and successes in following Him by faith. The many stories provide us principles of faith to live by and warnings of severe consequences for rebelling. The progressive revelation of God's nature and character is understood in some detail throughout the pages of Scripture. We also find hope in the OT because in the revelation of God's nature and character, we discover His faithfulness to His word, covenants, and promises. God's faithfulness to Israel is a comfort to Christian's that seek assurance in their own relationship with Jesus. The same God of the OT is the same God of the NT; therefore, He is the same when we think of both faithfulness and character. He does not change (His nature and character), though His covenants do, which brings a change of conditions to those living under them.

STRUCTURE OF THE OLD TESTAMENT

The structure of the OT regarding the basic layout of the Law will put the last paragraph in perspective. The Law makes up the first five books of the OT; Genesis, Exodus, Leviticus, Numbers, and Deuteronomy (Matt. 11:13). This is the foundation for the rest of the OT involving the historical narratives, prophets, and wisdom literature (Job, Psalms, Proverbs, Song of Solomon, and Ecclesiastes). The Law was essential to Israel (detailed in the chapters that followed it) and the first five books create a unit that is not divisible in any form. For example,

Genesis describes the creation of the universe and the creation of the nation of Israel. The book ends with Joseph reigning second to Pharaoh in Egypt and Jacob's family (comprising the nation of Israel at this point) being kept safe from a devastating famine.

Exodus tells of the history of Israel's exodus (exit) from Egypt, the giving of the Law at Mt. Sinai, and the building of the tabernacle with all its furniture.

Leviticus provides the giving of the Levitical (tribe of Levi) priesthood, sacrificial system, feasts, and accompanying laws to sanctify the nation. These would require the Tabernacle to perform all these functions.

Numbers starts with the numbering of the people of Israel (like a census), and the story of their wanderings in the wilderness until they reach the Plains of Moab where they will enter the Promised Land.

Deuteronomy (second law) is the restatement and expansion of the Law by Moses to those who would enter the Promised Land, and finally Moses' death.

This five-book unit provides the history of Israel in their creation and development until they reach the edge of the Promised Land. The book of Joshua continues the narrative as he leads them into the Promised Land. However, we must remember that after God accomplished all He did in getting Israel to the brink of the Promised Land, the majority of the people who came out of Egypt died in the wilderness and were not those who received Moses' address in Deuteronomy. The generation of Israelites who heard Moses restate and expand the Law in Deuteronomy were those who were under twenty years old when they left Egypt (Num. 14:29) and the rest were born in the wilderness – not having seen Egypt.

The layout of Deuteronomy will give light to the previous four books of the Law. As the nation of Israel developed in the wilderness, many issues had given rise to expand the existing laws so they could be clear on how to apply it to these new and future situations when in the land. Moses in Deuteronomy takes what he previously gave in the first four books, reiterates the history, gives the Ten Commandments again, and expands them for application and operation to those who will enter the Promised Land. He finally gives the blessings and curses of the Law and some prophetic warnings to Israel's future near the end of the book. The following chart is a high-level overview of Deuteronomy.

Reviewing History	Rehearsal and Expansion of the 10 Commandments	Revelation of the Covenant's Renewal
Chapters 1-4	Chapters 5-26	Chapters 27-34

The first four chapters in Deuteronomy reviewed the history of Israel and their deliverance from Egypt for those who were too young to understand the significance at the time of the

Exodus and for those born in the wilderness along with way. Imagine, you are part of a nation that has journeyed in the wilderness, all you know is life in the desert and now you are commanded to go into a new land and battle against people you have never seen before. Deuteronomy is a key book because it helped Israel with their national identity and God's long-term plan. The only way to make sense of the situation the nation was in at that point was for Moses to explain the history of why and how the nation of Israel exists in the first place. Without these connections to Israel's past they will not understand the future. Without the past connection, there is no national identity or ideology. These people needed to know that the God they worshiped and served was not just another god of the pagans in the land, but He is the creator of the universe and giver of all life. He was not a local god of hill and valley as the pagans worshiped, but the God of all creation and capable of providing Israel deliverance from Egypt and victory to gain the land promised to the father of their nation – Abraham.

A person's identity connects them to their history and provides the support for the ideology (i.e. doctrine) that is the foundation of their belief and operation. Thus, their national identity was the foundation of their ideology (belief system) and essential to their success in the land. These five books of the Law written to Israel specifically instruct them to understand their God, their covenants, and their development. Paul follows this method in his NT epistles; he tells us who we are in Christ before he asks us to apply the truth he taught. Until we know who we are in Christ, we cannot really apply the truth to our lives in a practical way. The history of Genesis through Numbers explains the Abrahamic and Mosaic Covenants along with how they came to be in the first place. The book of Numbers provides the nation's journey in the wilderness and why it needed to happen. Moreover, it makes clear God's intention for the nation to move into the Promised Land. Deuteronomy is a second giving of the Law, not that it is a different law, but expands on the Ten

Commandments (given twice – Ex. 20; Deut. 5). The expansion provides application for the laws and their practicality in various situations.

Chapters five through twenty-six is really the Ten Commandments and accompanying laws that relate to each commandment. Chapters five through eleven expand on various foundations for Israel as related to the Ten Commandments, Deut. 12:1-31 begins the expansion of the first commandment, "Thou shalt have none other gods before me" (Deut. 5:7). Moses provides laws that would naturally arise from the first commandment. Deut. 12:32 – 13:18 give laws that would naturally arise from the second commandment:

> Thou shalt not make thee any graven image, or any likeness of any thing that is in heaven above, or that is in the earth beneath, or that is in the waters beneath the earth: Thou shalt not bow down thyself unto them, nor serve them: for I the LORD thy God am a jealous God, visiting the iniquity of the fathers upon the children unto the third and fourth generation of them that hate me, And shewing mercy unto thousands of them that love me and keep my commandments. (Deut. 5:8-10)

What is interesting about this command is the beginning of Deut. 13:1-18 that falls under it. These verses are essential to the rest of the Bible and set a foundation for measuring whom to listen to and follow. They form a kind of error correction to future revelation. The instruction (Deut. 13) relates to a response to a popular leader (1-5), family and friends (6-11), and whole towns (majority opinion) influenced to commit idolatry (12-18). The key principle stated by Moses, "for the LORD your God proveth you, to know whether ye love the LORD your God with all your heart and with all your soul. Ye shall walk after the LORD your God, and fear him, and keep his commandments, and obey his voice, and ye shall serve him, and cleave unto him" (Deut. 13:3-4). In other words, God wanted Israel to decide whether they would take God at His word or listen to other influential people or movements that are contrary to revelation already given by Moses. This maturing process – obeying God's Word above all other voices – is easily observable in a nation or an individual. This chapter establishes a standard of measurement that must be applied to all those who claim to speak for God. It was clear through accompanying miracles God spoke through Moses. But that did not exclude Moses from the objective test; he and all others would be validated by the criteria in this chapter. Thus, competing "truths" or deceptive methods and their general influence were to be disregarded in light of God's Word.

This has strong correlation to what Paul wrote to the Galatians when he said, "But though we, or an angel from heaven, preach any other gospel unto you than that which we have preached unto you, let him be accursed. As we said before, so say I now again, If any man preach any other gospel unto you than that ye have received, let him be accursed" (Gal. 1:8-9). Though they wrote the Scriptures that would be used as an objective measurement for truth, they too were subject to what they wrote–as all others are since it is from God. There is only one Law given through Moses and as a prophet of God, he and all other prophets are judged by the Deuteronomy 13 criteria. Similarly, there is only one gospel and any human including Paul or "angel from heaven" who preaches a different gospel is "accursed." Those who claim to speak for God must pass these essential truth Tests. How often Christians are challenged with the same test of truth regarding God's Word when measured against popular opinion or particular experiences. Paul sets up this challenge with his teaching in Colossians chapter 2. There he lays out four "isms" for Christians to avoid,

> Gnosticism, the elevation of knowledge above Christ (Col. 2:8-10),
> Legalism, the elevation of laws above Christ (Col. 2:11-17),
> Mysticism, the elevation of experience above Christ (Col. 2:18-19), and,

Asceticism, the elevation of practices above Christ (Col. 2:20-23).

The word of God reveals the Christ of God, therefore to subject everything to God's word makes it subject to Jesus Christ. Making everything subject to the word of God is a consistent theme from Moses to the Millennial reign. For at that time all things will ultimately be subjected to the Lord Jesus Christ (1 Cor. 15:28). It is incumbent upon Christians to subject everything to Jesus now, since He is our Lord and Savior. This is a powerful measurement of our Christian maturity and loyalty to Him.

Finally, in chapters twenty-seven through thirty-four, Moses renews the covenant with Israel prior to their move into the Promised Land. The covenant blessings and curses are explained in relation to Israel's obedience. It is important to note in these chapters that the blessings and curses are related to the nation of Israel. Unfortunately, some pastors and church movements pull the blessings and curses out of these chapters and apply them individually to Christians at will. This is both a theological and covenantal error. The church was never under the national curses or blessings of Israel. Christian's are "in Christ," and Paul makes it abundantly clear that because of this position before God, that He has, "blessed us with all spiritual blessings in heavenly places in Christ" (Eph. 1:3). There is no place in the NT that believers are threatened with curses for lack of covenant obedience. This does not mean that Christians cannot make their life miserable; they certainly can and some do. However, it is not God's doing; on the contrary, God will chastise Christians, teaching them to avoid sinful living to work in their lives the "the peaceable fruit of righteousness to those who have been trained by it" (Heb. 12:11, NKJV). This is why picking and choosing Mosaic Law covenant conditions meant for the nation of Israel and threatening NT believers with them is reprehensible. Some do it ignorantly, which is understandable, but unfortunately can have the same results as those who do it with nefarious intent.

How many Christians have been extorted by greedy preachers who claim God will "rebuke the devourer" (Mal. 3:11) only if they will give to their ministry. How sad and unfortunate for those who are threatened by preachers after "filthy lucre" (1 Tim. 3:3, 8; Titus 1:7, 11; 1 Peter 5:2), taking advantage of them through verses ripped out of their context to achieve a selfish end. What these preachers tend to overlook is that they are extorting God's people using the name of Jesus. However, Jesus said, "Beware of false prophets, which come to you in sheep's clothing, but inwardly they are ravening wolves" (Matt. 7:15). The word "ravening" in this verse is the Greek word we translate the English word "extortion." These charlatans may enjoy the lavish lifestyle now with extorted wealth from God's people, but in the end, it will cost them far more than they realize. As Paul says, "whose end shall be according to their works" (2 Cor. 11:15). Manipulating God's Word for personal benefit is a very dangerous game, especially when it involves the mistreatment of people for whom Jesus died. Jesus did not give these strong warnings at the end of Matt. 7 for dramatic effect. "I never knew you: depart from me, ye that work iniquity" (Matt. 7:23) are very sobering words, and not ones that anyone wants to hear. No preacher is perfect, I can attest to that. But deliberate deceit, corruption, and manipulation has no place in Christian ministry. We all have feet of clay; the classic error is thinking the clay can be turned into gold. Pastor Chuck Smith taught the danger of claiming to speak for God when God is not speaking in his message on Jeremiah chapter 23:

> Now the final king of Judah is Zedekiah and it is felt that the 23rd chapter is addressed to Zedekiah. "Woe be unto the pastors that destroy and scatter the sheep of my pasture! saith the LORD" (Jer. 23:1).
>
> The word pastor is the same as shepherd. In the Old Testament it referred to the kings. As God intended that the kings should rule over the people with a shepherd's

heart. And that they have the interest of the sheep at heart. But this is not the case at the end of the kingdom before the Babylonian captivity. We were reading in the previous chapter how that the kings were taking advantage of the people. They were using their positions to enrich themselves. They were not seeking the welfare of the people but only their own gain. So God's indictment for enriching themselves rather than seeking the benefit of the people.

The interesting that God refers to them, the people as My pasture. I think that we need to realize in the New Testament the word pastor or shepherd applied to the leader in the church. And I think that every leader in the church needs to realize that we are shepherding over God's heritage. You are not my flock, you are His flock. But I have the responsibility of shepherding over His flock. Of taking care and concern for your spiritual welfare. Of seeing that you are well fed, and well taken care of. Because one day I am going to have to report to the Chief Shepherd of what I have done concerning the flock of God. His flock, you are His, His sheep. So the Lord looks upon you as His. And every pastor should look upon himself as one who is a caretaker over the flock of God. If I would be guilty of taking advantage, of fleecing the flock, then I am going to have to answer to God for that and it would be very very serious.

The false prophets usually have a lot of flare and a lot of flash. ...they are usually quite demonstrative and quite exciting and people go for that and they fleece the flock of God. It is interesting that Peter in warning concerning the false prophets gave as an earmark their attempt to make merchandise of you. Know that God is not broke. Know that God is not dependent upon your support. Know that God is not headed for bankruptcy if you do not go and borrow money to bail Him out. And any so called prophet of God who makes an emphasis upon giving and upon money according to Peter is a false prophet seeking by these feigned words to make merchandise of you.[61]

But this is not just the error of word-poor prosperity preachers and calculating swindlers; it is also encouraged by the theological failure of many Bible chapter headings. In some Bibles, it will have OT chapter headings that say, "Curses to Israel" and in the next chapter, it will say "Blessings for the Church." This is unfortunate for this practice captures the benefits of the Mosaic Covenant and transfers them to the church with no context or explanation, while leaving all the curses for Israel. This viewpoint has certainly fueled Replacement Theology;[62] the belief that the church has replaced Israel and there is no future for Israel in God's plan. It has also left Bible reading believers with a false sense that the headings are accurate, when in fact they are anything but. People will tend to believe the chapter headings of Bibles because they feel that they would not be there if inaccurate. However, nothing added to a Bible, from chapter heading to study notes, are part of the inspiration of Scripture. It is well-meaning editors and not the Holy Spirit who add reference notes, commentary, book outlines, and other information. The point is that poor theology has a direct impact on life application. Whether ill meaning or well-meaning promoters, a poor knowledge of the Bible in its context affects those who fall under its tutelage. God will evaluate the motive of those involved with teaching theology in its various forms in the end, but the damage to many believers' lives and the distortion of the Gospel to unbelievers is the current tragedy.

THE GOSPEL, THE LAW, AND CHRISTIANS

Considering all these matters, how are we to understand the Law? Does all this mean that Christians are under no moral, ceremonial, or civil obligations today? No, not at all. There are moral obligations under the Mosaic Covenant, many of which are taught to the church in the NT, however, under New Covenant conditions. Certainly, we do not have the same consequences for violations in the NT as under the Mosaic Covenant, which should be obvious. We do not stone people for working on a Sundays (Num. 15:32-36) or for the sexual sins that require capital punishment under the Law (Deut. 22:22). The conditions within the nation of Israel are starkly different from those within the nations that have been reached with the Gospel today. The Gospel is free to fly above the many variances in cultural practices, food choices, government systems, etc., and redeem those who believe. In each nation, people can follow Christ without the specific limitations placed on the nation of Israel, since many of the limitations existed to manage them to accomplish God's specific purpose through them. In other words, each covenant contained different purposes and therefore functioned differently. These distinctions correlate to the change in covenant, but it does not free NT believers from moral obligations. Paul instructs us that:

> ...the grace of God that bringeth salvation hath appeared to all men, Teaching us that, denying ungodliness and worldly lusts, we should live soberly, righteously, and godly, in this present world; Looking for that blessed hope, and the glorious appearing of the great God and our Saviour Jesus Christ; Who gave himself for us, that he might redeem us from all iniquity, and purify unto himself a peculiar people,

zealous of good works. (Titus 2:11-14)

Christians are to live pure, separated (not isolated) lives from the ungodliness that permeates the cultures that surround them as they wait for Christ to come and take the church to heaven in the rapture. This time on earth should be continually productive in advancing Christ's purposes in the world. Believers should be serving the Lord and fervently doing God's will in promoting the Gospel of His Son Jesus Christ. Immorality among Christians obstructs this goal.

Our focus as Christians should be our relationship with Jesus with the natural byproduct of our loving service to Him. We do not serve the Lord to establish our relationship with Him, but serve in appreciation of what He has already done – looking forward to the glorious future He planned for us. We should have an upward focus (Col. 3:1-4) as we wait for Him and an outward focus in our service to the Lord (Rom. 12:11). The proper balance of sitting with and serving Jesus was captured in a teaching that Dr. J. Dwight Pentecost gave before the Dallas Theological Seminary students and faculty on August 30, 2007. In his address entitled, "The Goal of Knowing God," Dr. Pentecost sublimely said, "it is more important to be occupied with Jesus, than for Jesus." I believe this statement captures the essence of the successful Christian life. It is impossible to be occupied properly for Jesus in service to Him, until we are intimately occupied with Jesus in our devotional life – sitting at His feet.

The NT epistles provide detailed instructions for Christians so they will know how to:

1. Live a life that is pleasing to God,
2. Work in the world and properly represent Christ,
3. Relate to family, friends, unbelievers,
4. Build the local Body of Christ where we worship,
5. Contribute financially to God's work in the world,

6.   Exercise the spiritual gifts given to us by the Holy Spirit, and,

7.   Remain in close fellowship with Jesus while awaiting His return.

There are a lot of "how to" books on the Christian market; however, we can go right to the source and exclude the middleman to find God's "how to" in His word. What a Christian should not do, is try to read the Law into the NT in a way that places believers under the Law as a means of "how to" sanctification, or worse, justification. Christians should learn the OT for a greater understanding of God's progressive revelation as mentioned above, but not to attempt to live under the Mosaic Covenant as a means of living the Christian life – the very opposite will be the result. Placing ourselves under the Law will short circuit our Christian spiritual development, not increase it.

As noted earlier, many of the moral commands we see under the Law for Israel are repeated in the NT for Christians. God did not change His nature in the NT He changed the covenant. For example, under the Mosaic Law, nine of the original Ten Commandments are restated for the Christian in the NT. The fourth commandment regarding the Sabbath Day observance is not restated. This is because the Sabbath day was a command given specifically to Israel as a sign of God's covenant with them (Ex. 31:12 -17). This is what made the violation so egregious when it came to Sabbath breaking.

Every covenant has a sign; the Abrahamic Covenant had the sign of circumcision (Gen. 17:10-11; Rom. 4:11), where the Mosaic sign was the Sabbath day (Ex. 31:12-18). Some of the clear statements of covenant signs are in the following chart:

COVENANT	SIGN	SCRIPTURE
Flood (Noah and his sons)	Rainbow	Gen. 9:8-17
Abraham	Circumcision	Gen.

and offspring (Promise)		17:7-14
Nation of Israel (Mosaic Cov.)	Sabbath Day	Ex. 31:12-18
The Church (New Cov.)	The Holy Spirit indwelling the believer	Jer. 31:33; Ez. 36:26-27; Joel 2:28-29; 1 Cor. 12:13; 2 Cor. 3:6-18

Regarding the Ten Commandments, some clarification is necessary. Of the ten, the Sabbath Day is related to Israel, but the remaining nine commands are moral obligations that everyone is to follow (OT and NT). To violate them results in committing sins no matter the covenant, OT or NT. Therefore, if a person violates these laws (nine commandments), they are committing sins. But to be clear, Christians are not under the Ten Commandments as they are given to Israel, they are under the NT commands given by Jesus or stated in the epistles that address the same nine sinful acts. The following chart will help clarify the nine commands, though these are not the only laws Christians are obligated to obey. The NT teaches many moral obligations in the epistles, though most commands exist in principle in the OT laws.

COMMANDMENTS (EXODUS 20)	REPEATED IN THE NT
1st commandment = Don't have other gods	Matt. 4:10; 1 Cor. 6:9-10, 8:6; Eph. 4:6; 1 Tim. 2:5
2nd commandment = Don't make images	1 Cor. 10:14; 1 John 5:21

3rd commandment = Don't take God's name in vain, or empty fashion (i.e. use God's name as if obeying God when not, a false representation)	Matt. 7:22, 25:11; Luke 6:46; 1 Cor. 15:2; James 2:1
4th commandment = Obey the Sabbath day	**No related NT command**
5th commandment = Obey parents	Rom. 1:30; Eph. 6:1; Col. 3:20
6th commandment = Don't murder	Rom. 1:29; 1 John 3:11-12
7th commandment = Don't commit adultery	1 Cor. 6:18; 1 Thess. 4:3; 1 Tim. 1:10; James 2:11
8th commandment = Don't steal	Eph. 4:28
9th commandment = Don't lie	Eph. 4:25; Col. 3:9; 1 Tim. 1:10
10th commandment = Don't covet	1 Cor. 10:6; 1 Thess. 4:4,5
Commandments 1-3	Rom. 5-8a
Commandments 5-10	Rom. 13:8-10

We can know what God approves of and disapproves of morally in both OT and NT. The *morality* is the same, but the *covenant* is different. Again, as previously stated, Christians are *not* under the Mosaic Law and its penalties (all or nothing proposition), but Christians are responsible to follow the moral commands in the NT. In both OT and NT, we observe similar moral requirements in many areas.

Understanding the OT Law provides a great advantage when learning NT truths. The NT apostles only had an understanding of the OT when they penned the NT scriptures. They realized that they had the same obligations morally as in the OT with regard to sins, but they were separated from the consciousness of being under the Mosaic requirements (Acts 15:10-11), being NT believers. Thus, they realized the need to be holy – as the Jews were holy under the Law (Lev. 11:44-45; 19:2; 20:7, 26; 21:8), but without the death penalty and curses (Deut. 27-30) attached to their failures (1 Peter 1:16).

For example, if a Christian commits idolatry (1 Cor. 10:14; Col. 3:5; 1 John 5:21), they won't be stoned as under the Law, but it will deteriorate their relationship with God and could incur God's chastisement (Heb. 12). Just as murder was sinful before the Mosaic Law came into effect in Israel (Gen. 9:6), and also the worship of other gods an abomination to God (Gen. 35:2; Joshua 24:2 with 24:19-20, 23), so these sins are wrong in the NT as well. The point is this: the Law is not the only dispensation of moral restrictions for people. Immorality was in the world prior to the Law (Gen. 6:5, 11-12) and after (Eph. 5:1-4). What the Law did was help clarify sin and assign specific definitions on many sins. It revealed the precision of the evil behavior attached to transgressions for both OT Jews and NT Christians.

We know that the Law cannot save anyone, for that was never its purpose. Therefore, keeping a law will not save a Christian any more than it would an Israelite. We should understand that a Christian is not under any aspect of the Mosaic Covenant because the church is not the nation of Israel. Moral commands for Christians in the NT come with inherent obligations because any moral command is *prescribing* how to live and not just *describing* how people live. However, even if there is the same command in the NT as found in the OT under the Law (such as the sin of murder), the NT command does not place the Christian *under* the Mosaic Covenant; it only imposes the same moral restriction by command because it is a sin whether under the Law or the Gospel. God has the same objection to His people sinning, no matter what covenant they live under. God's nature does not change (Malachi 3:6, Heb. 13:8); therefore, He hates the same immoral behavior no matter the time in human history. The consequences of sin differ under each covenant – hence the need to understand the covenant distinctions.

One example of this failure to distinguish the covenants would be the law against working on the Sabbath day under the Mosaic Covenant. Under the Law this was a capital offense requiring the death penalty (Exodus 35:2, Numbers 15:32-36). Are we to think that a Christian should be stoned for missing church on a Sunday (or Saturday for some)? Perhaps a Christian was called to their place of employment and was unable to attend church on a particular Sunday. This situation could be a common occurrence in a nation that does not respect any Christian holy days – i.e. Sundays. Should that Christian be stoned for the infraction? Of course not! Roy Aldrich offers valuable insight on this:

> The penalty for certain violations of each of the Mosaic Ten Commandments was death. No nation or church can honestly claim to be under the Mosaic Ten Commandments. But all people in every dispensation are under the moral law of God. Moses did not originate this law and it did not cease with the cross.

> To avoid confusion and legalism a careful distinction should be made between the moral law and the Mosaic Ten Commandments. When so many say that the Ten Commandments apply to Christians as fully as they ever did to Israel they mean that the moral principles of the law are still binding. But this is not what they have expressed. If the Ten Commandments of the law are still binding then all of the penalties must remain the same. The death penalties should be imposed for Sabbath-breaking, idolatry, adultery, rebellion against parents, etc. To change the penalty of a law means to abolish that law. A law without a penalty is an anomaly. A law with its penalty abolished is only good advice. That all of this is not pointless hairsplitting is as evident as the difference between life and death. It is just this difference that is

indicated by Paul's description of the Ten Commandments as "the ministration of death, written and engraven in stones" (2 Cor. 3:7a).[63]

This is why so many who try to include Christians under the Law have to divide the Law into different parts, otherwise they would be required to stone people for committing what the Mosaic Covenant describes as capital sins. They pick and choose what command to pull from the Law and how discipline is exacted for disobeying it – like a unique blend of covenants by their own making. This should indicate to them that they are in the wrong direction. However, when legalism is the road chosen, it seems to feed its own hunger to add more and more laws instead of limiting them. Those already with a propensity to incorporate OT laws into the Christian experience are more inclined to add their own convictions as additional rules to live by. This is an interesting phenomenon among legalists. Their addiction reminds us of the Pharisees who added to the OT laws from their own oral traditions. Their additions to the Mosaic Covenant caused them to have the majority of their arguments with Jesus and accuse Him of breaking the Law (ref. Matt. 12; Mark 3; John 5 and 9), which were really their own laws or a remake of OT laws.

It is currently popular to place Christians under Jewish traditions, practices, or festival participation (Lev. 23) as a means of sanctification and be closer to God. This is a dangerous error and represents classic legalism (condemned in Paul's letter to the Galatians). Paul's epistle to the Galatians should have solved this problem for Christians, but too many have ignored a proper study of that important and informative epistle. The Epistle of Paul to the Galatians alone reveals that Christians are not under the Law, and the Law cannot be divided into parts (more on this below). Gentiles can certainly learn from Jewish feasts and practices under the Law, not as a means of sanctification however. Learning these Jewish practices can better help Gentiles understand Jewish history and therefore the

Bible in general. But, to place a Christian (Jew or Gentile) under any aspect of the Law for sanctification is contrary to the NT teaching on sanctification (Rom. 6:1 - 8:17) and a spiritually deteriorating legalistic practice. Knowing the OT is vital to learning, living under the OT conditions is to arrest spiritual development, not develop it (Gal. 5:2-4).

This type of Bible teaching is the result of either poor Bible knowledge or great confusion in the Scriptures. However, most often an unwillingness to learn good theology or well-disciplined views as being discussed. These legalistic views are not just theological nuances, but are dangerous and can result in ruined Christian lives. Such twisted reasoning as we have discussed creates a distorted view of the Law and the Gospel, and are the foundational teachings of many cults misusing the Bible to place NT Christians under OT Laws – adding their own cultic psychological conditioning in the process. Cults are famous for their blend of OT and NT doctrines to come up with something completely different from either OT or NT teachings. All cults enslave their people into a system of psychological control by their unbiblical teachings, which is nothing new. Their twists of Scripture are almost endless, but the results are amazingly similar – bondage! When a cult's beliefs develop into a national political ideology, the results are Socialism, Nazism, Marxism, and Communism. Not a pretty picture of modern human history. Jesus came into the world to bear witness to the truth (John 18:37), because from the beginning Satan has filled humanity with lies (John 8:44). The Bible is the only source of absolute truth (Psalm 138:2; John 17:17; 1 Thess. 2:13). People will only learn the truth from the Bible taught from the church (1 Tim. 3:15). However, in contrast to the truth, human bondage is the result of sin and the sinful practices of cults and national political movements. Jesus came to set people free by knowing the truth (John 8:32). The truth is only known by knowing the Bible in context.

Christians have a great deal to look forward to as they await their eternal inheritance in Christ (Eph. 1:11, 14; 1 Peter 1:4). God the Father has "blessed us with all spiritual blessings in heavenly places in Christ" (Eph. 1:3), many of them to be enjoyed now and others when we enter glory (Rom. 8:23; Eph. 1:5). In the meantime, we should unreservedly offer ourselves to serve the Lord Jesus in loving response to all He has done – and is doing for us now (Rom. 12:1, 2). God desires that we enjoy a relationship with Him daily as He leads us by the Holy Spirit, who was given to us who believe in Christ (Rom. 8:2-4; Eph. 1:13). The Christian life is a life led by the Spirit of God as He takes the Word of God and makes it applicable to our lives as the people of God, for the glory of God.

THE LAW CANNOT BE DIVIDED

Quite often in Christian circles there is discussion of the Law being divided into segments such as the moral, ceremonial, and civil law divisions. However, though the Law covers these aspects of Israel's national life, the Mosaic Law itself is a whole and cannot be subdivided into sections for eliminating aspects that are unappealing or contrary to a theological perspective. When Jesus or the apostles refer to the Law, it is the whole without any subdivision. For example, Jesus in the Sermon on the Mount references "the Law" (Matt. 5:17-18, 7:12) and there is no way to understand His statement other than the entire Mosaic Law. Moreover, He continues His teaching to include aspects of all three areas of the Law – moral, ceremonial, and civil. John certainly incorporates the whole Law when he says, "For the law was given through Moses, but grace and truth came through Jesus Christ" (John 1:17). Whenever Jesus talks of a violation of the Law, He refers to the Law as whole and not certain aspects as if segmentation is somehow possible. For example, in His discussion with the Jews in Jerusalem during the feast of tabernacles, He said to them in response to His healing a man on the Sabbath:

> Moses therefore gave you circumcision (not that it is from Moses, but from the fathers), and you circumcise a man on the Sabbath. If a man receives circumcision on the Sabbath, so that the law of Moses should not be broken, are you angry with Me because I made a man completely well on the Sabbath? (John 7:22-23, NKJV)

Here Jesus makes a comparison of obeying the circumcision command (Lev. 12:3) even if it falls on the Sabbath day, and healing someone in need. These Jews followed a tradition they wrongly elevated to equal status with Moses Law. This tradition taught that healing on the Sabbath is a violation of the Law, that it was comparable to working on the Sabbath. Jesus did not refer to the ceremonial aspect of the Law when He addressed the circumcision of a child, but said it was the observation of the Law (as a whole). Circumcision is the sign of the Abrahamic Covenant (Gen. 17:10) for all male children. Later under Moses, the Law told the Jews *when* to circumcise the child (on the 8th day). The Jews that disputed with Jesus were wrong about their understanding that healing violated the Sabbath, and in His response, Jesus revealed their confusion and hypocrisy. He made it clear that a life made whole was more important than keeping a ritual. In doing so, He compared a ceremonial law (circumcision) with a moral law (Sabbath breaking) and never made a distinction between them, but just referred to them both as "the law of Moses." Moreover, if that healed person was a descendant of Aaron, it was only through physical restoration that they could have access to the temple to worship and serve God. Thus, without the healing they were barred from the temple for service (ref. Lev. 21:16-24). In another place, Jesus made it clear that the Law – the whole Law – covered an era in reference to the dispensation of Law when He said, "For all the prophets and the law prophesied until John [the Baptist]" (Matt. 11:13). In effect, He said the OT time period of the Law (which the prophets and Law fall under) ended at John the Baptist, who was technically the last OT prophet (Jesus the Messiah notwithstanding). Indeed, Jesus categorized the Law through a historical timeframe which included moral, ceremonial, and civil laws. Again, His understanding of the Law was the whole law and not subdivided parts (ref. Luke 24:44).

Likewise, Paul's use of the Law includes all aspects without subdivision (over 60 references in Romans, and almost 30 in Galatians). Paul's epistle to the Galatian churches was written to counteract the false teachers that attempted to bring believing Gentiles under the Law of Moses. Paul referred to ceremonial (Gal. 5:2), moral (Gal. 5:4), civil (Gal. 5:14) aspects, but simply referred to each as "the Law." Additionally, he made it clear that the Law cannot be divided when he says, "For I testify again to every man that is circumcised, that he is a debtor to do the whole law" (Gal. 5:3). In other words, one cannot choose what aspects of the Law to leave under the OT and what pieces to bring into the NT. Once any aspect of the Law is followed as a means of justification or sanctification, it must be taken as a whole and the person becomes indebted to fulfill the entire Law. Not an enviable position, nor even a possible one to accomplish. This Paul made clear when he said, "For as many as are of the works of the law are under the curse: for it is written, Cursed is every one that continueth not in all things which are written in the book of the law to do them" (Gal. 3:10). Indeed, James confirms that any attempt to keep the whole Law with a failure at one point makes a person a violator of the whole system, "For whosoever shall keep the whole law, and yet offend in one point, he is guilty of all" (James 2:10). The only reason James (the Lord Jesus' half-brother) can make that statement is that the Law is a unit, not a divisible list to fulfill particular aspects while leaving the others undone.

Civil, ceremonial, moral regulations, and statues combine to make up all that is in the Law regarding commands and instructions. When NT writers reference the Law, they never segment it into parts or divide it into separate pieces. The Law was understood as the entire legal code (civil, ceremonial, and moral), along with the historical narratives. They make up every aspect of what Moses gave in the Covenant. Jesus identified the entire Law (first 5 books of Moses or the Pentateuch) in Luke 24:44 when He said, "all things must be fulfilled, which were written in the law of Moses, and in the prophets, and in the psalms, concerning me."

Likewise, Paul had this same view of the entirety of Moses' revelation of the Law, but uses the phrase "the Law" in his epistles (Rom. 3:19-31, Gal. 2:16-21, 3:10-24), referring to all the commands of the Covenant the Jews received through Moses

(5 books of Moses). In my commenting on Paul's position on the Gospel of grace, that it is separate from Moses Law through videos on the internet, I have had legalists challenge me to the point they accuse Paul of being a heretic because he would not put Christians under the Law. They have even gone as far as trying to teach that Jesus taught that people can only be saved by keeping the Law. These are extreme unbiblical and problematic heretical positions. But what is interesting about those who hold to them is that they actually understand what Paul is teaching. They realize that he separates the Law and the Gospel, which is their main gripe with him (they are modern Judaizers). This is important to recognize because there are some in churches who try to put Christians under *certain parts* of the Law by discarding certain civil and ceremonial commands, leaving the moral parts for the Christian to follow as if bound to them with the Mosaic Covenant penalty for disobedience. Indeed, when heretical extremists seem to grasp the distinction of Paul's teaching and aspects of the church fails to, we have a serious problem. Frankly, some people that do teach the Bible should not. They cause more harm than good because of the overall confusion they have themselves. It would be better to observe what James taught, "My brethren, let not many of you become teachers, knowing that we shall receive a stricter judgment" (James 3:1, NKJV). Cults are famous for doing this and some Christian groups follow this similar heretical pattern to their own detriment, and those who hear and follow them (1 Tim. 4:16). Bad theology breeds bad practices and consequently some aspect of heresy, and unfortunately a poor dispensational approach to the Bible will result in the same.

The problem with this approach by some Christians is that it makes a distinction within the Mosaic Covenant of the Law that the NT writers do not. This alone should be instructive in itself, but it tends to be ignored. Paul is very specific in Ephesians 2:15 referring to moral commands under the Law when he says, "Having abolished in his flesh the enmity, even the law of commandments contained in ordinances." Also in Colossians 2:14, he says, "Blotting out the handwriting of ordinances that was against us." The word used in both verses translated *ordinances* (Greek=dogma) means a decree or edict. This gives the idea of an authoritative decision or ordinance, particularly when the legal ordinances of the Mosaic Law is in mind. Thus, the very parts of the Law that some try to place Christians under – ordinances – Paul says they are not under because Jesus removed them at the cross. The point is this, if Christians want to take sections of the Law to attempt to live under and think that pleases God, they will typically choose the moral commands and sometimes the ceremonial ones because they make sense to their carnal mind. However, Paul makes it clear in the two verses quoted that the moral commands of the Law were eliminated no different than ceremonial ones as a means of justification or sanctification for the Christian. Furthermore, since the Law cannot be subdivided into pieces, the ceremonies and civil commands are also part of those ordinances the Christian is free from. This is essential to comprehend, for we live in a time when the church in its spiritual deterioration is sliding back into Jewish legal practices and ceremonies to attempt to gain spirituality. This is exactly what Paul warned against in his epistle to the Galatians. Nothing in Judaism is going to help a Christian grow in sanctification. In fact, it has the opposite effect. Paul could not have been clearer:

> Stand fast therefore in the liberty wherewith Christ hath made us free, and be not entangled again with the yoke of bondage. Behold, I Paul say unto you, that if ye be circumcised, Christ shall profit you nothing. For I testify again to every man that is circumcised, that he is a debtor to do the whole law. Christ is become of no effect unto you, whosoever of you are justified by the law; ye are fallen from grace. (Gal. 5:1-4)

The bottom line – a Christian is not under any aspect of the Mosaic Covenant. Therefore, the church cannot arbitrarily impose on itself the requirements of the Law given to Israel with either the curses or blessings. If a Christian wants to put themselves under some aspect of the Law by this picking and choosing method, the laws they think they avoid they will actually violate, since the Law cannot be divided as we have seen. The Law is not like a bowl of fortune cookies that we can dig into and just pull the ones we think a Christian should observe. The Law is a system of legal requirements that a nation was covenanted to obey with heavy consequences for disobeying. To try to live under the Law is an all or nothing proposition, you either take the entire thing with all its aspects (civil, ceremonial, and moral), or you take what the NT writers tell us: that we were redeemed from its system of requirements to be fulfilled as a means of salvation (justification), or sanctification (Christian growth). We cannot have it both ways. The Law cannot be divided into sections to incorporate some of its aspects of it into the New Covenant. Theologians, not authors of Scripture, attempt to divide the Law into sections. Thus, the Holy Spirit gave the Law as a whole and the biblical authors understood this.

THE PURPOSE OF THE LAW

Why did God give the Law to Israel? It is important to note at the outset that the Law was never given to *save* people, but to *saved* people, not to *redeem*, but to the *redeemed*! The redemption of the Jews from Egypt was through blood by faith (Ex. 12), not through the keeping of laws. Paul the apostle said, "If there had been a law given which could have given life, verily righteousness should have been by the law." (Gal. 3:21). Moreover, prior to the redemption from Egypt, people like Abraham (Gen. 15:6) were saved by faith.

The Law was added for reasons other than redemption or salvation. The following descriptions should help to understand some reasons for the giving of the Law and make some distinctions from The Gospel of grace.

1. **The Law unified the Nation of Israel:** The nation of Israel came out of Egypt with the promises made to Abraham, but without any understanding of what it meant to function as a nation under the theocracy of God. They had more of a slave mentality without experience or understanding of how to operate as a unified nation. Much of their knowledge of how nations functioned came from observing the Egyptians, but this is not how God wanted them to operate under His care and guidance. Thus, the Law provided them instructions so they could know how to successfully live and thrive as a nation. In a sense, it functioned as their national constitution, foundational to their continued national success and prosperity. It provided them the spiritual, moral, and civil laws required to function under the oversight of God.

2. **The Law taught morality:** The Law imposed moral

behavior among those within the nation and those without. Israel was entering a land overrun with immoral and deadly pagan worship practices. Child sacrifice and filthy fertility rituals were a common part of daily pagan life. Disease and death were the consequences of their paganism. Archeological research has confirmed that cities were dying of diseases when Joshua marched Israel into the Land. God's Law would create a separation from these practices in every area of life to maintain the national morality, health, and dignity of God's people.

3. **The Law sanctified (*set apart for God*) the Nation:** The Law provided the means of approach to God through the five sacrifices in Leviticus chapters 1-7. These sacrifices were the means of fellowship and a relationship with God. They were not to bring a Jew to salvation, for the sacrifices were given to Jews who already believed. The seven festivals in Leviticus chapter 23 were the means of the nation *abiding* in their relationship to God. These feasts were annual celebrations of particular events in Israel's history that provided a reminder of what God had done for them. It provided annual remembrance of why they were, and how they became the nation that God created from Abraham, Isaac, and Jacob. The one annual sacrifice in Leviticus 16 called the Day of Atonement was a national offering. In other words, this offering sanctified the whole nation through the sacrifice by the High Priest and the required fasting on that day "afflict your souls" (Lev. 16:29); which was the expression of sorrow for Israel's national sins.

This shall be a statute forever for you: In the seventh month, on the tenth day of the month, you shall afflict your souls, and do no work at all, whether a native of your own country or a stranger who dwells among you.

For on that day the priest shall make atonement for you, to cleanse you, that you may be clean from all your sins before the LORD. (Lev. 16:29-30)

God managed the nation like an extended family which can be observed in many of the laws. One law in particular would not allow a Jew to charge interest to another Jew (Ex. 22:25; Lev. 25:36; Deut. 23:19-20) for they were "family." Leviticus in particular provides the bulk of the 613 laws God gave the nation to sanctify them and make them a holy (separate) nation. Their extensive laws regarding food, clothing, holidays, grooming, farming practices, etc. were given to maintain an understanding of this distinction between them and their pagan neighbors. This in turn would enable them to represent properly the Holy God they worshiped.

4. **The Law provided God's truth to the Nation:** The Law provided Israel the truth of God to know and live by. God's revelation in nature gives certain indications of His characteristics by deriving them from what we observe. For example, the awesome universe we observe is not eternal and therefore had a beginning. That said it is logically consistent that someone had to create it as discussed earlier. Thus, God has the power to create and sustain the entire universe (since it has been created and is currently sustained).

Another natural discovery is that creation has obvious design and complexity; this speaks to the intelligence and creativity of God. The fact that we can discover natural laws and formulas in the physical universe means that God created everything having these characteristics in them by design.

The ability of man to think, reason, use logic, and exercise discovery speaks to the purpose and intent of all that God created. Therefore, no matter what we can discover in the observable universe and what we can understand here on earth, it will never provide us the specific revelation of truth regarding God and ourselves – for that we need a special revelation that is God's Word – the Bible.

The Law provided Israel with the specifics of what God wanted known about His nature and character - things specific about God, which could not be deduced from observation of the physical universe. They certainly could not be discovered by watching cultural pagan worship practices of those in rebellion against God. Therefore, on one side there is God's truth, on the other are man's speculative inventions. Israel is a prime example of benefitting from the truth God revealed to them, while the pagan nations show the destruction of trying to live by man's speculative inventions and self-defeating relative truths.

5. **The Law foreshadowed Christ:** Everything in the Law, including the sacrifices, festivals, tabernacle layout, furniture, and materials that made up the tabernacle (with all their color significance), anticipated and foreshadowed Christ. The instruction in the Law, when understood, is a shadow to the real Christ, and this would help confirm Him at His arrival. Who He was and what He would accomplish in its fullness could be anticipated as the shadow is related to the Body. In other words, the NT's revelation of Christ would connect all the dots of the Law to the anticipated Messiah of Israel. When Israel eventually receives their Messiah, they will then comprehend the Law – for all the Law pointed to Him. Jesus not only fulfilled the Law (Matt. 5:17), but satisfied all the requirements of the Law regarding the payment for man's sin debt (Gal. 3:13). This is why Paul could say, "For Christ is the end of the law for righteousness to everyone who believes" (Rom. 10:4, NKJV). Placing faith in Jesus Christ satisfies the requirements of the Law (because

Jesus fulfilled the Law) and provides the complete redemption from sin. When a Jew comes to Christ, the Law has done its job.

6. **The Law taught man that he was a sinner in need of a Savior:** Since the Law required sacrifices for sin, it was necessary that instruction and definition of sin be contained in the Law. What sin is and how to make atonement for it is a major aspect within the Law. The Law is very specific and elaborate regarding this aspect of man in his relationship to God. Its many rules and laws made clear what sinful behavior was and was not. For example, a number of sinful violations required the death penalty, one of which was working on the Sabbath day (Ex. 31:14). Additionally, disrespecting God by worshipping and serving idols (idolatry, Deut. 17:2-7) – some of which destroyed life by human sacrifice such as the worship of Molech – invited the death penalty. Some other examples are blasphemy (Lev. 24:16), cursing parents (Deut. 21:18-21), adultery (Deut. 22:24), rape (Deut. 22:25), kidnapping (Ex. 21:16), trafficking with spirits (Lev. 20:27), incest and other unnatural sexual relations (Ex. 22:19; Lev. 20:10-16), and bearing false witness (Deut. 19:16-19) All these required the death penalty upon the guilty.

Since there was no redemption under the Law – it was a means of national sanctification – the Law required meticulous observance, so sinful man could come near to and keep fellowship with a Holy God. God was specific in how the Jews were to approach Him. The book of Leviticus prescribes specific details for them to follow so it would be safe to have sinners enter God's presence. For example, the book of Exodus ends with Israel at Mt. Sinai. They remained there until the cloud moved in Numbers 10. Moses built the Tabernacle with all the furniture as instructed by God in the book of Exodus. However, Moses stood at the door of the Tabernacle, but "was not able to enter the tabernacle of meeting, because the cloud rested above it, and the glory of the LORD filled the tabernacle" (Ex. 40:35). How were the Israelites going to enter the Tabernacle? The book of Leviticus provides the answer to this question.

The book of Leviticus begins with God speaking to Moses *outside* the Tabernacle, but God's presence was inside the Tabernacle. "Now the LORD called to Moses, and spoke to him from the tabernacle of meeting, saying, Speak to the children of Israel, and say to them: 'When any one of you brings an offering to the LORD...'" (Lev. 1:1-2, NKJV). The book of Numbers then begins with Moses *inside* the Tabernacle as God spoke to him, God's presence is also in the Tabernacle with Moses. "Now the LORD spoke to Moses in the Wilderness of Sinai, in the tabernacle of meeting..." (Num. 1:1, NKJV). This is the result of Moses (and Israel) following the laws in Leviticus so they can come safely into God's presence in the Tabernacle. They did not offend God or harm themselves by failing to follow the procedures required for their purity. Aaron's sons Nadab and Abihu failed to follow the prescribed method of approach spelled out and paid with their lives (Lev. 10). As the sun is necessary and beneficial to life on earth, getting too close to it can result in death without following proper procedures and without proper protection. Similarly, sinners cannot approach a holy God on their own terms, but must follow the specific procedures laid out by God for both their protection and benefit.

Thus, the Jews were instructed in matters of both sin and atonement. They were constantly educated that their sin caused the death of an innocent victim through animal sacrifice as they offered it for their own temporary atonement (Heb. 10:4). The continual offering of these sacrifices made it clear that the atonement was temporary and not permanent. In this way, the Law taught man he was a sinner and needed atonement by a sinless Savior, not an animal.

J. Dwight Pentecost, in an article entitled "The Purpose of the Law"[64] gives ten reasons for Moses' Law. The following is a summary list of his ten reasons from that article, appropriately ending this section:

1. To reveal the holiness of God (1 Peter 1:15)
2. To reveal the sinfulness of man (Gal. 3:19)
3. To reveal the standard of holiness required of those in fellowship with God (Psalm 24:3-5)
4. To supervise physical, mental, and spiritual development of redeemed Israelites until they should come to maturity in Christ (Gal. 3:24; Psalm 119:71-72)
5. To be the unifying principle that made the establishment of the nation possible (Ex. 19:5-8; Deut. 5:27-28)
6. To separate Israel from the nations to become a kingdom of priests (Ex. 19:5-6, 31:13)
7. To make provision for forgiveness of sins and restoration to fellowship (Lev. 1-7)
8. To make provision for a redeemed people to worship by observing and participating in the yearly festivals (Lev. 23)
9. To provide a test whether one was in the kingdom (theocracy) over which God ruled (Deut. 28)
10. To reveal Jesus Christ

CAN LAW AND GRACE
BE MIXED?

The simple answer to this question that heads this chapter is *NO!* Law and Grace cannot be mixed because they are contrasting methods of relationship. anymore than mixing the contrasting methods of earning wages and receiving gifts. If a person receives a gift, it means they have not earned it; otherwise it is an earned wage – the two concepts are mutually exclusive. It should be obvious that any contrasting truths, methods, models, systems, etc. that are opposite to each other cannot be equal and true at the same time, and in the same sense.[65] For example, someone that works for 8 hours earns a wage, the employer cannot correctly say it is a gift because it is an owed wage because it is earned. In the same way, if someone gives a gift, they do not consider the gift an earned wage. Paul the apostle uses these same contrasting concepts in Romans chapter 4. There he talks about how the righteousness of God is transferred or imparted (*imputed*) to man simply by *faith* and not by *works*. If it is of works, Paul reasons, then it is earned because it is owed. But, since *faith* in Christ results in a just standing before God by having His righteousness imparted – as in Abraham's example (Rom. 4:3) – any works or earnings have no relation to it. They are mutually exclusive.

Therefore, under the New Covenant, law and grace cannot be mixed or combined for salvation. *Faith* is always contrasted with *works* in Paul's theology as mentioned earlier. He links works and the Law (Gal. 2:16), but faith is coupled to grace (Rom. 4:16). Living by the Law brings a curse (Gal. 3:10), where believing by faith results in inheriting the promised blessing (Gal. 3:14, 22).

THE CONTRASTS OF LAW AND GRACE

The Law contrasts with the Gospel of grace in a number of areas. The *Law* was given to the nation of Israel and the Gospel of *grace* is related to the church, the Body of Christ. Listing the characteristics of both the Law and the Gospel shows the contrasts of each.

The **Law** given to the nation of Israel required *obedience* and has the following characteristics:

1. To the nation of Israel only
2. Requires obedience to fulfill it
3. Has curses for disobedience
4. Is incomplete
5. Was given by a prophet through mediation of angels
6. Identifying ritual is circumcision
7. Sabbath keeping is the sign of the Covenant
8. Law is written on stone, not hearts
9. Animal sacrifices offered were the means of sanctification (temporary offerings)
10. National feasts were the memorial practices to remember deliverance from Egypt
11. Had an anticipated end (New Covenant to follow)
12. Provided external laws that described how God wanted the promised descendants of Abraham to live and the land they were to live in
13. Jews had the priority under the Law as the covenant people, Gentiles were allowed to proselytize into Judaism
14. Israel and the Law were existing prior to the Body of Christ existing
15. Israel as a nation was put aside while the Body of Christ

is developed

16. Israel will be the nation God works through again after the Body of Christ (church) is removed
17. The Messianic kingdom is inaugurated through the nation of Israel
18. Israel's citizenship is on earth
19. Israel has its inheritance on earth
20. Ministry of death and condemnation
21. Conditional blessings
22. Conscious of their separation from God
23. Has dates, specific religious calendar, prophetic timetable

The *Gospel* is an individual message of salvation to anyone who will *believe* and has the following characteristics:

1. To the individual – "whomsoever"
2. Requires faith alone
3. Has blessings for all that believe
4. Is final and complete
5. Was revealed by the Son of God directly
6. Baptism is the ritual to identify with Christ
7. Seal of the Holy Spirit is the sign of the Covenant
8. Law is written on hearts, not stone
9. The sacrifice of the Son of God offered by God is the means of sanctification (one eternal offering)
10. The Lord's supper (communion) is the memorial to remember the completed redemption at the cross of Christ
11. Was expected as a New Covenant brought in by the Messiah
12. Provides commands and principles that believers in Christ are to obey through the inward power of the Holy Spirit, not by adhering to an external code
13. Jews and Gentiles are equal in the Body of Christ, and neither ethnic group had a priority over the other
14. The Body of Christ (church) didn't begin until after

Israel officially rejected Jesus as their promised Messiah and King

15. The Body of Christ (church) is developed from all nations around the world while Israel is set aside temporally
16. After the church is removed from earth in the rapture and taken to heaven, God will pour His Spirit on Israel during the tribulation
17. Bring in the Messianic Kingdom through Israel, the church is the bride of Christ
18. The church has citizenship in heaven
19. The church has its inheritance in heaven
20. Ministry of the Spirit and righteousness
21. Unconditional blessings
22. Conscious encouragement to draw near to God
23. Has no dates, specific religious calendar, prophetic timetable

The above list is organized into categories by characteristic and compared in the chart below:

CHARACTERISTIC	**THE LAW**	**GOSPEL**
Covenant for	Nation	Individual
Condition to Fulfill	Obedience	Faith
Contains Curses	Yes	No
Blessings Bestowed	Conditionally	Unconditionally
As a Covenant	Not Final	Final
Delivered Through	Angels/Prophet	Son of God
Identifying Ritual	Circumcision	Baptism
Sign of Covenant	Sabbath	Seal of Holy Spirit
Where Law Written	Stone Tablets	Heart
Sacrifices offered	Continually	Once
Memorial Ritual	7 Feasts	Lord's Supper
When Began	With Moses	With Christ
Ethnic Supremacy	Jews over Gentiles	Jews/Gentiles Equal
Citizenship Location	Earth	Heaven
Inheritance Location	Earth	Heaven
Ministry of (2 Cor. 3:7-9)	Death and Condemnation	The Spirit and Righteousness

PAUL THE APOSTLE TO
THE GENTILES

Paul is a fascinating character in the NT. He is initially introduced at the stoning of Stephen, the first Christian martyr (Acts 7:58). Not much is said about him other than he held the coats of those who threw the stones (Acts 22:20). The next time we hear of him he is spearheading a vicious persecution against the Christians (Acts 8:3; 9:1-2).

He "made havoc of the Church," invading the sanctuaries of domestic life, "entering into every house:" and those whom he thus tore from their homes he "committed to prison; or, in his own words at a later period, when he had recognised as God's people those whom he now imagined to be His enemies, "thinking that he ought to do many things contrary to the name of Jesus of Nazareth ... in Jerusalem ... he shut up many of the saints in prison." And not only did men thus suffer at his hands, but women also,—a fact three times repeated as a great aggravation of his cruelty. These persecuted people were scourged—"often" scourged, "—in many synagogues." Nor was Stephen the only one who suffered death, as we may infer from the Apostle's own confession. And, what was worse than scourging or than death itself, he used every effort to make them "blaspheme" that Holy Name whereby they were called. His fame as an inquisitor was notorious far and wide. Even at Damascus Ananias had heard "how much evil he had done to Christ's saints at Jerusalem." He was known there as "he that destroyed them which call on this Name in Jerusalem." It was not without reason that, in the deep repentance of his later years, he remembered how he had "persecuted the Church of God and wasted it," —how he had been "a blasphemer, a persecutor and injurious;" —and that he felt he was "not meet to be called an Apostle," because he "had persecuted the Church of God."[66]

He explained his actions when witnessing to the Jews in Jerusalem (Acts 22:4) and before Festus, King Agrippa, and the entourage of "chief captains, and principal men of the city" (Acts 25:23):

> I verily thought with myself, that I ought to do many things contrary to the name of Jesus of Nazareth. Which thing I also did in Jerusalem: and many of the saints did I shut up in prison, having received authority from the chief priests; and when they were put to death, I gave my voice against them. And I punished them oft in every synagogue, and compelled them to blaspheme; and being exceedingly mad against them, I persecuted them even unto strange cities. (Act 26:9-11)

Yes, Paul was determined to eliminate the Jesus movement, which he viewed as a heretical threat to Judaism. Yet, as with so many that try to strike down Jesus Christ and His followers, Paul ended up converted on the road to Damascus (Acts 9:3-18). He preached immediately after his conversion (Acts 19:22) and ended up three years in Arabia (Gal. 1:17-18), as Paul was being prepared to be the Apostle to the Gentiles. His situation with the Jews was dangerous, they constantly attempted to kill him (Acts 9:23-24; 13:50; 14:1-5, 19; 17:5-10a; 18:12-13; 21:23; 23:15; 25:3; 2 Cor. 11:26). However, many Christians initially were also leery of Paul (Acts 9:26), but the churches in Judea eventually embraced him (Gal. 1:21-24). Thus, for a time, Paul was between doubtful believers and Jews seeking his life. This difficulty continued with Paul, though he had a very successful ministry among the Gentiles. Even in Jerusalem, Jews in the church that were zealous to adhere to the Law had believed false rumors about Paul that put him in an unfavorable light (Acts 21:18-21). This motivated James (Jesus' half-brother and pastor of the Jerusalem church) and the elders to ask Paul to involve himself in a Nazarite vow with some other Jews to show he was not against Moses and the Law. There has been considerable debate as to whether or not Paul should have made this compromise, it was obviously a very tough spot for him. He always desired to be "made all things to all men, that I might by all means save some" (1 Cor. 9:22). And he acquiesced to James and the leaders in this case. However, in my own opinion, it was a mistake on the part of James and the others to ask this of Paul. Paul graciously accommodated them – it would have been very difficult not to – and God used it to accomplish His purposes nonetheless. G. Campbell Morgan had this comment,

> These elders seem to have had no conviction that the zealots of the law were wrong. They did not ask Paul for a concession, but for a vindication which is quite a different matter. They asked him to deny the rumor that he had abandoned rites and ceremonies, by observing these. The principle underlying their appeal was that of policy. Whatever their view, they must surely have known Paul's attitude. Their request for vindication before the believing Jews was dishonest. They knew that he had personally abandoned the observance of rites and ceremonies. These elders in Jerusalem had been in close touch with all his movements, they had read his letters, and certainly at this time the Galatian letter, and the two Corinthian letters were written. At Antioch he had rebuked Peter for dissimulation, and now they asked him to practise (sic) dissimulation.

> That leads us to consider the consent of Paul; and as in looking at the advice of the elders we observed the purpose and terms of the advice; so here let us consider the purpose of his consent, and the terms of that consent.

> Directly we turn from the advice of these men which was that of policy and of dishonesty withal, to the consent of Paul, and begin to look at the purpose of his consent, we have moved on to an entirely different level. I put that emphatically, because I hold that Paul made the greatest

mistake of his ministry on this occasion. Yet we have to recognize the fact that the reason of his consent was not that of expediency merely, not that of policy, but that of devotion. The reason of his consent was his desire to win his brethren.[67]

The curious question in all of this is why was Paul chosen to be sent to the Gentiles? Certainly, this is the choice of Jesus, for He told Ananias when he was apprehensive to go to Paul, "Go thy way: for he is a chosen vessel unto me, to bear my name before the Gentiles, and kings, and the children of Israel: For I will shew him how great things he must suffer for my name's sake" (Acts 9:15b-16). This is Paul's call to service, not salvation as read into the text by some. Jesus had a very specific call upon Paul's life – as He does upon every life – and it is clear that the Holy Spirit wanted Luke to make sure this is known to the church. This call upon Paul's life to "bear my name before the Gentiles" is confirmed throughout the book of Acts and Paul's epistles.

Acts 13:46-48: "Then Paul and Barnabas waxed bold, and said, It was necessary that the word of God should first have been spoken to you [Jews]: but seeing ye put it from you, and judge yourselves unworthy of everlasting life, lo, <u>we turn to the Gentiles. For so hath the Lord commanded us, saying, I have set thee to be a light of the Gentiles</u>, that thou shouldest be for salvation unto the ends of the earth. And when the Gentiles heard this, they were glad, and glorified the word of the Lord: and as many as were ordained to eternal life believed." (underline added, also in following verses)

Acts 18:5b, 6: "Paul was pressed in the spirit, and testified to the Jews that Jesus was Christ. And when they opposed themselves, and blasphemed, he shook his raiment, and said unto them, Your blood be upon your own heads; I am clean: <u>from henceforth I will go unto the Gentiles</u>."

Acts 21:19: "And when he [Paul] had saluted them [James and the elders at Jerusalem], he declared particularly what things God had wrought among the Gentiles by his ministry."

Acts 22:21: "And he [Jesus] said unto me [Paul], Depart: for I will send thee far hence unto the Gentiles."

Acts 28:28: "Be it known therefore unto you [Jews], that the salvation of God is sent unto the Gentiles, and that they will hear it."

Galatians 2:8: "For he [Jesus] that wrought effectually in Peter to the apostleship of the circumcision [Jews], the same was mighty in me toward the Gentiles."

Ephesians 3:1: "For this cause I Paul, the prisoner of Jesus Christ for you Gentiles."

Ephesians 3:8: "Unto me, who am less than the least of all saints, is this grace given, that I should preach among the Gentiles the unsearchable riches of Christ."

1 Thessalonians 2:16: "[Jews] Forbidding us to speak to the Gentiles that they might be saved, to fill up their sins alway: for the wrath is come upon them to the uttermost."

1 Timothy 2:7: "Whereunto I am ordained a preacher, and an apostle, (I speak the truth in Christ, and lie not;) a teacher of the Gentiles in faith and verity."

2 Timothy 1:11: "Whereunto I am appointed a preacher, and an apostle, and a teacher of the Gentiles."

2 Timothy 4:17: "Notwithstanding the Lord stood with me, and strengthened me; that by me the preaching might be fully known, and that all the Gentiles might hear: and I was delivered out of the mouth of the lion."

The above quotes make it very clear that Paul's call was among the Gentiles. The first quote is from Paul and Barnabas's first missionary journey. What is interesting in this missionary movement was its base of operation – Antioch in Syria. The book of Acts follows the outline established by Jesus, "But ye shall receive power, after that the Holy Ghost is come upon you: and ye shall be witnesses unto me both in Jerusalem, and in all Judaea, and in Samaria, and unto the uttermost part of the earth." (Acts 1:8). Thus, we observe the Gospel beginning at Jerusalem, moving to Judea, into Samaria with Phillip and with Paul's missionary journeys to the "uttermost part of the earth." However, within the movement is also the move of the Gospel's base of operation from Jerusalem to Antioch in Syria. It was the result of the ongoing persecution that Paul led which caused the Gospel to be spread initially to Antioch (Acts 11:19-20), and it was there "a great number believed, and turned unto the Lord" (Acts 11:21b). The Jerusalem church sent Barnabas to help the development at Antioch. Barnabas then went to Tarsus to find Paul and include him in the work God was doing in Antioch. Remember, it was Barnabas who initially brought Paul to the apostles (Acts 9:27), seeing Paul's preaching among the Gentiles at Damascus, and knowing the benefit Paul could bring to the Gospel effort.

Luke is very careful to provide the connections for all that the Lord was doing in the book of Acts. Luke joined Paul's missionary team (Acts 16:10) when they went to Macedonia, bringing the Gospel into Europe, since Paul was inclined to go east into Asia Minor (Acts 16:6-7). Therefore, Luke was with Paul from that point forward and was an eyewitness to the events that took place. Also he knew what happened before as he carefully investigated all the key aspects of Christ's life, ministry, and continued work in the establishment of His church and spread of the Gospel (Luke 1:1-4; Acts 1:1-2). Additionally, I believe Luke wrote apologetically since he understood the difficulty Paul faced from the slander of the Judaizers against his legitimate apostleship. This is clear from Paul's own comments:

1 Corinthians 4:15: "For though ye have ten thousand instructors in Christ, yet have ye not many fathers: for in Christ Jesus I have begotten you through the gospel."

1 Corinthians 9:1-3: "Am I not an apostle? am I not free? have I not seen Jesus Christ our Lord? are not ye my work in the Lord? If I be not an apostle unto others, yet doubtless

I am to you: for the seal of mine apostleship are ye in the Lord. Mine answer to them that do examine me is this…"

2 Corinthians 2:17: "For we are not as many, which corrupt the word of God: but as of sincerity, but as of God, in the sight of God speak we in Christ."

2 Corinthians 3:1: "Do we begin again to commend ourselves? or need we, as some others, epistles of commendation to you, or letters of commendation from you?"

2 Corinthians 10:12-16: "For we dare not class ourselves or compare ourselves with those who commend themselves. But they, measuring themselves by themselves, and comparing themselves among themselves, are not wise. We, however, will not boast beyond measure, but within the limits of the sphere which God appointed us—a sphere which especially includes you. For we are not overextending ourselves (as though our authority did not extend to you), for it was to you that we came with the gospel of Christ; not boasting of things beyond measure, that is, in other men's labors, but having hope, that as your faith is increased, we shall be greatly enlarged by you in our sphere, to preach the gospel in the regions beyond you, and not to boast in another man's sphere of accomplishment." (NKJV)

2 Corinthians 11:4-5: "For if he who comes preaches another Jesus whom we have not preached, or if you receive a different spirit which you have not received, or a different gospel which you have not accepted—you may well put up with it! For I consider that I am not at all inferior to the most eminent apostles." (NKJV)

2 Corinthians 11:12-15: "But what I do, I will also continue to do, that I may cut off the opportunity from those who desire an opportunity to be regarded just as we are in the things of which they boast. For such are false apostles, deceitful workers, transforming themselves into apostles of Christ. And no wonder! For Satan himself transforms himself into an angel of light. Therefore it is no great thing if his ministers also transform themselves into ministers of righteousness, whose end will be according to their works." (NKJV)

2 Corinthians 11:23: "Are they ministers of Christ? (I speak as a fool) I am more; in labours more abundant, in stripes above measure, in prisons more frequent, in deaths oft."

2 Corinthians 12:12: "Truly the signs of an apostle were wrought among you in all patience, in signs, and wonders, and mighty deeds."

Galatians 1:6: "I marvel that ye are so soon removed from him that called you into the grace of Christ unto another gospel: Which is not another; but there be some that trouble you, and would pervert the gospel of Christ."

Galatians 4:15-17: "What then was the blessing you enjoyed? For I bear you witness that, if possible, you would have plucked out your own eyes and given them to me. Have I therefore become your enemy because I tell you the truth? They zealously court you, but for no good; yes, they want to exclude you, that you may be zealous for them." (NKJV)

Galatians 5:7: "Ye did run well; who did hinder you that ye should not obey the truth?"

Galatians 5:12: "I would they were even cut off which trouble you."

The Judaizers constantly troubled Paul in his work of establishing churches. He would leave and they would come in like a band of termites eating away at the foundation of the Gospel of the Grace of God. Luke was well aware of this and made sure the book of Acts was an apologetic for Paul's apostolic legitimacy. It is clear from a casual reading of Acts that Peter is the leader among the apostles in Jerusalem and notable character of the first half of the book. Paul takes over in the second half as the lead apostle among the Gentiles. There is a comparison of both men throughout the book to reveal God working through them in equal fashion. For example, they both heal a man who is lame from birth (Acts 3:1-11; 14:8-18), they both have unusual miracles worked through them (Acts 3:15-16; 19:11, 12), they both had Jews come against them for their success in preaching Jesus (Acts 5:17; 13:45), they both confront sorcerers (Acts 8:9-24; 13:6-11), they both raise someone from the dead (Acts 9:36-41; 20:9-12), and they are both miraculously freed from prison (Acts 12:3-19; 16:25-34). Since Paul was not one of the original twelve, it made his ministry difficult as a late comer (1 Cor. 15:8). Yet, he made it clear in his ministry that the credit for his success was the Lord, "But by the grace of God I am what I am: and his grace which was bestowed upon me was not in vain; but I laboured more abundantly than they all: yet not I, but the grace of God which was with me" (1 Cor. 15:10).

Having said all this, I always wondered as a new Christian why Paul was sent to the Gentiles. He was clearly the most theologically educated among them all. He uniquely possessed Roman citizenship (Acts 22:28), another point Luke brings out. He was born in Tarsus, a Greek city giving Paul keen knowledge of that culture, thinking, and educational advantage. Also he was trained by the most eminent Rabbi (Acts 22:3, also see Acts 5:34) so we know his education as a Pharisee was stellar and his zeal beyond his contemporaries (Acts 23:6; 26:4-5; Gal. 1:14; Phil. 3:5, 6). So would not Paul be a better witness to the Jews? He obviously had a tremendous theological grasp of the Messianic prophecies and supportive scriptures; we observe this in his constant witnessing to the Jews in Acts and what Peter writes about him (2 Peter 3:15-16). However, it was necessary that God use someone like Paul, with his education, knowledge, and revelation (2 Cor. 12:7; Eph. 1:9; 3:3, 4; Phil. 3:8), championing the protection necessary to save the Gentile church from the tenacious legalism of misguided Jews. Paul was uniquely suited for this task with his keen understanding of the Law to prevent the Gospel from any confusion by any theological or cultural attacks against it. That he protected the Gentile believers against the onslaught of Judaizers who constantly threatened their liberty in Christ is borne out in his epistles. To this point, Paul was the master in the Master's hand. As he said to the Ephesian church, "For this cause I Paul, the prisoner of Jesus Christ for you Gentiles" (Eph. 3:1). Paul was imprisoned for the defense of the Gospel (Phil. 1:7, 12, 17) as he preached the Gospel to the Gentiles. It was his life (Phil. 1:21) and the fulfilling of his call from that point on the Damascus road, until he was a martyr under Caesar Nero in 64 A.D.[68]

Yes, it was vital that Paul protect the Gospel from legalistic contamination in the first century so that all succeeding centuries of Christians would benefit. His service and epistles have been both an example and instruction to the church through the centuries. When the church moves away from Paul's instruction, it begins to add to the Gospel and legalize the sanctification process. Instead of church rituals having a place of relevant observance reflecting a greater reality, they are brought into the place of ultimate reality, being incorporated into the Gospel itself. This contamination of the Gospel has been a constant threat from Jesus' initial work through Paul's ministry until today. Men and devils (many times working in concert) will do anything possible to pervert the pure Gospel of the grace of God. As Paul was called to prevent that contamination and reduce the Gospel to an aspect of human effort and filthy works, we must stand our ground. We must not allow the modern day Judaizers to ruin the work of Christ on the cross by mixing it with man's filthy sin. Our sin put Christ on the cross; let us not profane the only sacrifice that can save us from our sins. In any aspect of Christian endeavor, the Gospel is polluted with laws and human works, we know "This persuasion does not come from Him who calls you" (Gal. 5:8, NKJV). For there is only one true gospel (Gal. 1:6-7), and those (men or angels) who preach a different one other than revealed through Paul will be accursed

(Gal. 1:8-9).

The grace of God worked hard through Paul to keep the Gospel free and pure. It required a keen understanding of the Law and the differences with the Gospel. As Paul said to Timothy, "Be diligent to present yourself approved to God, a worker who does not need to be ashamed, rightly dividing the word of truth" (2 Tim. 2:15, NKJV). The ability to divide between the Law and the Gospel is essential. But it requires our diligence and effort to make sure we understand what is at stake and how to respond. This book is dedicated to that understanding and desire to keep the Gospel free from those who want to pervert it. Some will try and change it deliberately because they cannot stand that their own efforts are eliminated. They cannot stand the fact that they have no contribution to the cross of Christ – a heretical and silly concept indeed. And others will ruin the Gospel because of their own biblical ignorance and want to hear something novel, but it will be a myth (2 Tim. 4:3-4). They do not realize that if it is not the pure gospel of God's grace, it is no gospel at all. It is simply the words of men, the imagination of their own hearts (Jer. 23:17, 21), "intruding into those things which he hath not seen, vainly puffed up by his fleshly mind" (Col. 2:18). The church is flooded with this nonsense today because its members learn from the culture and bring it into the sanctuary and pulpits. It would take an entire book to delve into the specifics of how these dangerous trends are bringing constant deterioration to the Gospel and neutralization to the word of God. Paul's attitude toward popularity and wealth is observed in his letter to the Corinthians. He would not even take financial support from them because they were so carnal that they would have taken credit for Paul's ministry. Though Paul was in his right to accept support from them, he declined to both keep them from misunderstanding their involvement and receive his own reward before Christ in glory for the work of God's grace in his life.

But I have used none of these things, nor have I written

these things that it should be done so to me; for it would be better for me to die than that anyone should make my boasting void. For if I preach the gospel, I have nothing to boast of, for necessity is laid upon me; yes, woe is me if I do not preach the gospel! For if I do this willingly, I have a reward; but if against my will, I have been entrusted with a stewardship. What is my reward then? That when I preach the gospel, I may present the gospel of Christ without charge, that I may not abuse my authority in the gospel. For though I am free from all men, I have made myself a servant to all, that I might win the more. (1 Cor. 9:15-19, NKJV)

This should be our attitude as well. We should do all for the glory of God and keep the Gospel free of the legalism of works. We must stand fast in the liberty that Christ has made us free, or we will once again be brought into bondage. Instead of freeing the sinner from their yoke of bondage to sin and self, we will only add to their burden and dishonor Christ who died to set them (and us) free. It is time to hold the line and not waver on this truth. If we are going to contribute anything to the Gospel, let it be the effort in God's grace to keep it free of contamination. No wonder Jesus picked such a great Jewish theologian to keep the Gentile church free from bondage. It needed someone particular enough to establish that defense in the first century when the church was starting and its initial attacks came roaring in.

I have grown in my appreciation of Paul over the years. When I was a young Christian, Paul was an apostle that penned most of the NT letters. Now, my appreciation of how Jesus used him is beyond words. I cannot wait to meet Paul and thank him. I am sure he will point to Jesus for all the glory, and that would be where the credit is due. But there are many that begin their service to the Lord and fizzle out or get sidetracked, never reaching the specific potential that Jesus has called them to. That never happened with Paul, and as a Gentile that has learned the importance of what he accomplished, I want to tell him as one sinner to another that I appreciate his loyalty and diligence to Christ. Jesus selected Paul, a responsible rabbi, in charge of protecting the Gospel to the Gentiles. Jesus is glorified because Paul kept the pure gospel from the threatened contaminants. Ultimately, we should honor our Savior who did all the heavy lifting to accomplish our redemption alone on the cross – there would be no gospel of grace without it. He alone was separated from the Father for a moment, so we did not need to be forever (Matt. 27:46). All the glory goes to Him, all the praise, all the honor, and the Gospel of the good news offered to all is by grace alone, through faith alone, accomplished by Christ alone for us. God only asks that we enter a relationship with Him through faith alone, plus nothing. It is all about Him as seen in this hymn:

Rock of Ages, cleft for me,
Let me hide myself in Thee;
Let the water and the blood,
From Thy wounded side which flowed,
Be of sin the double cure,
Save from wrath and make me pure.

Not the labor of my hands
Can fulfill Thy law's demands;
Could my zeal no respite know,
Could my tears forever flow,
All for sin could not atone;
Thou must save, and Thou alone.

Nothing in my hand I bring,
Simply to Thy cross I cling;
Naked, come to Thee for dress;
Helpless, look to Thee for grace;
Foul, I to the fountain fly;
Wash me, Savior, or I die.

While I draw this fleeting breath,
When my eyes shall close in death,

When I rise to worlds unknown,
And behold Thee on Thy throne,
Rock of Ages, cleft for me,
Let me hide myself in Thee.[69]

CONCLUDING APPLICATION

How Should a Christian View the Law?

Though a Christian is not under the Law for sanctification, much of the Law (Genesis – Deuteronomy), and the rest of the OT is quoted in the NT for warning, example, insight, perspective, instruction, knowledge of the truth, and application by the NT authors. The whole Bible is written *for* Christians, but not *to* Christians. Gaining an understanding of the OT texts within their respective contexts is of the utmost value for Christians, even though their original address is to Israel. Limiting Bible knowledge to the NT alone will result in a limited understanding of God's revelation and the inability to apply fully what God meant for all believers.

Having said that, the NT is fully adequate - and necessary - to educate Christians on their relationship with the Lord Jesus Christ. However, to gain further depth of who Jesus is and what He has accomplished, knowledge of the OT is mandatory. The types and shadows in the sacrifices of the Law and principles behind the various ceremonial commands given by Moses are invaluable to understanding the Person of Christ. Understanding the laws given by Moses provide invaluable insight to how God sanctified Israel and kept them from sin. This foundation and comparison to the NT is essential and cannot be overemphasized. Comprehending OT laws enable Christians to draw principles of truth, which enhances insight to aid application for daily living. Who has not been encouraged by the Psalms or gained wisdom from the book of Proverbs? Though the book of Proverbs is written by and *to* Jews under the Law (some verses make that very clear when speaking of kings, of sacrifices, or references to Mosaic commands), the profound truths taught therein become timeless in their wisdom and application to anyone who will listen to "Wisdom's voice." The narrative portions of the OT are immensely instructive for Christians; we find NT writers using them continuously as the basis of instruction, warning, and encouragement.

For example, in 1 Corinthians 10, Paul writes to warn the Corinthian believers to avoid idolatry and its resulting immorality. He used the OT books of Exodus and Numbers as the foundation to his teaching (1 Cor. 10:1-10). In verses 5 and 6, Paul speaks of the Israelite experience of wandering 40 years in the wilderness because of their unbelief, "But with many of them God was not well pleased: for they were overthrown in the wilderness. Now these things were our examples, to the intent we should not lust after evil things, as they also lusted." This generation of wandering Israelites were constantly falling into sin because of their struggle to trust God; this caused them to be vulnerable to attack through their wicked desires. Paul made a direct application to the desire of the Corinthians based on the evil desires of the Jews from Exodus and Numbers. The Jew's evil desires brought judgmental consequences and Paul applied the spiritual danger these same sins would be to the Corinthians. The Corinthian believers were lusting after evil things no different from the wandering Israelites. Paul had already addressed their carnal divisions in chapters 1-3, their lack of humility and responsibility in chapter 4, sexual immorality in chapter 5, taking other Christians to secular courts, and visiting temple prostitutes in chapter 6. We can go on, but the point is that the Corinthian church had some serious moral problems. Paul was using the OT as an example of how God viewed such behavior through the consequences visited upon the Jews. However, he was *not* placing the Corinthians under the same covenant as the Jews, nor imposing any curses or recommending capital punishment for any such violations. However, he brought the principle into the NT and applied the warning comparing the destructive nature of sin no matter the covenant. Though NT believers are under a different *covenant*, they are not under a different *God*.

Let me provide a personal illustration. I currently work for my best friend, our Senior Pastor. My job as the assistant pastor requires me to fulfill certain obligations and follow particular policies of our church. I am expected to fulfill all directives and responsibilities of my position as a staff pastor at our church in order to continue serving at our church. However, when we get together as friends, "job obligations" or "directives" are not required. In other words, as an employee, I am shown no favoritism; but as a friend, at times I am. He is the same person (Senior Pastor, friend), but when I am under the obligations of my employment, the Senior Pastor cannot show favoritism. If he did, it would violate Scripture by showing partiality (James 2:1). However, in our interactions as friends, we both show favoritism. Many problems would result if I tried to bring the favoritism of friendship into our working relationship, and it would be a strange friendship if I brought work conditions into our friendship. A similar problem often happens with Christians and the Law of Moses. They try to bring aspects of Moses Law into their relationship with Christ and it becomes a confusing and strange type of Christianity – certainly not, what we see in the NT. Thus, I can have the same friend with two different aspects of our relationship – boss and friend. Similarly, the God of the OT law can have different covenants by which He relates to different people, one group under Moses Law (nation) and others under the Gospel of Grace (Body of Christ).

Continuing his teaching in 1 Corinthians, Paul says, "Now all these things happened to them as examples, and they were written for our admonition, upon whom the ends of the ages have come" (1 Cor. 10:11, NKJV). What does Paul mean by "examples"? He means that we can gain an understanding of how God views various sins or behaviors as we look at how He dealt with Israel. We can use the examples of how God addresses sins under the Law, to know at a minimum how He views the same behavior in Christians, though not under the

Law's punishment. As NT Christians, we are not free to commit the same immoral acts at OT Jews and think God views them differently, just because the punishment under the Law was more severe. On the contrary, NT believers have the indwelling presence of the Holy Spirit to enable them to live above the mere negative legal restrictions of rules and laws. Israel was baptized into (identified with) Moses (1 Cor. 10:2), Christians are baptized into (identified with) Christ (Gal. 3:27), and by that union the power of the sin nature in our lives has been broken – literally *made idle or rendered powerless* (see Romans 6:3-7). Moreover, if the Corinthians continued this immoral behavior, God would step in with chastisement that can be very severe, as exampled in their sinful behavior in abusing the Lord's supper (ref. 1 Cor. 11:30). All sin results in death (Rom. 6:16, 23; James 1:15), whether it is a deadening of our relationship with Jesus, relationships to others, or the overall deadening of our Christian experience and joy. It can also result in the death of our bodies in extreme cases, whether the natural results of certain sinful behavior or a chastisement from the Lord. John talked about a sin that led to the death of a "brother" (1 John 5:16), which is a severe chastisement. God has all the tools in His toolbox He needs to work in a believer's life for chastisement or blessing. We can limit Him by our unbelief (Psalm 78:41), but we remove those limits by our sin (1 Cor. 11:31, 32).

The following chart may help to understand the differences discussed above.

Covenant	Command	Consequence	Verse
Law	Don't murder	Stoning	Ex. 21:12
Grace	Don't murder	Accountable to civil authorities	Rom. 13:1-5
Law	Don't blaspheme	Stoning	Lev.

			24:16
Grace	Don't blaspheme	Delivered to Satan for discipline	1 Tim. 1:20
Law	Idolatry	Stoning	Ex. 22:20
Grace	Idolatry	Call to repent	2 Cor. 6; 1 John 5:21
Law	False Prophecy/ teaching	Stoning	Deut. 13
Grace	False Prophecy/ teaching	Correction	1 Tim. 1:3-11

Therefore, as a NT believer, I can – and must – read the OT and utilize it to the fullest advantage. If we read the NT with no understanding of the OT, a possibility exists of imposing an interpretation of quoted OT passages into the NT that are foreign to them, and thus misunderstand the whole text. The Law is not a twenty-first century writing; it has an entirely different background and culture than ours. To read our present cultural concepts back into the passages quoted by NT writers almost ensures a misunderstanding of various texts. This has caused a lot of confusion among Christians because they have imposed their own ideas into certain OT quotes, having never studied the original OT context. Our approach to the Bible is extremely important when trying to get the most out of our OT and NT studies!

HOW CAN I APPLY THE OLD TESTAMENT TO MY CHRISTIAN LIFE?

We can all find tremendous application to our lives from the Old Testament. Though Christians are not under the Mosaic Covenant, the verses of the OT speak significantly to us as they did to the NT writers. All the writers under the New Covenant drew on the OT for theology and life application. For example, after Peter laid the foundation for the reliability of prophetic inspiration in chapter 1 of his second epistle, then in the second chapter he immediately drew on the OT and provided application. What is interesting concerning his use of the OT is that without reference to dispensation or covenant, he masterfully quoted the OT and brought light to the NT situation by his use of OT history and examples. He seamlessly wove a message of stark warning to his audience guarding them from the false teachers that threatened their Christian liberty and morality. He laid out the seductive craft and characteristics of false teachers (2:1-3), started at the fall of angels (2:4), moved on to the days of Noah (2:5), and followed on to the destruction of Sodom and Gomorrah and Lot's deliverance with a descriptor of their ungodliness and pompous attitude (2:6-11). He continued and spoke of their immoral character that drove them as if by animal instincts alone and brought others through evil persuasion into their bondage (2:12-14). Like Balaam, their insatiable love of money consumed them to the point of irrational behavior (2:15-16), which revealed their spiritual emptiness (2:17). This however did not deter them, for they had mastered the art of word psychology to fleece all they could from thier victims. To fill their own desires, they influenced as many unstable souls as possible, brought them into the same bondage, and returned to the fleshly filth from which they sprang with only the judgment of God as their final course (2:18-22). Thus, Peter started at the fall of angels, moved right through the OT, and drew application after application to make his very poignant argument. Why was this possible? The answer is because none of the examples he gave required a covenant connection that restricted his application. He brought the entire biblical theme of morality and spirituality right into the NT for important and strategic life application.

Many Christians have what they consider life verses, which are typically those verses they cherish because of how they speak to them personally, even though many times they come from the OT. They are not selected with respect of covenant or context necessarily, but because of the nature and principle of the truth they reveal. These verses are typically timeless truths that permeate the Scriptures like Peter's example above, making their point and speaking loudly. At times, they are used metaphorically which does not necessarily mean inappropriately. Those who choose them normally understand this, but not always, which can be very misleading if the original meaning is not understood before attempting to apply it. Any reading from the classic authors in Christianity–especially those of long ago–wrote with this metaphorical use of various texts. Spurgeon was a master at this. I will never forget the example he gave as a warning to those teachers that borrow from the experience of others in their sermons, of which he was not a fan:

> Fictitious experience is dangerous to the forger of it. Experience borrowed from other people is like the borrowed axe, sure to fall into the ditch and make its user cry, "Alas."[70]

This metaphor is both instructive and funny if you know the story of the axe head that Elisha had to recover (2 Kings 6:1-7). In the story, the young men of the school of prophets were too poor to buy tools of their own, but wanted to enlarge the place where they lived which had become too cramped. Thus, they got a loan of an axe head that they might cut down some trees to build. "But as one was felling a beam, the axe head fell into the water: and he cried, and said, Alas, master! for it was borrowed" (2 Kings 6:5). Applying that to preachers becomes very instructive though it has nothing to do with that subject or context. The metaphor is of great use and education when addressing those who are too lazy to do the necessary study for their own sermons. When they fail because of borrowed sermons or experiences, they may in the end cry out "Alas! for it was borrowed." Really, how do you improve upon this?

I have had so many verses speak to my situation and life it would be difficult to choose just one. But if I had to, it would probably be the following:

> This I recall to my mind, therefore have I hope. It is of the LORD'S mercies that we are not consumed, because his compassions fail not. They are new every morning: great is thy faithfulness. The LORD is my portion, saith my soul; therefore will I hope in him. The LORD is good unto them that wait for him, to the soul that seeketh him. It is good that a man should both hope and quietly wait for the salvation of the LORD. Lam. 3:21-26

Historically in these verses, Jeremiah was lamenting the destruction of Jerusalem and deportation of Judah and Benjamin to Babylon as he watched from the hill outside the city. His heart was broken and the pain was evident in his cry. Nevertheless, in the midst of this pain he remembers the promise of God to return and fulfill His word to Israel through both the Abrahamic and Mosaic Covenants that were still to be accomplished. I understand the context and its significance in the plan of God specifically for Israel. However, the viewpoint of Jeremiah regarding the mercy and faithfulness of God is so clearly expressed; it has spoken to my own heart time and time again. Over the past forty plus years of my Christian walk, I have had painful times when I believe I failed the Lord or was at least not as faithful as I could have been. In those times, these verses have spoken to me because they remind me of

God's daily mercies and His faithfulness–even when we are not faithful. Now, is this principle of God's character isolated to the OT? No! We have the same principle repeated in the NT by way of God's mercy and faithfulness many times (Matt. 9:13; 2 Tim. 2:13; Heb. 2:17 among many other verses). The truth reflected concerning God's mercy expressed in Lamentations 3:21-26 are grounded in His nature and character, which is the same in every covenant and dispensation because of God's immutability (Malachi 3:6; Heb. 13:8). How God exercises His mercy through each covenant and or dispensation is based on the particulars of each as explained earlier in this book. This must remain the important distinction when drawing OT verses for life application. Conflating the covenants will confuse the application because it ignores the original context and interpretation.

The point is this: Christians obviously use the entire Bible for life application. It would be a tragedy and terrible oversight to limit applicable verses to just the NT. Having said that, it is important that we understand the context of the OT verses so we are not conflating covenant promises in our personal application. God's words to Joshua (see Joshua chapter 1) when preparing to enter the Promised Land can be of great encouragement and personal application to believers today. Are Christians entering the land of Canaan to take it over and expel the occupants? Of course not! But as God said to Joshua, "Be strong and of a good courage" (Joshua 1:6) in his endeavor to obey God and take the Promised Land. God can use those words to speak to Christians in their endeavor to follow through on the call of God upon their lives and the ventures in faith they believe God has opened to them. When God said, "Only be thou strong and very courageous, that thou mayest observe to do according to all the law, which Moses my servant commanded thee: turn not from it to the right hand or to the left, that thou mayest prosper whithersoever thou goest" (Joshua 1:7), this again is applicable in principle to Christians. We need to be "strong and very courageous" to obey (not Moses' Law particularly); we should not turn "to the right hand or the left," in other words do not deviate from the NT instruction so that we may fruitfully fulfill whatever endeavor the Lord has called us to perform. Drawing this type of application from the OT into the Christian life is normal and encouraging. As discussed in the previous chapter, warnings are also there and should be heeded as in 1 Corinthians chapter 10. At times, warnings can speak louder than encouragements if the Lord is trying to get our attention.

Knowing the covenant and context provides the secret to avoid misapplication of the OT in our lives as NT believers. In other words, if certain promises made to Jews under the law are applied to Christians in the NT in an equally literal way, disappointment and potential disillusionment may result. For example, Christians have no covenant land promise as the nation of Israel does (Gen. 13:14-15, 17), and any attempt to apply that type of claim is simply mistaken. The church has a heavenly inheritance (Phil. 3:20) that the NT writers encourage believers to look forward to. Moreover, Christians have no curse (Deut. 27:9-26) upon them because they are not under the Mosaic Covenant. On the contrary, Christians are blessed "with all spiritual blessings in heavenly places in Christ" (Eph. 1:3) and thus cannot be cursed. NT believers can be chastened and disciplined (Heb. 12:5-11) for their benefit so that "afterward it yieldeth the peaceable fruit of righteousness" (Heb. 12:11), but never cursed. Moreover, Christians have no "generational curse" (promoted by some of the charismatic extremes) upon them, nor can they be demon possessed, for the Holy Spirit is in them (1 Cor. 6:19-20) and He is not into timesharing. If Christians see a demon behind every tree, and heavily weight their focus toward demonic involvement rather than the Holy Spirit's work, there is no longer correlation with NT practices. These types of doctrinal errors and theological confusion are avoidable.

Establishing the proper context of verses (OT and NT)

provide proper understanding so they can be correctly applied. It will also free people from the nonsense interpretations out there that create weird doctrines by stringing similar words or subjects together between the OT and NT. When examined with sound interpretive principles, these type of shallow word or idea connections between covenants many times reveal they conflict rather than connect. Sound methods of Bible study and good interpretive principles yield the fullest benefit for all of God's people and deliver the entirety of the Scriptures properly into the hands of those looking for solid life application. Haphazard cherry picking of verses or treating the Bible like a bowl of fortune cookies is disrespectful to the Word of God and the God of the Word. We would not do it with any other book, why would we do it with the most important book on the planet? Glen Davis stated the true reason why we should read the Bible carefully and respectfully:

Every verse of Scripture, from Genesis 1:1 - Revelation 22:20, has as its theme the Person and work of the Lord Jesus Christ. The verses below are some that express this:

"Search the Scriptures; for in them ye think ye have eternal life: and they are they which testify of Me" (John 5:39).

"And beginning at Moses and all the prophets, He expounded unto them in all the Scriptures the things concerning Himself" (Luke 24:27).

"And a certain Jew named Apollos, born at Alexandria, an eloquent man, and mighty in the Scriptures, came to Ephesus. This man was instructed in the way of the Lord; and being fervent in the spirit, he spake and taught diligently the things of the Lord, knowing only the baptism of John. And he began to speak boldly in the synagogue: whom when Aquila and Priscilla had heard, they took him unto them, and expounded unto him the way of God more perfectly. And when he was disposed to pass into Achaia, the brethren wrote, exhorting the disciples to receive him: who, when he was come, helped them much which had believed through grace, for he mightily convinced the Jews, and that publicly, showing by the Scriptures that Jesus was Christ" (Acts 18:24-28).

This is a vital point, that all Scripture is valuable to the believer because it all points somehow to the glory and revelation of the Lord Jesus, and to His Person and work. The covenantal, dispensational, attitudinal, behavioral, verbal, historical, soteriological, and prophetic matters of the Bible all somehow commence, continue, and culminate in Him.

"All Scripture is given by inspiration of God, and is profitable for doctrine, for reproof, for correction, for instruction in righteousness" (II Timothy 3:16).

Paul clearly writes to NT believers, for believers, and about believers as the audience he addresses. He declares "all Scripture" to be profitable.[71]

As this chapter ends, think about the value of the whole Bible to the NT believer. What Christian that has spent any significant time in the Scriptures has not been motivated and encouraged by the OT saints? Who has not found great encouragement through David's Psalms or his stories of faith and victory? Who has not taken the words spoken to Joshua entering the Promised Land (Joshua 1) to heart as their own? Who has read of the heroes of faith in Hebrews chapter eleven and not been personally inspired to a stronger faith in God–especially in the midst of trying and uncertain circumstances? I cannot adequately explain the value of the OT to its fullest capability in the life of a Christian. God can use the OT stories, examples, principles, truths, and revelation of Himself to encourage, inspire, and direct NT believers in ways only the Holy Spirit knows. Even though Christians are not under the Mosaic Covenant, the truths expressed and characteristics of God revealed to the OT saints still remain consistent with the NT revelation (Heb. 13:8). The difference is covenant requirements. Though covenants change, God remains the same in nature and character (Malachi 3:6). This is where maintaining the distinction becomes important for the Christian in a successful walk with the Lord.

WHAT IS THE NEW TESTAMENT AGE OF GRACE?

The NT age of grace is the current period in which we are living. God is calling out from all nations those who will place their faith in his Son Jesus Christ. The Gospel is the simple message that Jesus Christ paid the sin debt of the world and God now calls all to be reconciled to Him through His Son (Acts 17:30). Paul describes this in his explanation of the ministry of reconciliation (2 Cor. 5:11-21). He makes a key point in verses 18-21 when he says:

> And all things are of God, who hath reconciled us to himself by Jesus Christ, and hath given to us the ministry of reconciliation; To wit [that is], that God was in Christ, reconciling the world unto himself, not imputing their trespasses unto them; and hath committed unto us the word of reconciliation. Now then we are ambassadors for Christ, as though God did beseech you by us: we pray you in Christ's stead, be ye reconciled to God. For he hath made him to be sin for us, who knew no sin; that we might be made the righteousness of God in him. (2 Cor. 5:18-21)

The current dispensation of grace is a time where God is not imputing people's sins against them, but Jesus has taken "the sin of the world" (John 1:29) upon Himself at the cross, "Blessed is the man to whom the Lord will not impute sin" (Rom. 4:8). The cross has solved the sin problem from God's side, now it is up to man to respond by faith – believing this good news (gospel), which has the power to save whoever believes it. Thus, God initiated this work of redemption by sending His Son to pay the price for man's sin (payment made in full, see John 19:30), which is why He does not impute sin to those who are "in Christ."

"Blessed is the man to whom the Lord will not impute sin."

This is a fascinating truth, isn't it? I love the emphatic *"will not* impute sin." In other words, a trillion devils could not entice God to jeopardize the saving relationship He freely gives to all who trust the Lord Jesus. Why? Because the work of Christ on the cross is so huge, significant, and effectual in the Father's sight. He knows how perfectly and completely His Son's death on the cross atoned for our sins. He sees His trusting sons and daughters through the lens of Calvary. He sees us "in Christ" because He saw our sins upon Christ, and even more wondrously, "made Him to be sin for us, who knew no sin." Wondrously, He also sees the entire human race through that lens (1 John 2:2). Thus, all can be saved, although not all will be saved. The atoning work is that precious, extensive, and effectual to the Father - "for the sins of the whole world." Little wonder. He poured out His own wrath on the Son of His love to make possible our redemption. In this holy magnitude of how much the Lord Jesus accomplished at Calvary, how can He not offer to all the free gift purchased there? And how could He ever impute sins to His children when He imputed them all to Christ? How safe we are, and how saved we are! And how genuine and powerful is the offer of redemption to all! This Christ-centered emphasis has a powerful effect of grace when shared with the redeemed and the lost.[72]

The message of the Gospel, which has the power of God in it to save those who will believe it (simple message, to which all are capable of response, Rom. 1:16-17), and this is only possible because of the work of redemption accomplished by Christ. In addition, the convicting work of the Holy Spirit (John 16:9) takes the Gospel and reveals the need to have saving faith in Jesus Christ. This is what Paul is speaking about when he is pleading for people to be reconciled in the text of 2 Corinthians 5:11-21.

This dispensation of Grace could not work with Mosaic restrictions. The Gospel of Jesus Christ is designed to avoid all the cultural variations each nation possesses that differ from what Israel had under the Law. It would not be possible for various cultures to accommodate the Mosaic legislation - it was designed specifically for Israel and their particular call to service in the world, not nations that are pagan or secular in nature. This is not to say that nations will not benefit if they take the principles taught in the OT and incorporate them. We see much of the principles of the Bible (OT and NT) reflected in the founding documents of our own country (United States of America). But we would expect this, because "Righteousness exalteth a nation: but sin is a reproach to any people" (Prov. 14:34). Unrighteousness has destroyed many nations in human history. Wicked rulers have committed atrocious sins upon their own people, to the point of genocide. Again, "When the righteous are in authority, the people rejoice: but when the wicked beareth rule, the people mourn" (Prov. 29:2). These are prime examples of how the OT can be very applicable to modern day living, without incorporating the Law of Moses upon the people.

As discussed earlier, the *nation* of Israel is a specially made people that were to carry the word of God to the world. Understanding their creation by God, they (Israel) were to function under the Mosaic restrictions that kept them genealogically pure and enabled them to trace the messianic line. The moral purity also enabled them to keep in fellowship with God by obeying the laws. This prevented the nation from ultimate deterioration through sinful behavior and positively accomplished much of what has been detailed in the chapter entitled "The Purpose of the Law." Israel had a great responsibility and also great privilege in the purpose of God in their call to serve Him in the world. Paul spells this out in Romans chapter 9.

However, the Gospel is for the *individual* to change each life from the inside out, including deliverance from paganism and idolatry. The Gospel is a message for the *individual*, not for a *nation*. It can change a nation by changing individuals, but that is a result of the individual people changing from the ground up and their involvement in government positions and obeying society's laws. Placing moral people that have a Christian ideology in governmental positions can change a nation. However, a nation will not change by the imposition of the Mosaic Law code imposed on people that are not Israel. It will actually create more of a problem than it will solve. I know there are some Christians that think this type of Mosaic government system is the solution for a country's success, but it would be a colossal mistake. This topic is beyond the scope of this book, but in the age of grace, God is interested in changing people in all nations, no matter what system of government they live under. Hence the need for a "New Covenant" (Jer. 31:31-33).

WHY GOD WORKS THROUGH THE CHURCH TODAY

During this current time, because of Israel's continual self-hardening (Romans 9-11), they have been judicially blinded. God has temporarily put them aside while He works through the Body of Christ (Church, Bride of Christ) to reach all nations. Therefore, Jesus is currently building His church from all ethnic groups around the world. Israel is judicially set-aside because of their national rejection of Jesus as their Messiah; this is a result of their own hardness of heart and self-righteousness (Rom. 9:30-33; 11:11-25). Why were the Jews hardened to the Gospel? The answer is found in Rom. 9:30-33 and 2 Cor. 3:14-16; the Jews sought righteousness through keeping the Law and not by faith in Christ. Paul referred to this self-hardening in Acts 28:23-29 (note the underlined phrase):

> ...[Paul] expounded and testified the kingdom of God, persuading them concerning Jesus, both out of the Law, and out of the prophets, from morning till evening. And some believed the things which were spoken, and some believed not. And when they agreed not among themselves, they departed, after that Paul had spoken one word, Well spake the Holy Ghost by Esaias the prophet unto our fathers, Saying, Go unto this people, and say, Hearing ye shall hear, and shall not understand; and seeing ye shall see, and not perceive: <u>For the heart of this people is waxed gross [lit. grown callous], and their ears are dull of hearing, and their eyes have they closed</u>; lest they should see with their eyes, and hear with their ears, and understand with their heart, and should be converted, and I should heal them. Be it known therefore unto you, that the salvation of God is sent unto the Gentiles, and that they will hear it. And when

he had said these words, the Jews departed, and had great reasoning among themselves.

No ethnic group has any priority in the church. Everyone is equal in Christ (Gal. 3:28)--this has no equal comparison within the Mosaic Law! A person is a member of Israel because they are an ethnic Jew or a Gentile proselyte. A person is a member of the Body of Christ because they believe in Jesus. Once God has called all who will make up the Bride of Christ (Church), the Holy Spirit will be poured out on Israel again. They (Israel) will then be converted (Rom. 11:25) to belief in Jesus as their Messiah. The final event is the inauguration of the Messianic Kingdom with Israel having priority in that promised Kingdom on earth, as prophesied.

In Romans 9, Paul expressed this hardening to the recipients of the letter when he explained the status of Israel. This was necessary since he just encouraged the church in Romans 8 that God was faithful to accomplish His redemptive plan for those "in Christ" and he would then ask in Romans 12 to unreservedly offer themselves to God for service in the Gospel. The obvious question anticipated by Paul that would be on the minds of the Roman believers is, "but what about Israel? Did not God give promises to them also? Look at where they are today in unbelief! Did the Word of God fail?" This would be eerily similar to what the Jewish interlocutor questioned in Romans 3:1-8 and 9:4-5, 14. Paul needed to address this issue before proceeding to chapter 12. Thus, he answers the questions about the nation of Israel in Romans 9-11.[73]

Paul describes in Romans 9 how Israel received great privilege as a nation starting from Abraham, Isaac, and Jacob (9:4-5). However, just because the majority of Jews did not personally benefit from these privileges, does not mean that God's Word failed because not every Israelite had faith in God's promise (9:6-9). Paul is careful to connect believing God's promise with the exercise of faith (ref. Gal. 3). The righteousness resulting from works is a righteousness that is self-produced and valueless when it comes to a salvation relationship with God. As mentioned earlier, works righteousness would equate to earning of a wage, since it would require a reward for something earned or "worked for." However, the Bible teaches that a relationship with God is by faith (Hab. 2:4) which is the opposite of works. Therefore, the belief in God's promise of a son to Abraham through his wife Sarah (9:8) was the basis of relationship, not works, for works have no connection to believing a promise. Remember, promises are not earned (worked for); promises are received by faith not earned by works – works and faith are mutually exclusive!

As God chose the line of people (Abraham, Isaac, Jacob - Rom. 9:7-13) through which His redemptive program would be accomplished, it did not mean that all the offspring of Abraham would receive the benefit of the national privileges – salvation is always by faith, never by genealogy. Thus, Paul asked the key question in Romans 9:14: "What shall we say then? Is there unrighteousness with God? God forbid!" In other words, is it right for God to use Israel to bring about the world's redemptive program, yet not save all of them based on their involvement or connection to the nation? Paul's answer is, God extends mercy and compassion to those He chooses in order to bring about His program of redemption based on His initial promise to Abraham (Gen. 12:1-3). We also must recognize that those to whom God extends His mercy and grace is not a mystery. It is those who humbly believe and respond by faith to His offer (Ex. 10:3-4; Isaiah 57:15, 66:2; Prov. 3:34; James 4:6; 1 Peter 5:5). The Scriptures repeatedly reinforce this. Furthermore, we know that Jesus delights in giving mercy (Hosea 6:6; Jonah 4:2; Matt. 9:13), and as with God's response to Moses (Rom. 9:15-16), it is clear that the working of God's redemptive plan has nothing to do with man's effort. Only the exercise of God's mercy and compassion could fulfill His loving promise in bringing redemption to the world (Gen. 18:18, 26:4).

Thus, when Israel grew hardened (to the Gospel) in their

refusal to respond by faith, and held on to their good works under the Law for acceptance with God (self-righteousness), He then used their unbelief to further His redemptive plan. Paul uses Pharaohs' self-hardening to explain Israel's self-hardening (9:17-29). God offered Pharaoh multiple chances to respond to His offers, but Pharaoh continued to harden his own heart until God *judicially* hardened him in his stubborn position of rebellion. If we closely examine the Exodus passages Paul refers to regarding Pharaoh, we can see why Frédéric Louis Godet came to the conclusion he did in his commentary on Romans when he said:

> But what must not be forgotten, and what appears distinctly from the whole narrative, is that Pharaoh's hardening was at first *his own act.* Five times it is said of him that he himself hardened or made heavy his heart (Ex. 7:13-14, Ex. 7:22, Ex. 8:15, Ex. 8:32, Ex. 9:7; we do not speak here of Ex. 4:21 and Ex. 7:3, which are a prophecy), before the time when it is at last said that God hardened him (Ex. 9:12); and even after that, as if a remnant of liberty still remained to him, it is said for a last time that he hardened himself (Ex. 9:34-35).

Likewise, it is through this continual refusal to receive the Gospel by faith that made Israel enemies of it (Rom. 11:28). Again, Paul tells us the reason was based on their attempt to gain their righteousness from the Law and not through faith as the Gentiles did in their response to the Gospel (Rom. 9:30-33).

God used Pharaoh's hardness to bring about the deliverance of Israel from Egypt; He used the hardness of self-righteous Jews to bring the Gospel to the nations of the world. They might complain about how and who God redeems (i.e. Gentiles), but they have no claim in His redemptive plan. God is the potter and they are the clay (Rom. 9:20-21). He formed Israel to serve Him and accomplish the plan prepared before the foundation of the world (Rev. 13:8). He has a right to extend mercy when it meets with His redemptive purpose for the world and withhold it to those attempting to thwart His will (Rom. 9:15). Therefore, He has a right to withdraw mercy and allow the self-hardening of Israel (or anyone else) to be used for His purposes if it aids in accomplishing the same. Did not Pharaoh witness the miracles performed by God's messengers (Moses and Aaron), and have multiple opportunities to respond by faith? – Absolutely! Did not the Jews witness miracles performed by God's messengers (Apostles) and have multiple opportunities to respond by faith (Heb. 2:3-4)? – Absolutely! However, just because Israel failed to take advantage of the privileges afforded to them (Rom. 9:4-5), does not mean that God's Word failed in accomplishing God's purpose (Rom. 9:6). God brought His word to full effect (Isaiah 55:7-11)! God is not obligated to the physical offspring of Abraham simply because of their genealogical connection (Rom. 9:7). God used Israel to bring His word and Messiah to the world (Rom. 3:1-4; 9:4-6), but they are no different from any other people when it comes to saving faith. Everyone needs to respond by faith to take advantage of the offer of the Gospel of the Grace of God.

Matthew (Matt. 12) reveals this hardening of Jews with the rejection of Jesus by Israel's leadership. It became official in Matthew chapter 21 as the Jews publicly rejected Jesus riding into Jerusalem on a donkey (ref. Zech. 9:9). Jesus' last words to the Herodians, Sadducees, and Pharisees is given to us in Matthew chapter 22; and the final pronunciation of condemnation to the Scribes and Pharisees is given in Matthew chapter 23. At the end of that chapter, we have this critical statement from Jesus, where He said:

> O Jerusalem, Jerusalem, thou that killest the prophets, and stonest them which are sent unto thee, how often would I have gathered thy children together, even as a hen gathereth her chickens under her wings, and ye would not! Behold, your house is left unto you desolate. For I say unto you, Ye shall not see me henceforth, till ye shall say, Blessed is he that cometh in the name of the Lord. (Matt. 23:37-39)

In Matthew 24, Jesus explained the tribulation period that

Israel would enter and bring them to the point where they will call upon Jesus of Nazareth as their Messiah. This is described as the "time of Jacobs trouble" (Jeremiah 30:7) and Daniel's 70th week (Daniel 9:24-27), among other names given by the OT prophets. The world will then experience seven years of tribulation (Rev. chapter 6-18), ending with the second coming of Jesus Christ (Rev. 19), and upon His return establish His Kingdom on earth (Rev. 20). Just prior to this seven year tribulation period, Jesus will rapture (1 Thess. 4:13-18) His church (Body of Christ) from the world and pour the Holy Spirit upon the nation of Israel. This explains why God is working through the church (a mystery) in this dispensation, yet is not explained by the prophets in the OT, but is revealed by the NT apostles and prophets (Eph. 3:1-7; note verse 5).

The following chart provides a simplified timeline overview:

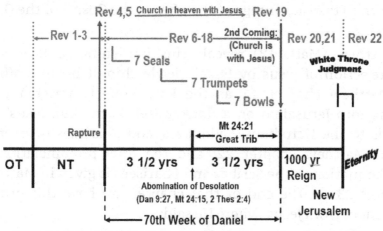

(AKA 7yr <u>Tribulation Period</u> = Jer. 30:7 "Time of Jacobs trouble")

The church is a *mystery* (something not prophesied in the OT but revealed in the NT, Eph. 3:1-6), it is a body of people that Jesus would create – Jews and Gentiles together - without any ethnic or class distinctions. A Body separate from that of Israel – which was already in existence at the time of the creation of the church. Who could have even guessed at a plan like this? As Paul expressed his heart when he said, "O the depth of the riches both of the wisdom and knowledge of God! how unsearchable are his judgments, and his ways past finding out!" (Rom. 11:33). What can we say to this? Amen!

HOW SHOULD CHRISTIANS LIVE UNDER GRACE?

This key question has a simple answer but requires explanation. The simple answer is Christian's are to live by the leading and power of the Holy Spirit (Rom. 8:4). The explanation requires a bit of detail since this book already addressed the complications added to the Christian life by mixing it with OT laws. This book shows in multiple ways how Christians are not under the Mosaic Covenant, but how various Christian leaders, groups or denominations attempt to do it nonetheless. The concept of faith can be difficult for some and people seem addicted to pleasing God by observing laws, no matter the dispensation. This is not to say that God does not want man to observe laws, for each dispensation has them. However, salvation is always by faith (trust) and never by the observance of particular rules. No true relationship can exist by the rule principle. What husband and wife could have success in their marriage if the relationship was based on a list of daily rules and not trust in who the other person is? The activities that extend from a trust relationship have their proper place in that relationship, but they do not create it. In other words, trust (faith, belief) is the foundation of the relationship and obeying certain principles (rules, laws) are the result of it, not the basis of it. Indeed, it is no different with the Christian life, the relationship begins with faith (belief, trust) in Christ, and obedience to the NT laws is the result of that relationship.

Many times Christians face the challenge of trying to live the Christian life by obeying either the OT laws or rules they establish for themselves. This propensity is not uncommon among Christians, for Paul the apostle gave his own autobiographical situation regarding this issue in Romans 7.

I was alive once without the law, but when the commandment came, sin revived and I died. And the commandment, which was to bring life, I found to bring death. For sin, taking occasion by the commandment, deceived me, and by it killed me. Therefore the law is holy, and the commandment holy and just and good. Has then what is good become death to me? Certainly not! But sin, that it might appear sin, was producing death in me through what is good, so that sin through the commandment might become exceedingly sinful. For we know that the law is spiritual, but I am carnal, sold under sin. For what I am doing, I do not understand. For what I will to do, that I do not practice; but what I hate, that I do. If, then, I do what I will not to do, I agree with the law that it is good. But now, it is no longer I who do it, but sin that dwells in me. For I know that in me (that is, in my flesh) nothing good dwells; for to will is present with me, but how to perform what is good I do not find. (Rom. 7:9-18, NKJV)

Paul discovered that the Law of Moses (or any law in principle) cannot save a sinner, and cannot sanctify a Christian. The Law brings the knowledge of sin, but offers no solution for it. There is no redemption in laws of any kind. Redemption is by blood, not by command. The Mosaic Law provided the means of sanctification for the nation of Israel, unrelated to Christianity and the New Covenant. Other laws that a Christian may use as a means to grow in Christ will in fact undermine their sanctification, which Paul makes clear. "For the good that I will to do, I do not do; but the evil I will not to do, that I practice" (Rom. 7:19, NKJV). The seemingly enigmatic living situation Paul expresses is part of the inherent problem with any law. A law establishes what acceptable and unacceptable behavior is by declaring one behavior right and the other wrong. In the Bible, the wrong behavior is sin. Using a biblical law does not make a Christian more able to grow spiritually, it only reveals their inability to consistently keep that law, revealing their sin. The more laws, the more sin (Rom. 5:20). Paul saw this inability to mature by keeping laws when he said, "Now if I do what I will not to do, it is no longer I who do it, but sin that dwells in me. I find then a law, that evil is present with me, the one who wills to do good" Rom. 7:20-21; NKJV). Paul went on to declare, "For I delight in the law of God according to the inward man. But I see another law in my members, warring against the law of my mind, and bringing me into captivity to the law of sin which is in my members" (Rom. 7:22-23; NKJV). Thus, Paul agreed with the Law of God that they were holy and he should obey them, but he had a sin nature that consistently undermined his ability to keep them. Indeed, agreement with the truth of God's laws receives an overwhelming Amen from our minds, but our sinful natures do not possess the capability of obeying them in any consistent manner, nor do they want to. As Glen Davis observes,

> Unlike Pharaoh, who demanded that the Israelites make bricks without straw, God provides abundant supply for born again believers in the Lord Jesus Christ to live in a manner pleasing to Him (Exodus 5).
>
> The commands of the New Testament, far greater in measure and scope than the mandates of the law of Moses, would be a cruel joke were it not for the Christ of the New Testament. We would find ourselves more strawless, as it were, than the Israelites of old. Thankfully, God never acts cruelly, and He most certainly does not jest about our doing His will. Thus, He sends His Spirit to inhabit the innermost being of those who trust the Lord Jesus, birthing a "new man, created in righteousness and true holiness" (Ephesians 4:24). hereby, Christians become supercharged vessels of faith and obedience in our innermost Christ-inhabited being. "I delight in the law of God after the inward man" declared the Apostle Paul, an affirmation every believer can and must make about ourselves in the light of promise: "It is God which worketh in

you both to will and do of His good pleasure." (Romans 7:22; Philippians 2:12)[74]

This being the case, any attempts to grow by keeping certain laws or rules will always end in failure. It will put us in a tailspin, as the focus will be more on how well we obey the laws more than a focus on our relationship with Jesus in thanks of His delivering power. This is why Paul ends Romans 7 by acknowledging, "O wretched man that I am! Who will deliver me from this body of death? I thank God—through Jesus Christ our Lord! So then, with the mind I myself serve the law of God, but with the flesh the law of sin" (Rom. 7:24-25; NKJV). Christians have been set free from the Law, thus Paul in his overview says:

> Therefore, my brethren, you also have become dead to the law through the body of Christ, that you may be married to another—to Him who was raised from the dead, that we should bear fruit to God. For when we were in the flesh, the sinful passions which were aroused by the law were at work in our members to bear fruit to death. But now we have been delivered from the law, having died to what we were held by, so that we should serve in the newness of the Spirit and not in the oldness of the letter (Rom. 7:4-6, NKJV).

It is in the "newness of the Spirit" that Christians are to live, not in the "oldness of the letter." The "oldness of the letter' is a reference to the Mosaic Law. Writing to the Corinthians in explanation of the higher value of the New Covenant that surpassed the old, Paul declared:

> [God] who also made us sufficient as ministers of the new covenant, not of the letter but of the Spirit; for the letter kills, but the Spirit gives life. But if the ministry of death, written and engraved on stones, was glorious, so that the children of Israel could not look steadily at the face of Moses because of the glory of his countenance, which glory was passing away, how will the ministry of the Spirit not be more glorious? For if the ministry of condemnation had glory, the ministry of righteousness exceeds much more in

glory. (2 Cor. 3:6-9; NKJV)

The letter that kills of which Paul speaks has been the target of some appalling Bible interpretation. In the context, Paul uses the phrase for the Mosaic Covenant and its representative laws. There is no way to misunderstand this once we read and follow the context. However, that has not stopped some weird and speculative views as MacDonald points out:

> Paul gives several striking contrasts between the law and the gospel. He begins here in verse 6 with the first by saying, **Not of the letter, but of the Spirit; for the letter kills, but the Spirit**, or **spirit** (NKJV mg.) **gives life**. This is widely interpreted to mean that if you just take the outward, literal words of Scripture and try to be obedient to the letter without desiring to be obedient to the full spirit of the passage, then it harms you rather than helps you. The Pharisees were an illustration of this. They were scrupulous in their tithing to the very minutest extent, but they did not show mercy and love to others (Matt. 23:23). While this is a valid application of this passage, it is not the interpretation. In verse 6 the letter refers to the Law of Moses, and the spirit refers to the gospel of the grace of God. When Paul says that the letter kills, he is speaking of the ministry of the law. The law condemns all who fail to keep its holy precepts. "By the law is the knowledge of sin" (Rom. 3:20). "Cursed is everyone who does not continue in all things which are written in the book of the law, to do them" (Gal. 3:10). God never intended the law to be the means of giving life. Rather it was designed to bring the knowledge of sin and to convict of sin. The New Covenant is here called spirit. It represents the spiritual fulfillment of the types and shadows of the Old Covenant. What the law demanded but could never produce is now effected by the gospel.[75] (bold in original)

Christians mature through the work of the Holy Spirit in their lives empowering them to abide in Christ (John 15:4-5). The NT provides the knowledge of how Christians are to live, but the Holy Spirit provides the power to live it and thereby follow the Lord. There is no law that develops relationship or advances discipleship – which is the denial of our own will that is mastered by our sin nature. Which is why "Then He said to them all, "If anyone desires to come after Me, let him deny himself, and take up his cross daily, and follow Me" (Luke 9:23; NKJV). It is the daily bearing of the cross that identifies this passage with discipleship, "And whosoever doth not bear his cross, and come after me, cannot be my disciple" (Luke 14:27). Sanctification, discipleship, spiritual maturity, and spiritual development all are done in submission to the Holy Spirit's leading and empowering in our lives. This means that there is a choice on our part to "deny ourselves," i.e. deny our will and replace it with His will. The choice is made by us, the power is given by Him. There is no other method of Christian maturity, "He must increase, but I must decrease." (John 3:30)

All disciples are Christians, but not all Christians are disciples. This has caused another form of legalism among Christians. Many of the Reformed community tend to identify the decision for discipleship with salvation. However, I am not saved by my self-denial, I am saved by my faith in Jesus Christ. The self-denial is a decision I make as a believer and is part of the sanctification process as just mentioned, thus it is not automatic. I must willingly submit my life to Christ on a continual basis as I did when I initially believed in Him. As Paul says, "As ye have therefore received Christ Jesus the Lord, so walk ye in him" (Col. 2:6). We received Him by faith and we walk in Him by faith. For, "For we walk by faith, not by sight" (2 Cor. 5:7).

Are there laws God wants me to follow as a NT Christian? – Yes! Are some of these laws the same in the OT? – Yes! Do I grow as a Christian by following these NT laws? – Yes and No! I grow as a Christian as I live empowered by the Holy Spirit to present myself to Christ; in doing that I follow His will for me. Remember, the relationship is based in trust, the growth is doing what I know pleases the Lord. As I continually please the

Lord, His will is incorporated into my life and my will is put aside (denied). This process develops spiritual maturity because it is exercising faith (trust) in Him and relying on the power of the Holy Spirit consistently as I embrace His will. God's will for the Christian is primarily taught in the NT epistles, and the epistles are the result of Jesus promise to the apostles:

> These things have I spoken unto you, being yet present with you. But the Comforter, which is the Holy Ghost, whom the Father will send in my name, he shall teach you all things, and bring all things to your remembrance, whatsoever I have said unto you. (John 14:25-26)

> I have yet many things to say unto you, but ye cannot bear them now. Howbeit when he, the Spirit of truth, is come, he will guide you into all truth: for he shall not speak of himself; but whatsoever he shall hear, that shall he speak: and he will shew you things to come. (John 16:12-13)

These promises by Jesus at the last supper ensure that the rest of the NT will both be completed and be a work of the Holy Spirit through these men and their associates (2 Tim. 3:16; 2 Peter 1:21). We follow the instructions of the Holy Spirit given by the NT epistles because of our love for Jesus. He set me free to follow Him, not just perform certain laws or commands. That is not to say there are not laws and commands in the NT, but they are there to prevent me from the errors and lies that will ruin my relationship with Jesus. For example, I do not cheat on my wife because I love her; I made a vow to honor her and to not dishonor her by committing adultery. But the basis of my relationship is love, not the sinful behavior of adultery. Just as committing adultery will ruin my relationship with my wife, the NT commands me to refrain from committing sin that will ruin my relationship with Jesus. If I woke up each morning and recited certain behaviors that I will not perform so I can have a relationship with my wife, my marriage would become more of a prison because the focus of my relationship would be the rules and the regimen. It is similar to my relationship with Jesus. If it is just a list of daily rules to follow, it is reduced to a religion of repetitive devotion and not a relationship with the living Christ. My wife would not appreciate it, so why would Jesus?

ANSWERING THE CHALLENGE OF SKEPTICS

People who are critical of the Bible tend to attack it by contrasting a quote from under the Mosaic Law with a verse that is an apparent contradiction from the NT. As mentioned, the different covenants have different consequences for sinful acts. A person could be stoned for committing adultery under the Mosaic Covenant, but the consequences are not equal under the New Covenant. Thus, to criticize the Bible by correlating the same sin under the Law and gospel, while ignoring the consequences because of covenant differences, is making an unequal comparison. This is a classic misuse of Scripture from people who ignore the context. I put up a series of responses to atheism[76] that address these very issues from the atheists.org website.[77] They make many out of context accusations against the Bible and claim they are contradictions. Many of the Scriptures used on their website simply contrast a verse from the Law and a verse from the NT and they believe that makes their case. In reality, it is the ignorance of what the Bible teaches that results in these erroneous apparent contradictions.

For example, Atheists make a claim about the Sabbath Day[78] as if it contradicts what Paul writes. "Remember the Sabbath day, to keep it holy" (Ex. 20:8) is positioned as if it contradicts Paul's teaching in Rom. 14:5, "One man esteemeth one day above another: another esteemeth every day alike. Let every man be fully persuaded in his own mind." The alleged contradiction is between keeping a specific day (Ex. 20) and having the choice to esteem days differently (Rom. 14). In response, the nation of Israel under the Mosaic Covenant was required to keep the Sabbath Day because it was the *sign* of the Mosaic Covenant (Ex. 31:13, 17). The New Covenant has no requirement for a day of worship. The church typically met on Sundays (Acts 20:7, 1 Cor. 16:2); however, Christians have liberty to choose, which Rom. 14 explains.

This type of charge is very typical of the skeptics' attack upon the Bible. Indeed, it is drawing a conclusion without actual evidence or proper investigation. This should not shock anyone since we live in a culture where this is done all the time politically, socially, professionally, and spiritually. Claims are targeted against people based on opinion without any actual evidence with the result of having their careers and livelihood destroyed apart from any actual evidence or investigation. Often people are treated as criminals based on public opinion alone, without ever being tried for a crime or having their case before a jury. This type of public practice has become welcomed in our culture, but it is unjust, unfair, and done out of pure ignorance. When it comes to criticisms of the Bible, it is this same practice of unjust treatment made by people through ignorant claims. Surface arguments tend to turn the uninformed away from the Bible because the culture is accustomed to listening to this type of unsubstantiated claim. As with the study of any history book, the Bible is no different and requires some effort to read it objectively, and not just to find apparent contradictions by looking for sentences that appear to contradict each other.

Indeed, it would reveal the height of ignorance to find sentences in the US Constitution that appear to contradict each other if I did not actually read and understand the document in its context. However, we see this today among many both in and out of professional politics. Many people do not actually understand the Constitution, Declaration of Independence, or Bill of Rights. Thus, when claims are made regarding these documents, much of the public think the statements are correct – even if inaccurate – because they do not actually know what the documents teach. For example, the Constitution has the phrase "We the People" in it. To read this phrase as those holding government positions (elected representatives) as opposed to the represented citizens would be to read that meaning into the phrase, and thus to *misread* the Constitution. The context must be specifically ignored to identify the government in that statement. For example,

> In the Constitution, on the other hand, by opening up with "We the People", it immediately affirms that the Constitution is of the people, for the people, and by the people of the United States. This interpretation, which arises most strongly from the presence of "We the People", leads to an understanding of the Constitution as affecting the people directly and not through regulations imposed on the States. In other words, those words define the interaction between the Constitution and the citizens of the United States is direct and immediate, meaning that the Constitution and the government it creates supersedes any State government.

> The words "We the People" in the Preamble are often considered the strongest links between the Constitution and the Declaration of Independence, in that the Declaration of Independence was written from the perspective of the people, not of specific individuals or of government. In beginning the Preamble of the Constitution with "We the People", The constitution is immediately emphasizing the significance of the people and is also ensuring an understanding that the people are the ones giving power to the Government. This is also a critical element to the American Constitution in that the power of the Government mandated by the Constitution comes not from God or from itself, but from "We the People."[79]

In a commentary on the legal weight of the preamble of the Constitution, this commentary referencing Justice Joseph Story (1833) gives further insight to the meaning of "We the People."

> As Justice Joseph Story noted in his Commentaries, the Preamble never can be resorted to, to enlarge the powers confided to the general government, or any of its

departments.8 The Supreme Court subsequently endorsed Justice Story's view of the Preamble, holding in Jacobson v. Massachusetts that, while the Constitution's introductory paragraph indicates the general purposes for which the people ordained and established the Constitution, it has never been regarded by the Court as the source of any substantive power conferred on the federal government.9 Nonetheless, while the Court has not viewed the Preamble as having any direct, substantive legal effect, the Court has referenced the broad precepts of the Constitution's introduction to confirm and reinforce its interpretation of other provisions within the document.10 As such, while the Preamble does not have any specific legal status, Justice Story's observation that the true office of the Preamble is to expound the nature, and extent, and application of the powers actually conferred by the Constitution appears to capture its import.[80]

What this example teaches us is that if there is any question as to who "We the people" are, it is answered by the statement in the Declaration of Independence when it says, "Governments are instituted among Men, deriving their just powers from the consent of the governed." In this quote, the "government" is not the "governed." It is impossible not to understand who is referred to in both the Constitution and Declaration of Independence. For this is what the founding fathers both wrote and intended.

This ignorance of the Constitution is eerily similar to that of the Bible. While ignorance of the Constitution has a temporary effect in the lives of the American people's ability to understand the power the Constitution gives them. Ignorance of the Bible has an eternal effect in the individual lives of those who misquote, mistreat, and misinform, along with the recipients who blindly believe them. Indeed, taking things at face value in areas of great importance – especially the documents in consideration – can drastically affect the lives of people now and eternally.

It would seem that in an era of massive amounts of information at people's fingertips, that this ignorance would not be possible. However, people have used the internet and other information mediums mostly for entertainment and not for learning. Truly, it is a difficult task to fact check claims made on the internet and social media, not to mention the media itself. But the diligence must be done to know what is true and what is not. If Americans remain ignorant of the documents used to create the country they live in and form the very government that rules them, how will they ever vote knowledgably? How will they remain a free people enjoying the benefits of the Constitution if they do not actually know what it says? Likewise, how can people know what is correctly stated from the Bible if they have never read it, or never read it in the context of which it is written? Unfortunately, Christians that Jesus wants to live freely in His grace will be subject to bondage by their ignorance (Hosea 4:6).

Every day preachers misquote the Bible to congregations and some of those people blindly believe them. I am not talking about doctrinal nuances of various orthodox beliefs, I am speaking of specific misquotes to teach a belief that is foreign to the Bible. Many beloved preachers are taken at their word and never "fact checked" by their congregation. On the contrary, some of these preachers have told their congregations that if they challenge their statements, they are coming against "the LORD's anointed" (2 Sam. 1:14). However, in a case like this, the preachers have put themselves above the word of God, when in fact they are subject to that very word. If people are afraid to use the Bible to check what a person teaches, they think with a cultic mentality and this is dangerous. Jesus and the apostles checked and validated all through by what the Scriptures say. As Paul stated to the Corinthians, "Let the prophets speak two or three, and let the other judge" (1 Cor. 14:29). How can others "judge" unless there is something absolute to measure the words spoken by prophets? The absolute reference Paul refers to is the word of God. It is no different today; the word of God is to have the final authority, not any human speaker. I have appreciated our pastor and some of the other pastors I know personally in this regard. They instruct the people they teach to go home and make sure that what they taught is accurate, not to take their words as absolute, but measure their words against The Word (Bible). This is a safeguard for the Bible teacher and for the people listening. But none of this evaluation can be properly done if people are not willing to put the time in and study the Bible instead of reading it like a novel or toying with it like a fortune cookie.

CONCLUSION

All the necessary points have been made, so I will summarize the key items that were addressed. We started with laying a foundation about the importance of understanding the Bible in its given context. I gave some examples of how the cults distort the Bible, using their own definitions and supplying their own context. Christians can do the same if they are not careful; thus it is essential that we lay a proper foundation when discovering what the Bible teaches. Once the foundation is established for how we approach the Bible, we can then read it with confidence and conclude what the Bible teaches about God and every other subject it addresses. This helps us avoid any deviation from orthodox teaching about God and understand His nature and characteristics. This is the essential background for the revelation from God, taught throughout the Bible. Knowing His nature prevents the misunderstanding of His actions when there are situations that might alter our view of God. In other words, because I know God's nature and character, I will not walk away from the Bible with a distorted view of God that skeptics tend to impose by their interpretation of Scripture. It will also prevent my own biases from influencing my own interpretation of Scripture. It is similar to knowing someone well enough to realize that it would be against their nature to perform an action that is out of character for them. Unfortunately people can disappoint us and perform actions against their better judgment, but God cannot (Num. 23:19; Titus 1:2). I can prevent my own disillusionment with God if I do not impose my own artificial expectations on Him. This is only accomplished by understanding the Bible in its context. I know, I have made the point repeatedly, but I want you to hear it every time you pick up the Bible (believe me, it rings in my own ears).

We next began with some covenants in the Bible and

related them to dispensations. I realize that not everyone is a "dispensationalist," but the fact that Paul uses the word (Eph. 1:10, 3:2) to describe current and past eras of God's working makes the use of it legitimate. Having said that, the more obvious dispensations were described to explain various conditions man is placed under while God gives progressive revelation; however salvation is always by faith. This is important to recognize, for though we did not enter a discussion on various views like Covenant Theology,[81] serious theological errors have resulted from this view imposed on the Bible. To ever place man under a covenant of salvation by works is in this author's opinion an eisegesis resulting in theological error. There is no place in the Bible that salvation is said to be by works. Even under the dispensation of promise and law, Abraham is to only have works credit before man, but and never before God (Rom. 4:2). Moreover, his "justification by works" (James 2:21) mentioned by James has to do with the maturity of Abraham's faith manifesting fruit near the end of his life (Gen. 22). He was already justified by faith before God when he believed early in his life (Gen. 15:6), which is before his faith bore any fruit. James addresses this issue in the second chapter of his epistle. The theology of Paul and James are not in contradiction but are complementary. Some try to pit Paul and James against each other because of a purely surface reading of each of their epistles (context, context, context). However, Paul provides the root of faith when he uses Abraham as the example from early in his life (Gen. 15:6), where James provides the fruit of Abraham's life near the end (Gen. 22). The main point being that our approach to the Bible should be through exegesis and not eisegesis.

The next section explained the relationship between the Christian and the Law. Ultimately, this is the focus of the book since it is where Christians live. As discussed, much of Christianity is still undermined by an inaccurate view of the Law. As an example, some denominations do not allow women to wear pants, not because the NT teaches anything about clothing, other than, it should be moderate (1 Tim. 2:9) and to wear something! Some think women must wear dresses because Deut. 22:5 says, "A woman shall not wear anything that pertains to a man, nor shall a man put on a woman's garment, for all who do so are an abomination to the LORD your God." However, if we apply this to the context of Moses Law and the history of where Deuteronomy is in relation to Israel's progress toward the Promised Land, we get a different application. God did not want Israel mixing with the pagans in Canaan. One of the pagan cultural practices was the elimination of gender in their worship. Much like our current culture, pagan worship and sinful living involves a confusion of genders and a perversion of them. Thus, there was what we call cross-dressing among pagans that distorts any gender distinctive. But when Moses wrote, everyone wore wrapped clothing, i.e. no one was wearing "pants." The only Levi's were an Israelite tribe, not a jean label. Identifying pants as male is a bit of a stretch today. Attempting to pull Deut. 22:5 into the NT is applying a Mosaic Law inappropriately. The principle is clear: God has made man and woman distinct and we should not confuse the genders. But pants in and of themselves is a bit of an overstatement for gender distinctiveness. Many women's slacks are not designed for men and vice versa. But style is not necessarily equal to form when it comes to attire. Though a Christian woman might have a legitimate conviction against wearing pants, there is no Bible command she can quote to support her conviction; it is her preference and nothing more. I do not want to overstate this issue, I am trying to make a point that we should not create NT laws where they do not exist – especially by borrowing them from Moses. Thus, we should not move specific Mosaic legal codes into the NT as if they were meant for Christians. It is clear in each culture what men and women's styles are, in pants, shirts, and other items. Imagine the difficulty if somehow long sleeve shirts were moved into the "pants" category? This would not be an advantage for Christian women in colder climates. I think you see the point.

In these next verses, the particular law given was to prevent Israel's identification with paganism when they entered Canaan. There were many restrictions to avoid because of Canaanite practices:

> When thou art come into the land which the Lord thy God giveth thee, thou shalt not learn to do after the abominations of those nations. There shall not be found among you any one that maketh his son or his daughter to pass through the fire, or that useth divination, or an observer of times, or an enchanter, or a witch. Or a charmer, or a consulter with familiar spirits, or a wizard, or a necromancer. For all that do these things are an abomination unto the Lord: and because of these abominations the Lord thy God doth drive them out from before thee. Thou shalt be perfect with the Lord thy God. For these nations, which thou shalt possess, hearkened unto observers of times, and unto diviners: but as for thee, the Lord thy God hath not suffered thee so to do. (Deut. 18:9-14)

Not only were they to avoid these practices, they were not to allow their curiosity to motivate them to seek out how and why the Canaanites practiced such things:

> When the Lord thy God shall cut off the nations from before thee, whither thou goest to possess them, and thou succeedest them, and dwellest in their land; Take heed to thyself that thou be not snared by following them, after that they be destroyed from before thee; and that thou enquire not after their gods, saying, How did these nations serve their gods? even so will I do likewise. Thou shalt not do so unto the Lord thy God: for every abomination to the Lord, which he hateth, have they done unto their gods; for even their sons and their daughters they have burnt in the fire to their gods. What thing soever I command you, observe to do it: thou shalt not add thereto, nor diminish from it. (Deut. 12:29-32)

Christian groups that restrict pants for women as if it is

a Bible command in the NT have to artificially identify pants as a male-only piece of clothing. This becomes problematic on many levels and teaches Christians that holiness is mainly in choice of specific church accepted attire – poor Bible exposition notwithstanding. The main issue with the Law is that Christians are not under it in any form. As discussed, the principles from the OT can be applied to Christians because we actually see this done by the NT writers. However, what we do not see is NT writers placing Christians under any OT restrictions, we see the opposite (Acts 15). Therefore, if the NT writers do not place Christians under the Mosaic Covenant, neither should the church.

Finally, application in the Christian life became our focus. Various aspects should be considered in reference to a Christian's perspective on the Law. But none is more important than that of the direct addressing of this issue by Paul the apostle. Regarding a Christian's perspective on Moses Law, Paul said:

> Stand fast therefore in the liberty wherewith Christ hath made us free, and be not entangled again with the yoke of bondage. Behold, I Paul say unto you, that if ye be circumcised, Christ shall profit you nothing. For I testify again to every man that is circumcised, that he is a debtor to do the whole law. Christ is become of no effect unto you, whosoever of you are justified by the law; ye are fallen from grace. For we through the Spirit wait for the hope of righteousness by faith. For in Jesus Christ neither circumcision availeth any thing, nor uncircumcision; but faith which worketh by love. (Gal. 5:1-6)

Judaizers taught Gentile Christians they needed to be circumcised and obey Moses Law to be saved and sanctified made the Galatian churches their target. Their focus was circumcision as the entry point for these Gentiles, thus Paul is very direct in Gal. 5:1-5. He says Christ is no profit to someone who decides to live under any aspect of Moses Law, since as we have seen, the Law cannot be divided so there is an obligation to keep the entire Law and not selective parts. Faith is the only true connection to Christ and the basis of relationship. Paul goes on to say, "For all the law is fulfilled in one word, even in this; Thou shalt love thy neighbor as thyself" (Gal. 5:14). This is because the Law taught how to live in proper relationship to others within Israel, but if a person loves their neighbor as the Bible teaches, all the laws are covered and more (Rom. 13:9). In other words, if I love my neighbor,

I will not kill them (6th commandment), I will rather protect their life and help them.

I will not commit adultery with them (7th commandment), I will help strengthen their marriage.

I will not steal from them (8th commandment), I will voluntarily give them to help their need.

I will not lie about them (9th commandment), I will protect the truth and be honest. And,

I will not want what they have for myself (10th commandment), but will be happy God has blessed them with what they have and be content with what God has provided me (Heb. 13:5).

The NT emphasizes the loving aspects of how to relate to others, though it also commands us to refrain from these sins. When love is the focus, no one needs to use laws to restrict wrong behavior when right behavior is exercised.

Legalism is a destructive philosophy as Paul warned, "But if ye bite and devour one another, take heed that ye be not consumed one of another" (Gal. 5:15). People that try to live in relation to each other by legalistic codes become miserable. The rules become the focus as well as those who do not properly observe them. This results in everyone becoming a spiritual police officer or as my pastor says, "a sin-sniffer," and this is where the biting and devouring begins. Over the past 40 years of my Christian life, I have watched this occur time and time again. Once a Christian is focused on what they think everyone else should be doing and the moral manager of other's lives, it never ends well. It divides family and friends, relationships are destroyed, and at times, churches are ruined by this attitude and behavior. Legalism is not a help to anyone, it is purely a destructive endeavor. The irony is those who become legalistic believe their zeal for rules and laws will aid spiritual growth, when in fact the opposite is always the case. Grace and love go right out the window once the legalism begins. I have watched it and experienced its destructive power.

This is why Paul emphasized *how* to live the Christian life:

> This I say then, Walk in the Spirit, and ye shall not fulfil the lust of the flesh. For the flesh lusteth against the Spirit, and the Spirit against the flesh: and these are contrary the one to the other: so that ye cannot do the things that ye would. But if ye be led of the Spirit, ye are not under the law. (Gal. 5:16-18)

The flesh is destructive and connects to legalism in that it reduces Christianity to rules. The flesh is responsible for the following sins and the desire to live by the rules of law for righteousness. The Pharisees made this error of rules righteousness and many follow in their path today. Thus, Paul makes it clear:

> Now the works of the flesh are manifest, which are these; Adultery, fornication, uncleanness, lasciviousness, Idolatry, witchcraft, hatred, variance, emulations, wrath, strife, seditions, heresies, Envyings, murders, drunkenness, revellings, and such like: of the which I tell you before, as I have also told you in time past, that they which do such things shall not inherit the kingdom of God. (Gal. 5:19-21)

In other words, when human strength and wisdom becomes the source of the Christian experience, the nature of the flesh drives it. The ultimate evidence of this is the manifestation of the sins listed by Paul. However, Paul goes beyond the effects of legalism in these verses to show that the conduct of those who practice these sins are not Christians. Indeed, the list is how people live that have no relationship to God and His kingdom. The practices are indicative of those who are not believers in Christ. What Paul is not saying is that if a person continues to practice these sins that they are not Christians. The KJV is a bit misleading in verse 21 translating "do such things." Of this, A. T. Robertson says,

> *Practise (prassontes)*. *Prassō* is the verb for habitual practice (our very word, in fact), not *poieō* for occasional doing. The *habit* of these sins is proof that one is not in the Kingdom of God and will not inherit it.[82]

Moreover, MacDonald makes the insightful comment,

> The passage does not teach that a drunkard cannot be saved, but it does say that those whose lives are *characterized* by the above catalog of fleshly works are not saved.[83]

I want to be clear here. A believer can fall into sin, appear to be an unbeliever while sinning, no differently than an unbeliever can at times live like a believer, and yet not be a Christian. However, both will eventually return to what their true nature is. In other words, the prodigal son returned home because he was not a pig (Luke 15:11-32), and the unbeliever returns to the pigpen because he is not a son (2 Peter 2:22). In behavior, people can temporarily act differently than who they are, but not permanently (1 John 3:9). People will eventually reveal their true character; this was the case in the life of Judas Iscariot.

In the end, Christians are instructed to follow commands or laws in the NT. However, Paul says, "If we live in the Spirit, let us also walk in the Spirit" (Gal. 5:25). The life of the believer is to be characterized by a life led by the Holy Spirit. The Spirit of God who lives in the believer teaches (1 John 2:27) through the instruction of the word of God. Thus, the Holy Spirit empowers the believer to obey the word of God as they abide in Christ (John 15), which is the true expression and dynamic of the Christian life. Paul gave the principle of living the Christian life in Romans 8. As Scofield notes, "Hitherto, in Romans, the Holy

Spirit has been mentioned but once; (Rom. 5:5); in this chapter, He is mentioned nineteen times. Redemption is by blood and by power."[84] Thus, the Christian life is a life walking in the power of the Holy Spirit. Paul writes:

> For the law of the Spirit of life in Christ Jesus hath made me free from the law of sin and death. For what the law could not do, in that it was weak through the flesh, God sending his own Son in the likeness of sinful flesh, and for sin, condemned sin in the flesh: That the righteousness of the law might be fulfilled in us, who walk not after the flesh, but after the Spirit. (Rom. 8:2-4)

These verses follow Paul's autobiographical section in Romans 7 and his failure to live the Christian life by observing laws, and his declaration in verse 1 that there is "no condemnation." Why is there no condemnation? Verses 2-4 explain the reason. Godet makes this comment regarding verse 2:

> It is strange that Paul should speak of the *law of the Spirit*. Are these two expressions not contradictory? We shall not understand the phrase unless we bear in mind what has been said (Rom. 3:27, Rom. 7:21, etc.) of the general sense which the word *law* often takes in Paul's writings: a controlling power imposing itself on the will, or, as in the case before us, appropriating the very will.[85]

Referencing "the law of sin and death", the Cambridge Bible NT has this comment:

> In other words it is the Divine Law, (instanced in that of Moses,) which, as a Covenant, is by its very holiness the sinner's doom. The word "law" is (though not at first sight) used in the sense of a fixed process in both parts of the verse: the "new covenant" is linked, *by the chain of cause and effect*, with the Spirit of Life; the "old covenant," with sin and death.[86]

Thus, the use of law by Paul here refers to a principle of power acting within. Newell further adds to this insight:

> It is on account of the Spirit's acting as a law of life, delivering the believer from the contrary *law* of sin and death in his yet unredeemed members, that there is no condemnation. It is of the utmost importance to see this. The subject here is no longer Christ's work for us, but the Spirit's work within us. Without the Spirit within as a law of life, there would be nothing but condemnation: for the new creature has no power within himself apart from the blessed Spirit,--as against a life of perpetual bondage to the flesh,--"the end of which things is death" (Rom. 6:21).[87]

Paul declares in verse 3 that the Law could not accomplish this in our lives because of the inability of our flesh to obey it. The solution? God sent His Son and He condemned sin in the flesh.

> Having stated the fact of freedom, Paul then explained how it is achieved. He declared again the impossibility of attaining freedom over sin through **the** (Mosaic) **Law**. It **was powerless** to free from sin. Not that the Law was weak in itself (as many translations suggest), for it was good (Rom. 7:12). But because of sinful human nature, the Law could not deliver from sin.[88] (bold in original)

The Cambridge Bible NT adds this:

> *what the law could not do*] Lit. **the Impossible of the Law**. What was this? The answer lies in ver. 4. The Law could not procure the "fulfilment" of its own "legal claim;" could not make its subjects "live after the Spirit." This was beyond its power, as it was never within its scope: it had to prescribe duty, not to supply motive.—Here, obviously, the Law is the Moral Code; just alluded to as inseparably connected with sin and death in its effects (apart from Redemption) on fallen man.[89] (bold in original)

Macdonald provides a key note on verse 3:

> As a sacrifice for sin, Christ **condemned sin in the flesh**. He died not only for the sins which we commit (1 Peter 3:18)

but also for our sin nature. In other words, He died for what we *are* just as much as for what we have *done*. In so doing, **He condemned sin in the flesh**. Our sin nature is never said to be forgiven; it is **condemned**. It is the sins that we have *committed* that are forgiven.[90] (bold in original)

Again, the Cambridge Bible NT provides some overall insight regarding what "condemned sin" encompasses:

condemned sin] i.e. *in act:* He *did* judgment upon it. Perhaps the ideas of disgrace and deposition are both in the phrase: the sacrifice of the Incarnate Son both exposed the malignity of sin and procured the breaking of its power. But the idea of *executed penalty* is at least the leading one: Christ as the Sin-offering bore "the curse;" (see Gal. 3:13;) sin, in His blessed humanity, (representing our "flesh of sin,") was punished; and this, (as is immediately shewn,) with a view to our deliverance from the *power* of sin, both by bringing to new light the love and loveliness of God, and by meriting the gift of the Holy Ghost to make the sight effectual.[91]

Finally, verse 4 declares, "That the righteousness of the law might be fulfilled in us, who walk not after the flesh, but after the Spirit" (Rom. 8:4). Notice Paul does not say that the Law is fulfilled "by us" but "in us." I do not fulfill the Law by just following the outward rules and commands. As Paul tells us later in Romans, "For Christ is the end of the law for righteousness to every one that believeth" (Rom. 10:4). The law is fulfilled "in us" because of what Jesus did for us and we experience that life as we walk after the Spirit and not after the flesh. David Guzik gives a great explanation:

That the righteous requirement of the law might be fulfilled in us: Because Jesus fulfilled the **righteous requirement of the law**, and because we are in Christ, we fulfill the law. The law is fulfilled in us in regard to *obedience*, because Jesus righteousness stands for ours. The law is fulfilled in us in regard to *punishment*, because any punishment demanded by the law was poured out upon

Jesus.

> Paul does not say that *we* fulfill the **righteous requirement of the law**. He carefully says that the righteous requirement of the law is **fulfilled in us**. It isn't fulfilled *by* us, but **in us**.

> Simply put, Jesus is our substitute. Jesus was treated as a sinner so we can be treated as righteous.

> **In us who do not walk according to the flesh but according to the Spirit**: The people who enjoy this are those **who do not walk according to the flesh but according to the Spirit**. Their life is marked by obedience to the Holy Spirit, not by obedience to the flesh.[92] (bold in original)

Thomas Constable says further:

> He fulfills them if and as we walk by the Spirit rather than walking according to the flesh. Walking by the Spirit means walking in submission to and dependence on the Spirit (cf. Gal. 5:16). Walking according to the flesh means behaving as the flesh dictates and allowing our sinful nature to govern our lives.[93]

Therefore, through the power of the Holy Spirit, believers actually live above any law's requirements and in doing so, by default fulfill the Law's requirements. That is *not* to say believers are under the Mosaic Law, but the ministry of the Holy Spirit in the New Covenant enables living that is not even comparable to the Law's requirements.

This inner working power results in a both freedom from the guilt of sin through forgiveness and justification,[94] and joy because of the indwelling Holy Spirit's presence (Rom. 8:9; 1 Cor. 1:22; Eph. 1:13, 4:30). This is the result of regeneration (Titus 3:5) by the Holy Spirit when a person comes to saving faith in Christ. A completely new life in Christ (2 Cor. 5:17) changes the believer and their experience in relation to and walk with Jesus. This privilege was not part of the experience of believers in the OT. Only after Jesus' ascension and the coming of the Holy Spirit on the day of Pentecost (John 14:16-17, 16:7; Acts 1:11, 2:1-4) was this the experience of believers under the NT. This advent of the Holy Spirit was promised by God the Father (Luke 24:49; Acts 1:4, 2:23) and is now the experience of all believers in Jesus. This new dynamic is the effective difference in application for living between the OT and NT. The Laws written in stone in the OT are now written on the heart under the New Covenant (Ez. 36:25-27; Jer. 31:33; 2 Cor. 3:3). This is the ideal experience of NT believers when they walk with the Lord – i.e. "after the Spirit." Thus, we listen to one voice of the Holy Spirit speaking through the word of God in order to walk with God. The Holy Spirit also confirms through that word what we sense He writes on our hearts through this New Covenant relationship. Further, when our hearts are at variance to the written word of God we have the opposite confirmation – that the leading from our own nature and not "after the Spirit." We have this safeguard of absolute truth in the word of God. All of this new relationship is possible because of the work of Christ on the cross, His resurrection and subsequent ascension to heaven. Jesus fulfilled all necessary that the Law – or any law – required. In His incarnation "He did no sin (1 Peter 2:22), He knew no sin (2 Cor. 5:21), and there was no sin in Him (1 John 3:5)."[95] Believers are "in Christ," thus they fulfill all requirements by virtue of being "in Christ."

Much more can be said about walking in the Spirit, which is living the Christian life as reflected in the NT. We should be the most stable, content, and joyful people on the planet. Think about it, we have the Holy Spirit of the living God dwelling (1 John 4:13) in us! We are new creations in Christ (2 Cor. 5:17), our old lives have passed away. We were bound by sin, but set free and changed (Rom. 6:17-22; 1 Cor. 6:11). We have a future inheritance that is literally out of this world (Eph. 1:10-14). Moreover, we look forward to glory with Christ (Rom. 8:18). This is not to say that we do not face problems and trouble in this world, and it can be even more troubling because we are Christians (John 16:33; 2 Tim. 3:12). Yet we have Jesus to call on and provide the help we need in our hour of trouble (Heb. 2:18). But when we put all these benefits together, there is no position or condition better for time and eternity than being a believer in Jesus. How glorious!

We entered into this topic of walking in the Spirit by the quote from Galatians chapter 5, which sums up the contrasts between the Law and Gospel of Grace for Christian application. MacDonald insightfully comments:

> The last verse of [Galatians] chapter 4 describes the believer's position—he is free. This first verse of chapter 5 refers to his practice—he should live as a **free** man. Here we have a very good illustration of the difference between law and grace. The law would say: "If you earn your freedom, you will become free." But grace says: "You have been made free at the tremendous cost of the death of Christ. In gratitude to Him, you should **stand fast therefore in the liberty with which Christ has made you free**." Law commands but does not enable. Grace provides what law demands, then enables man to live a life consistent with his position by the power of the Holy Spirit and rewards him for doing it.[96] (bold in original)

I do not think the matter can be summed up any better than that. "Stand fast therefore in the liberty wherewith Christ hath made us free" (Gal. 5:1a). Let us thank Jesus for the cost He paid to set us free and walk in that freedom provided. The Law will not help us, but will weigh us down. If you are a believer in Jesus Christ, He freed you and should live free in Christ and enjoy every aspect of your relationship with Him. It will take you this lifetime to exhaust the riches and resources of spiritual endowment He made available to His own. This should be the focus of all believers. It is so easy to get side tracked and wonder what happened. The work of God in our lives and the glorious experience we can enjoy should be our daily anticipation. Imagine waking up to talk to the living God, the Creator of the universe, and we call Him Father. How intimate and wonderful that privilege is, and we should not overlook it but take every advantage of it. It is all because of Jesus – "All to Him I owe! Sin had left a crimson stain; He washed it white as snow!"[97]

Freedom is an interesting experience. It must be safely guarded or it can be easily lost. It is the second half of Galatians 5:1b that gives the warning, "and be not entangled again with the yoke of bondage." Many have used their freedom to end up in the same or worse chains than when they started. How many have been set free from one or another form of substance abuse to only end up back in the same situation. Why? Because when we are free, we tend to get the false sense that we now can control that, which previously controlled us. The heavy bondage is gone, the difficulty of managing the problem is behind me, but that does not mean I cannot return. Paul said, "But put on the Lord Jesus Christ, and make no provision for the flesh, to fulfill its lusts" (Rom. 13:14, NKJV). Those who have been set free by Jesus Christ must protect that freedom, lest the "yoke of bondage" once again overtakes them. This admonition of Paul in Galatians 5:1 is directly applicable to legalism. Once free, the sense of that freedom is wonderful, but our sin nature is like a Benedict Arnold. There is a constant assault of this traitor and the lies, schemes, and manipulation of this seductive voice is dangerous. The Holy Spirit does not unnecessarily warn us; the danger is real and lurking. However, if I walk after the Spirit, I will not fulfill the lusts of the flesh. This is the key to continually enjoying the victory in Jesus Christ.

If you do not know Jesus Christ, He paid the price for your freedom from sin and its debt. You can bow down your heart to Him today and enter a relationship with Him by faith (trust). Believing in Jesus is not a matter of simply acknowledging His existence; it is entering a relationship with Him through trusting He is who the Bible says He is and that He accomplished what the Bible says He accomplished for you. He redeemed you, will you believe that and trust Him? It is much like a marriage when you say "I do." You may believe *that* your fiancée would make a great wife, but she is not your wife until you say, "I do." At that moment, you enter a relationship with her, believing she will be the wife in which you commit to trust. It is no more complicated than that. Your freedom awaits, Jesus paid it all – for you, because He loves you! Do not put it off, ""In an acceptable time I have heard you, and in the day of salvation I have helped you." Behold, now is the accepted time; behold, now is the day of salvation" (2 Cor. 6:2, EMTV).[98]

---

[1] Geisler, Norman. *Systematic Theology in One Volume*, The Final State of the Saved (Heaven). Minneapolis, MN: Bethany House Publishers. 2011, p. 1259.

[2] Davis, Glen. *The Orange Moon Café*, http://www.orangemooncafe.com/, Daily email and online devotional.

[3] *Awake!* (Magazine), May 22 issue, 1994, p.2.

[4] MacDonald, William. "Leviticus 17:10-14."*Believer's Bible Commentary*, ESword ed., Thomas Nelson, 2008.

[5] Casper The Friendly Ghost, Cartoon, 1945, https://www.imdb.com/title/tt6280432/

[6] JW.ORG. *After Jesus' Resurrection, Was His Body Flesh or Spirit?*, https://www.jw.org/en/bible-teachings/questions/jesus-body/.

[7] Day, Mike. "Ezekiel 37-39 Dry Bones, Sticks and War", LDS Scripture Teachings, 5 May 2012, https://www.ldsscriptureteachings.org/2012/05/05/ezekiel-37-39-dry-bones-sticks-and-war/.

[8] Smith, Chuck. *2000 Series Bible Commentary*, Ezekiel 36-39 (c2000), 1979-1986, https://www.blueletterbible.org/Comm/smith_chuck/c2000_Eze/Eze_036.cfm

[9] To explain from the text of Scripture, i.e. allowing the text to explain itself.

[10] To read into the text of Scripture what the text does not explain, i.e. introducing an idea not that is not there.

[11] Orr, James. *Progress of Dogma*. London Hodder and Stoughton, Printed by R. & R. Clark, Limited. 1901, p. 21.

[12] Dependent on other conditions or circumstances. i.e. God did not need creation for His own existence.

[13] Harris, Ralph W., M.A. "Genesis." *Complete Biblical Library Commentary*, executive editor, Stanley M. Horton, Th.D. Dagengruppen AB. Database, 1995, WORDsearch Corp. World Library Press, Inc., 2009.

[14] Ibid.

[15] From the Latin ex "from" and nihilo "nothing".

[16] Turek, Frank. *Stealing from God: Why Atheists Need God to Make Their Case*. NavPress. Kindle Edition.

[17] https://www.barna.com/research/competing-worldviews-influence-todays-christians/

[18] Barna, George. *Perceptions about Biblical Worldview and Its Application*, May 2021. https://downloads.frc.org/EF/EF21E41.pdf

[19] https://www.christianitydaily.com/articles/11996/20210527/only-6-percent-of-americans-believe-biblical-worldview-barna-survey-reveals-family-research-council.htm

[20] Barna, George. *Perceptions about Biblical Worldview and Its Application*, May 2021, Table 1, p.9 https://downloads.frc.org/EF/EF21E41.pdf

[21] Davis, Glen. Author of *The Orange Moon Café* Devotional, http://www.orangemooncafe.com/, quote from personal email dialog with Glen, July 2022, (I highly recommend Glen's devotional I receive his emails daily).

[22] This belief known as Chrislam, since it attempts to combine Christianity with Islam as if they worship the same God.

[23] https://mormonfaq.com/mormon-beliefs/what-is-mormonism/why-do-mormons-think-they-can-become-gods

[24] Geisler, Norman. *Systematic Theology in One Volume*, Bethany House Publishers, 2011, p.790.

[25] Ibid. p. 796

[26] Lewis, C. S. *The Case for Christianity*, Collier Books Macmillan Publishing Company, NY, 1989, p.32

[27] Sir Fred Hoyle was a British mathematician and astronomer who coined the term "Big Bang" as a mockery of the concept. He rejected the concept and also rejected Darwinian evolution. He was not a Christian or Biblical Creationist, but through evidence believed that the fine-tuning of the universe required a designer.

[28] Turek, Frank. *Stealing from God: Why Atheists Need God to Make Their Case*, NavPress, 2014

[29] The law of *non-contradiction* states simply that two things cannot be opposite and true at the same time in the same sense. For example, in the discussion of various religions, not all can be true at the same time in the same sense since they make opposite claims. In other words, either all religions are wrong or only one of them is right, but they can't all be right since they contradict.

[30] The law of the *excluded middle* states simply that with two opposites, there is no middle position. For example, in the discussion of theism and atheism, since they state opposite and contradictory truths, there can be no middle position. In other words, God either does or doesn't exist, He doesn't

partly exist or almost exist – the middle position is excluded.

[31] The law of *identity* simply states that the claim of a truth that is true in reality is true. For example, the identity of an object is known by its identifying characteristics and is not something different. In other words, I know I'm me and someone else is not me.

[32] Based on charts in various PowerPoint presentations by Dr. Norman Geisler.

[33] Constable, Thomas. "Luke 23:8-9." *Expository Notes of Dr. Constable*, ESword ed., Tyndale Seminary Press, 2012, 12 vols.

[34] This is what is involved in the movement known as Chrislam discussed earlier in the chapter entitled, *The Seven Major Worldviews*.

[35] Discussed above in explanation of the JWs views of Jesus Christ.

[36] Schaff, Phillip. *History of the Christian Church*, Vol. III, chap 9, sec 132, WM. B. Eerdmans Publishing Company, Grand Rapids, Michigan, 1910, p. 690-695.

[37] Robertson, A.T. *Word Pictures in the New Testament*. vol. V, Baker Book House, 1931, p. 4

[38] My own paraphrase.

[39] Vincent, Marvin R. *Word Studies in the New Testament*, 2nd ed., Vol. 2, MacDonald Publishing, 1975, p. 34.

[40] Heresy means a *chosen* view that is at variance, from what the Bible properly teaches.

[41] Schaff, Phillip. *History Of The Christian Church*, Vol. II, Chapter 12, Section 141. WM. B. Eerdmans Publishing Company, Grand Rapids, Michigan, 1910, p. 537

[42] Girdlestone, Robert Baker. Entry for 'Jehovah', *Synonyms of the Old Testament,*, https://www.studylight.org/lexicons/eng/girdlestone/e/elohim.html, also E-Sword version in Dictionaries.

[43] Ibid.

[44] Girdlestone, Robert Baker. Entry for 'Jehovah', *Synonyms of the Old Testament,*, https://www.studylight.org/lexicons/eng/girdlestone/e/lord.html, also E-Sword version in Dictionaries.

[45] Girdlestone, Robert Baker. Entry for 'Jehovah'. *Synonyms of the Old Testament*, https://www.studylight.org/lexicons/eng/girdlestone/e/jehovah.html, also E-Sword version in Dictionaries.

[46] Tozer, A.W. *Knowledge of the Holy*. Electronic ed., Harper & Row, 1961, p. 76.

[47] For a more detailed study, see my book, *Rediscovering Romans 9, How Calvinism Distorts the Nature and Character of God*, https://www.amazon.com/Rediscovering-Romans-Calvinism-Distorts-Character/dp/B08W7SNJYK/ref=tmm_pap_swatch_0?_encoding=UTF8&qid=1657509940&sr=8-1

[48] Constable, Thomas. "John 1:17." *Expository Notes of Dr. Constable*,

ESword ed., Tyndale Seminary Press, 2012, 12 vols.

[49] *The Scofield Study Bible*, NY, Oxford University Press, 2002, p. 1621.

[50] *Classic King James Study Bible with C.I. Scofield Study Notes*, TX, Church Bible Publishers, 1917, Note #1 The Fourth Dispensation, p. 20.

[51] Vine, W.E. *The Expanded Vine's Expository Dictionary of New Testament Words*. Bethany House Publishers, Minneapolis MN, 1984, p. 313.

[52] *Classic King James Study Bible with C.I. Scofield Study Notes*, TX, Church Bible Publishers, 1917, Note #1 The Third Dispensation, p. 16.

[53] The term *Palestinian* is a derogatory term I prefer to avoid and is only used because of the pervasive use in Study Bibles and commentaries, so to change it may create a misunderstanding of what is meant. The term is typically used for the land of Israel. For more information, see https://www.britannica.com/place/Palestine.

[54] *Classic King James Study Bible with C.I. Scofield Study Notes*, TX, Church Bible Publishers, 1917, Note #1, p. 362.

[55] *Classic King James Study Bible with C.I. Scofield Study Notes*, TX, Church Bible Publishers, 1917, Note #4, p. 5.

[56] Walvoord, John. *"Reflections on Dispensationalism"*, (https://walvoord.com/article/151)

[57] Chafer, Lewis Sperry. *Systematic Theology*, Vol. IV, p. 170.

[58] Pentecost, J. Dwight. *Things to Come*. "Chapter 5, The Abrahamic Covenant, The Importance of the Abrahamic Covenant", Zondervan Academic. Kindle Edition.

[59] Pentecost, J. Dwight. *Things to Come*. "Chapter 5, The Abrahamic Covenant, Introduction", Zondervan Academic. Kindle Edition.

[60] Pentecost, J. Dwight. *Things to Come*. "Chapter 5, The Abrahamic Covenant, Introduction", Zondervan Academic. Kindle Edition.

[61] Smith, Chuck. *3000 Series Bible Commentary*, Jeremiah 23 (Tape# 7291), https://robertcliftonrobinson.com/jeremiah-by-chuck-smith/jeremiah-23/ .

[62] The teaching that the church has replaced Israel regarding the promises and prophecies originally given to the Jewish nation. Many prophecies must be changed to metaphorical statements; since the church was never promised any land or other earthly-based tangibles that were clearly promised to the nation of Israel.

[63] Aldrich, Roy L. *Holding Fast to Grace: What Is the Relationship between Law and Grace?* (p. 35-36). Grace Gospel Press. Kindle Edition.

[64] Pentecost, J. Dwight. *Bibliotheca Sacra Journal article*, (July 1971), https://www.galaxie.com/article/bsac128-511-04

[65] Ref. Law of Non-Contradiction.

[66] Conybeare, W. J. & Howson, J. S. *The Life and Epistles of St. Paul*, WM. B. Eerdmans Publishing Company, Michigan, 1987, p. 64-65.

[67] Morgan, G. Campbell. *Acts of the Apostles*, Fleming H. Revell Company, 1924, p. 484-485

[68] Tradition informs us Paul was beheaded at a place now called Tre Fontane in Rome, and that the church of St. Paul stands
over his grave.

[69] Toplady, Augustus Montague. *Rock of Ages*, https://library.timelesstruths.org/music/Rock_of_Ages/, Public Domain, 1776

[70] Spurgeon, Charles. *A Delicious Experience*, Sermon No. 2090, The Metropolitan Tabernacle Pulpit, https://www.spurgeongems.org/sermon/chs2090.pdf, pg. 7.

[71] Davis, Glen. *Personal correspondence with the author*, June 1, 2023.

[72] Davis, Glen. Author of *The Orange Moon Café* Devotional, http://www.orangemooncafe.com/, quote from personal email dialog with Glen, August 2022.

[73] Ch. 9: The Election of Israel, Ch. 10: The Rejection of Israel, Ch. 11: The Restoration of Israel.

[74] Davis, Glen. *The Orange Moon Café Devotional*, "Straw and Bricks", http://www.orangemooncafe.com/2021/12/orange-moon-monday-december-6-2021.html, December 6, 2021.

[75] MacDonald, William. "2 Corinthians 3:6 note." *Believer's Bible Commentary*, E-Sword ed., Thomas Nelson, 2008

[76] https://www.youtube.com/watch?v=7h1IgUBIAbI&list=PLcwC7B6G2AFH5Jr5Oerz032V1S03svKf4&index=4

[77] https://www.atheists.org/activism/resources/biblical-contradictions/

[78] https://www.atheists.org/activism/resources/biblical-contradictions/

[79] https://constitution.laws.com/preamble/we-the-people

[80] https://constitution.congress.gov/browse/essay/pre-1/ALDE_00001231/

[81] Covenant Theology (CT) is not a form of "systematic theology," but is a predetermined context for interpreting the Scriptures. It attempts to do what the dispensational view provides, a framework for interpretation. However, the difference is that CT assumes too much and already interprets covenants as either works or grace. The inherent problem with this perspective and approach is that salvation under particular covenants is by works, while the ultimate covenant of grace is the NT. Dispensationalists view salvation from start to finish always being by faith and never by works. The dispensations create the conditions for faithful living laid out progressively, but do not change the criteria of faith for salvation. CT imposes either works or grace into various covenants, which in this author's opinion is begging the question theologically (assuming what is trying to be proved). Dispensationalists look at various conditions within the context of progressive revelation and interpret covenants as they relate to each dispensation and or covenant. This

is why dispensations are not always equal to covenants under this view.

[82] Robertson, A.T. *Word Pictures in the New Testament.* vol. IV, Baker Book House, 1931, p. 313

[83] MacDonald, William. "Galatians 5:21 note." *Believer's Bible Commentary,* E-Sword ed., Thomas Nelson, 2008.

[84] *Classic King James Study Bible with C.I. Scofield Study Notes,* TX, Church Bible Publishers, 1917, Note #1, p. 1201.

[85] Godet, Fredric Louis. *St. Paul's Epistle to the Romans.* Funk & Wagnalls, New York, 1883, p. 296.

[86] Perowne, J. J. S. General Editor, *The Cambridge Bible for Schools and Colleges,* "The Romans", 8:2 note, Cambridge University Press, 1891, ESword ed.

[87] Newell, William R. *Romans Verse-by-Verse,* Kregel Publications, MI, 1994, p. 288.

[88] Walvoord, John and Zuck, Roy. *Bible Knowledge Commentary,*

[89] Perowne, J. J. S. General Editor, *The Cambridge Bible for Schools and Colleges,* "The Romans", 8:3 note, Cambridge University Press, 1891, ESword ed.

[90] MacDonald, William. "Romans 8:3 note." *Believer's Bible Commentary,* E-Sword ed., Thomas Nelson, 2008.

[91] Perowne, J. J. S. General Editor, *The Cambridge Bible for Schools and Colleges,* "The Romans", 8:3 note, Cambridge University Press, 1891, ESword ed.

[92] Guzik, David. *Romans Verse by Verse Commentary,* Rom. 8:1-39 - A NEW AND WONDERFUL LIFE IN THE SPIRIT, ESword ed.

[93] Constable, Thomas. "Romans 8:4." *Expository Notes of Dr. Constable,* Tyndale Seminary Press, ESword ed., 2012. 12 vols.

[94] Justification is the act whereby God declares the sinner righteous and establishes their standing in the perfection of Christ – based on His merit alone – before God. This is one of the many benefits of the believer's position before God "in Christ". Forgiveness removes sin, but does not remove the fact that the offense was committed. Justification by position in Christ is as if the offense was never committed, since Jesus never sinned (Matt. 1:20; John 8:46; 2 Cor. 5:21; Heb. 7:26; 1 Peter 2:22; 1 John 3:5).

[95] MacDonald, William. "Romans 8:3 note." *Believer's Bible Commentary,* E-Sword ed., Thomas Nelson, 2008.

[96] MacDonald, William. "Galatians 5:1 note." *Believer's Bible Commentary,* E-Sword ed., Thomas Nelson, 2008.

[97] Hall, Elvina M. *Jesus Paid it All,* https://library.timelesstruths.org/music/Jesus_Paid_It_All/, Public Domain, 1865.

[98] *English Majority Text Version,* E-Sword ed., also https://www.bibliatodo.com/en/the-bible/english-majority-text-

version/2corinthians-6

ABOUT THE AUTHOR

Scott Mitchell

Scott Mitchell is the assistant pastor of Calvary Chapel of Boston since it began in 1989. He has written multiple pamphlets on various Bible subjects. He teaches high school Bible, apologetics, and ethics classes at Calvary Chapel Academy, and a weekly discipleship class focused on various Bible topics and Christian apologetics. He has been married since 1983.

BOOKS BY THIS AUTHOR

Rediscovering Romans 9, How Calvinism Distorts The Nature And Character Of God

Romans chapter 9 has become a dividing point between competing theologies for years. Calvinistic authors ground much of their interpretation of the Bible and understanding of God's nature and character from this particular chapter. Christians that are unaware of the theological traps they can fall into by blindly following Calvin's theological determinism can result in a distorted view of God's nature and character. The consequence of this is surely problematic when applying a predetermined view of God to the rest of the Bible that the Scriptures simply will not support. This has at times resulted in confusion among God's people through an inconsistent approach to the Bible, as attempts to harmonize the biblical themes cannot be accomplished through the lens of theological determinism. Rediscovering Romans 9 provides a sound and systematic approach to Bible study – Romans 9 in particular. The book challenges the Calvinistic interpretation of Romans 9, informs the reader of Calvinistic theology and answers nagging questions surrounding this wonderful and glorious chapter of Paul's epistle. Some history of Calvinism, a look into context, an examination of sound hermeneutics, and fundamental principles of logical thinking are all combined to bring the reader to a place where Romans 9 can be approached without deterministic bias. Romans 9 is a theological chapter that deserves the attention provided in this book. If you are investigating Calvinism and considering that theological direction, this book can be a tremendous help. If you are convinced Calvinistic determinism is how to approach the Bible, this book will test the soundness of your theology and challenge your position. Either way, the church needs a sound biblical view of Romans 9, since it reveals much of God's nature and character. All this can be achieved by Rediscovering Romans 9.

Made in the USA
Monee, IL
03 October 2024